Growing Up in Indiana

The Culture & Hoosier Hysteria Revisited

Donna,
The best to you in the
years ahead. Your pal,
Norm Jones
1954

— Dr. Norman Jones —

authorHOUSE™

1663 LIBERTY DRIVE, SUITE 200
BLOOMINGTON, INDIANA 47403
(800) 839-8640
WWW.AUTHORHOUSE.COM

First published by AuthorHouse 09/27/05

ISBN: 1-4208-7235-4 (sc)

Library of Congress Control Number: 2005907321

Printed in the United States of America
Bloomington, Indiana

This book is printed on acid-free paper.

CONTENTS

DEDICATION

I would like to dedicate this book to three special groups of people. The first group is the many legions of people who, for whatever the reason, never had the thrill of representing their schools on the athletic field. Most boys in Indiana who got cut from their high school basketball teams can recall that exact disheartening moment. Many physically and mentally challenged young people never even had the chance to make the team. I'm thinking also of a friend who many said it looked as though he had All-Star potential in basketball. He was deprived of playing by contracting the dreaded disease of our childhood...polio. His legs, at middle school age atrophied to half the size they should be and he used crutches the rest of his life. Another friend had his dreams of playing end when he got hit by a truck in the fifth grade shattering his leg and his dreams. Others had parents whose value systems would not allow them to play.

The above group of people, for the most part, are America's real heroes for they moved ahead and followed the slogan to do the best you can, with whatever you have, wherever you are. May others so disabled have the courage to move ahead and lead meaningful lives. May all those to follow develop similar courage within themselves and work hard to lead meaningful lives and contribute to our society.

I don't think near enough appreciation has been shown to those African-American athletes who endured sickening forms of discrimination in the 1930s and was still rampant into the 1960s. Famous athletes like Jesse Owens, Jackie Robinson, Bill Russell, Hank Aaron and Oscar Robertson endured bigotry, hatred and harassment that reached its zenith during the turbulent times from the 1930s to the 1960s. They all handled those times with dignity, class and grace, opening doors so others could play without such tension to overcome. Younger people in today's America, born in the 1960s and beyond can never know how bad the discrimination really was in the early part and middle of the 20th century. Try to imagine an African-American going to an arena to play in those turbulent times and being shown a rope with a noose signifying a lynching. Or try to understand what it was like when the team could not be served in a restaurant because it had black players. Or what it was like when white fans wanted to know if the black players had their shoeshine kits, called them names and made racial slurs.

African-American players in high school and college not as well-known as the above listed stars, often suffered similar discriminatory acts that made them question whether or not they lived in a democracy. Many of them were my teammates. I cannot apologize for a country...but I would like to. I hope this book helps add to the understanding of the racial strife our country has endured.

The third dedication goes first to Pat, my wife of forty-five years. She is as beautiful on the inside as she is on the outside. Pat has shown a tremendous amount of patience during my writing career that has often taken substantial time away from my family. Pat had more input into this book than the other books and I thank her for her valuable suggestions.

My three married daughters, Denise Luksetich, Diane Stratton and Deborah Struck cannot know how proud I am to be their father. They also know that I have told them often it is more important that they be proud of themselves than it is for me to proud of what they do. The book is also dedicated to my three son-in-laws whom I enjoy very much. They are Rick Luksetich, Eric Stratton and Bob Struck. Last, but by no means least, my writing is dedicated to my grandchildren, Eric and Adam Luksetich and to Jack, Danielle and Jamie Stratton. To all of these family members I am indebted to their insights and warm, loving relationships.

ACKNOWLEDGMENTS

Writing a book about events that happened long ago is more of a challenge than I thought. Since this book, *Growing Up in Indiana: The Culture and Hoosier Hysteria Revisited*, focuses on things that happened while I was growing up in Indiana in the 1950s, I had to rely a great deal on memory. I began checking facts as I thought I knew them with friends from my early years. We found that our memories played tricks on us. I found that to validate contents of the book became a cumbersome task, but worked hard to make certain the facts are accurate. I am pleased with the result, but suspect even now that readers will tell me of errors. If anyone is offended by those errors, please accept my apology here beforehand as this was not my intent.

In a non-fiction book it is per-usual that many people contribute to its content and this book is no different. Many people gave of their time and patience while others contributed in just a short comment or note. Nevertheless, all contributions add up to the final outcome.

Perhaps the people who gave of their time more than others are five of my Marion, IN. high school classmates of the class of 1954. John Roush went so far to take pictures, sent many e-mails that answered questions about Marion and attended to other details for me. Sharon Riddle clued me in to phone numbers and informed me about important facts as I pursued permissions to quote copyrighted material and use sources. She also helped to accumulate other important information as did other classmates, Barbara Archey and Sandra Nukes and Gari Peterson. For their contributions I am grateful and send a sincere "Thank you."

Other classmates told me things that are included in the book. Some, like Larry "Wid" Mathews, Wynston "Wynn" Lynn, Bill Abdon, Al Harker and Ed Wilkinson and Sally Phillips made special contributions. Classmates Jim Harmon, Gary McKillip, Jan Davis, Bob Kittle, Don Melnik, Larry Hickman, Jim Hensley and Frankie Wehrly verified dates, events and other important items that helped to enhance the book.

Marion High School grads, although not in my class, also helped me insert valuable material into the book. They are Oatess Archey, Tommy Nukes, Jerry Hamm, Bob France, Jules Walker, Don Weber and Judy Solms. Thanks also to Marion grads B. Sue Miller and David Allison Miller for their timely contribution.

Thanks to Dr. Don Park, Vice President, University Advancement, Ball State University in granting permission to use Ball State yearbook photos. Also to Ernie Krug, Director, Alumni Activities, Ball State University for his special contribution. Most helpful were the comments of my friend and fellow Ball State alum, Tom Hilgendorf. Fraternity brother and long time golf coach at Ball State, Earl Yestingsmeier, made meaningful contributions to the book. Also a heartfelt "thank you" goes out to Gary Montel, Executive Director of the Alumni Association at Manchester College in North Manchester, IN. who granted me permission to use a Manchester College photo. In the Marion, IN. school system my thanks goes to Patty Barney, Executive Assistant to the Superintendent, who tracked down permission for me to use photos out of the *Cactus,* the Marion High yearbook. Most helpful in obtaining information and permissions to use photos from the *Marion Chronicle-Tribune* was sports editor Adam Wire.

Several men deeply immersed in the game of basketball in Indiana made timely donations to the book. A sincere "thanks" goes to Roger Dickinson, Executive Director of the Indiana Basketball Hall of Fame. He advised me of several things that helped the book take shape. Under his watch, the Web sites of well-known players and coaches who have been inducted into the Indiana Basketball Hall of Fame served to verify facts for me as the book took shape. Phil Raisor, a former opponent on the hardwood and Muncie Central star deserves mention. Phil played in the famous Milan-Muncie game that inspired the movie *Hoosiers.* As an Associate Professor of English at Old Dominion University, he gave me a tip that helped to make the book read better. A debt of gratitude is owed to my friend, my mentor and Indiana All-Star, Jim Barley from Marion High School. Jim played at Indiana University and is a member of the Indiana Basketball Hall of Fame. He contributed last second material I wanted, but didn't have.

My long time friend, Marc Denny, named in 1960 to the Indiana All-Star basketball team from Bedford, IN., clarified several things for me that took place during our time together in Indiana. Dick McAvoy, from Marion, was a good player in 1954 for what was then known as St. Paul high school. Dick told me about things of yesteryear that are found in the book and he deserves a big "thank you." I worked at North Vernon, IN. high school with Athletic Director Don Pelkey and head basketball coach, Orville Bose. Both supplied me with valuable information for this project and I am grateful for the contributions. Hank Weedin, head basketball coach at Salem High School (IN) where I once coached, supplied dates and records used in the book. Thanks Hank!

Dick Davis, a rival Anderson Indian, and husband of Marion classmate Jan Davis, helped to verify some facts as did my former neighbor Jim Ward. Two pretty fair "country shooters," Dave and Don Waymire both sent material I found worthwhile to include.

Bob Struck, my son-in-law, made so many quick fixes concerning my computer ignorance it probably saved me many hours from having to sit at the computer. He helped me find information on the Internet that I needed, but was having trouble finding. He is a wizard and I appreciated his help along the way. Having similar computer expertise, my daughter, Diane Stratton, contributed a great deal by helping to enhance pictures found in the book. Her able assistance is appreciated.

Many Hoosier basketball fans are indebted to Mr. Herb Schwomeyer of Butler University who dedicated a big part of his life to compiling a record book about Indiana high school basketball. He authored several editions of *Hoosier Hysteria-A History of Indiana High School Boys Single Class Basketball*. I consulted this book to verify player and team records, scores of games and other statistics. Accolades should also go to Gary K. Johnson and Sean W. Straziscar who compiled the book titled *Official 2001 Men's NCAA Basketball Records*. This book also helped me verify important information concerning college basketball.

CHAPTER ONE
On Becoming A Hoosier

THERE ARE TWO SEASONS IN INDIANA:
THERE IS BASKETBALL SEASON AND
GETTING READY FOR BASKETBALL SEASON.

Family photos reveal that my mother was an All-State basketball player in Mississippi. She was born in Tishomingo, Mississippi and my father in Ft. Wayne, Indiana. This makes my father a born Hoosier. I was born in Battle Creek, Michigan on June 4, 1936. Many Hoosier families place a basketball in the cribs of newborns in sort of a voodoo attempt to someway influence basketball greatness as their offspring develops. My parents did not place a basketball in my crib, or so they told me, so even with possible genetic links to basketball skills and a bloodline to the Hoosier state I was not a Hoosier from day one. However, one can become a transplanted Hoosier.

The trials and tribulations of young boys growing up in Indiana and striving to play basketball at a high level are often fascinating stories. Such were the dreams of almost every boy in Indiana in the late 1940s and in the 1950s. I was no different. My own story can be traced back to what has become known as the Golden Era of Hoosier Hysteria. It is also an account of me as a youngster learning through bits and pieces about a culture riveted with racism and prejudice. It is about battles between people about segregation and integration and the effect this had on me as a youngster.

When I was around age two my parents moved to Anderson, Indiana. We lived in Middletown for awhile and moved again to Kokomo, Indiana where I attended kindergarten. A graduation with caps and gowns was one

1

of my earliest recollections. My folks then moved to Marion, Indiana. My next memory is of our house on West 6th Street in Marion and my brother, Wendell, who is seventeen months younger, and I playing in our yard. We did not venture out much since we were new in town and did not know anyone. I started first grade in August of 1942. I remember my first day in Miss Milan's room at Horace Mann Elementary school was a disaster. The school had to call my dad to come and get me because I would not stop crying. I don't remember what caused this episode, except everything was new to me, I didn't have many friends yet and I was scared. I know I went back the very next day and settled into that first grade and Marion, Indiana came to be my hometown.

In the second grade Mrs. Palmer finger thumped our heads if we weren't doing what we were supposed to be doing. Mrs. Ballard danced a jig, as promised, at recess because all of us in the fifth grade scored perfect spelling papers. We played marbles at recess and my friend David Phillips entertained us by eating crayons. In the sixth grade Mrs. Gardner sent me to the office because my friend, Larry "Wid" Mathews made me laugh out loud and disrupt the class. The principal, Mr. Stephens, gave me one whack on my fanny with his paddle. When I closed the door to his office I said, "Thank you," but I don't know why since it was Wid's fault in the first place. It seems as though basketball was first brought to my attention during the fifth grade.

Two important events took place in Marion well before World War II began in December 1941. Marion is a town of about 30,000 people located about seventy miles northeast of Indianapolis. Many Indiana towns have a courthouse and a town square where many businesses are located and Marion was no different. In 1926 Marion High School won the Indiana state basketball championship before 15,000 fans in the Exposition Center or the "Cowbarn" in Indianapolis. In the state final game they beat a Martinsville team that included John Wooden who most basketball fans recognize as the legendary coach who later guided UCLA to ten NCAA crowns. He was the first player to be named consensus All-American three times while at Purdue.

Marion was led by 6' 7" Charles "Stretch" Murphy, Bob and Everett Chapman and Glen Overman. The coach was Gene Thomas. "Stretch" Murphy went on to become a two-time All-American at Purdue with Wooden and both were eventually named to the Indiana Basketball Hall of Fame. Both played professionally when pro basketball came to Indiana.

It would be difficult for anyone to live in Marion very long without becoming aware of the accomplishments of the 1926 Marion Giants. Hoosier Hysteria was already fifteen years old and towns that won state titles usually made that fact known by painting the town water tower with an inscription like MARION GIANTS-1926 STATE CHAMPS. Added to that was the fact that pictures of the team or individuals were visible in barbershops, restaurants, bars, schools, offices of town officials, homes and other establishments. Winning the state championship was a source of pride...and still is for basketball crazy Indiana.

There is no doubt that the 1926 team set a standard for every Marion team to follow. Even as this is being written, I can promise you that young boys are shooting baskets somewhere in Marion and dreaming of playing for the Giants and winning the state championship. Proof of that is the fact that Marion has, to this date, won seven state basketball titles which puts the school just one title behind the Muncie Central Bearcats. These schools are only about thirty miles apart. It is basketball country of legendary proportions.

The second event shattered some of the pride the people in Marion had built up. It happened on August 7, 1930 when two black men were hung just outside the Marion courthouse where the jail was located. The best way to describe what happened is perhaps best reported in a book titled *A Lynching in the Heartland: Race and Memory in America*. In the first chapter titled A Night of Terror, author James H. Madison wrote:

> The first sounds the prisoners heard were murmurs and bits of conversation. Beginning around 6:30 P.M. on Thursday, August 7, 1930, the words grew louder as more and more people gathered on the sidewalk, street, and yard in front of the Grant County Jail in Marion, Indiana. "Get'em," some shouted. "Kill the niggers." Louder and louder, the sounds of vengeance cut between the bars of the three-story jail and into the cells where Tom Shipp, aged 19, Abe Smith, 18, and James Cameron, 16, listened and waited
>
> The three black teenagers were in separate cells, connected by the crime they had confessed to the night before. On August 6, they had ambushed a young couple parked in the local lovers' lane along the Mississinewa River. Claude Deeter, aged 24, a Marion factory worker, fought the three assailants heroically,but could not resist the bullets fired from a revolver by one of the three. His companion, 18-year-old Mary Ball, was pushed down in the weeds and thorns along the riverbank and raped, press stories reported.

Further accounts of this racially charged event reveal that Claude Deeter died. His death made the three teen-agers liable for murder. That night a mob of Marion people attacked the jail and pulled Smith and Shipp from their cells. They lynched the two by throwing a rope over a maple limb on the northeast corner of the square. A calming voice in the crowd spared Cameron his life and he was returned to the jail.

Many in the area at the time blamed the Ku Klux Klan because their enemies were known to be Catholics, Jews and blacks. However, no one was ever convicted of the lynchings. Cameron was convicted of being an accessory to voluntary manslaughter and was released after spending four years in jail.

The lynchings are only a part of the history of Indiana and the mid-west as racial relations continued to be strained from time to time. In the years since I was born I have learned that the summer of 1936 was when Jesse Owens, an African-American track star from Ohio State University, upset the plans of Adolph Hitler. The notorious Hitler wanted to use the Berlin Olympic games to prove that German "Aryan" people were the dominant race. In the so called "Hitler Olympics" Jesse won the 100-meter and 200-meter dashes and the broad jump and ran on the gold medal relay team. He was the first American to win four gold medals. Jesse Owens was even cheered by the German people and made Americans proud to be Americans.

Back home in the United States, the discrimination against blacks did not seem to be diminishing. Jesse Owens could not live on the Ohio State campus. He could eat in "blacks-only" restaurants, could use only the back door or stairs instead of the elevator if he was allowed to stay in a white managed hotel.

It wasn't only blacks who were discriminated against in our culture in these years. It was the summer of 1941 that I have a very fond memory of visiting relatives back in Michigan. My uncles and my father were Detroit Tiger fans. They took my brother and I to our first Major League Baseball game at Briggs Stadium in Detroit. I will always remember Tiger slugger Hank Greenberg, a big Jewish lad out of New York, hit his 21st homer of the season. I can still see that ball landing in the green seats in the upper deck in left field. It was my first real big time sporting event and I loved it. I think it was one of the events in my life that got me excited about sports.

As with Jesse Owens, I learned later in my life how Hank Greenberg was discriminated against in his own country. Hank had 58 homers with five games left in the season. Babe Ruth had set the homerun record of 60 playing with the New York Yankees in 1927. Hank was walked several times and was not given many good pitches to hit and many baseball fans saw this as a form of discrimination against a Jewish boy. Years before this incident, in 1935, Hank had 100 RBIs at the All-Star game break in mid-season and *did not make the American League All-Star team.* His season finished up so well that he was named MVP in the American League and led the Tigers in winning the World Series.

After the Japanese sneak attack on Pearl Harbor the government rounded up most of the Japanese who had immigrated to the United States and placed them in internment camps throughout the country. Government officials determined this was for their own safety as many Americans were angry with the Japanese for attacking Pearl Harbor. There were very few incidents between Japanese and Americans regarding this situation and the Japanese were released at the end of the war. In many parts of the country Japanese were even treated better than native African-Americans. Of course, as youngsters, my friends and I were kept in the dark when it came to racial problems. We didn't know it then, but we were living in a culture of deceit, a society that kept silent about bigotry, prejudice and hatred.

Despite such problems, the first few years at Horace Mann Elementary seemed to fly by and the next thing I knew all of my friends and I were beginning to play basketball and baseball. Baseball was mainly pick-up games, often with three or four on a side. Little League had not yet started so there was no organized baseball for us. Basketball seemed to be the best game to play because two guys could play or you could play by yourself.

As I remember it in the beginning getting started in learning to play the game of basketball seemed difficult because the basket was so high. Since Marion had won the state championship in 1926 everyone seemed to agree that youngsters coming up should shoot at the regulation ten-foot high basket. I don't recall ever seeing a lower basket. It was hard to shoot over handed and get the ball up to the basket, but that started coming around before we got too much older. Many of us had to shoot free throws underhanded just to get them up to the rim. Many coaches were still teaching the underhand free throw methods used by "Stretch" Murphy and John Wooden.

We began to get some coaching in the fifth grade. Martin Boots Jr. High School was located right beside Horace Mann Elementary and it had a gym. This school held grades seven through nine. Marion High School held ten through twelve. Fifth and sixth graders interested in playing basketball eventually had to report to the Martin Boots gym. I think it was the first gym I ever saw. It didn't have seats as the walls came almost to the edge of the floor.

The ceiling was so low if a player arched a shot too high it would deflect off of the ceiling. There was one spot on the ceiling players learned about that was so placed if they could hit it perfectly with the ball when taking it out of bounds the ball would go in the basket. The floor was marked and what is now known as the "lane" or "the paint" was then called the "key" because it was shaped like a key. Some radio and TV announcers until just recently referred to the key and younger people had no idea what they were talking about.

When school was out for the summer my friends and I all knew that we would have to tryout for the Horace Mann team if we were to play basketball the next school year. For that reason, we played almost every day in the summer months. Parents put up goals and we would soon be calling these "courts" by the name of the people whose property they were on. We would say for example, "Let's go to Miller's," or "Let's go to McClain's." Usually the places that we knew had nets would get priority. Parents wanting to help build the next state champions would pay more attention to the goals being the proper height and not bent.

Those really into Hoosier Hysteria would keep nets in good shape. Some of the courts were cement and later on a new surface called asphalt appeared on courts around town. Martin Boots had two outside goals placed apart about the distance of a regulation floor so we were able to play a full court game. It was a dirt court and we could not dribble the ball very accurately on dirt so we usually limited games to the half-court variety.

Basketball was so important to my friends and I that we would check the calendar anytime in the year to see when a full-moon was to appear. This meant on a clear night we could see the basket well enough to shoot. Sometimes after playing all day we would eat dinner and rush back out of the house because we knew on that full-moon night we would get to play longer…and dream our dreams. Pretending to be a radio announcer we would yell out, "Five seconds to go, the score is tied, Jones fires a one-hander from the right side…that's all brother." One legendary announcer in central Indiana coined the phrase, "That's all brother," when the ball swished into the basket. In the winter when it snowed we would have to find a cement court to play on so we could shovel off the snow. We would play until our hands got so raw we would have to go inside and warm them up.

Excitement about basketball reached new heights in Indiana in the early to mid-1940s. Indiana University, coached by former Indiana star Branch McCracken, won its first national championship in 1940. Two years later Stanford won the NCAA title with coach Everett Dean who was the first

All-American from Indiana University. Dean coached at Indiana from 1925 to 1938 and had coached McCracken at the school located in Bloomington. McCracken, who first coached at Ball State, introduced a fast-paced game at Indiana and the fans fell in love with his running style. Someone named the team The Hurryin' Hoosiers. In 1937 a rule was changed whereby the ball was taken out of bounds after each basket. This rule eliminated the boring jump ball at center court after each basket and helped to speed up the game.

Coach Dean's assistant, Woodrow Weir, came to Marion High School to take over the head coaching position shortly after they won the national title at Stanford. It is noteworthy in basketball history that Dean coached a great player at Stanford named Hank Luisetti. Luisetti is generally given credit for introducing the one-handed shot and was the first player to ever score 50 points in a game. Most shots before 1940 were launched either underhanded or were of the two-handed set shot variety or a lay-up. The one-handed shot helped to increase accuracy and speed up the game. Basketball was getting exciting for spectators and the game was well on its way to it current popularity.

Adding even more to the excitement of Indiana basketball, it was about this time in the mid to late 1940s that professional basketball was overcoming turbulent years getting started in the state. In 1948 the town of Anderson, Indiana was now sponsoring a team known as the Anderson Duffy Packers. They played in the National Basketball League (NBL). The Ft. Wayne (Indiana) Zollners had already won several championships, including the Chicago World Tournament. In an attempt to beat Ft. Wayne, the Chicago Gears signed 6'10" DePaul star George Mikan to a lucrative contract. Mikan had led DePaul, coached by the legendary Ray Meyer, to the National Invitational Tournament (NIT) title in 1945. (At that time the NIT was a more prestigious tournament to be invited to than the NCAA)

Even the great Mikan could not upset the Ft. Wayne Zollners in the World Tournament held in the spacious Chicago Stadium. Due to the quick success of high school basketball and Indiana University and Ft. Wayne winning on a regular basis, Indiana was establishing its reputation as "the basketball state." Other cities fielding teams about this time were Oshkosh, Baltimore, New York, Syracuse, Detroit, Toledo, Rochester and a team from the Tri-Cities of Moline and Rock Island in Illinois and Waterloo in Iowa.

Years before, in 1926, the Harlem Globetrotters were founded on the South Side of Chicago by Abe Saperstein, a Jewish businessman. The "Trotters" played serious basketball in the beginning and even won some worldwide tournaments. They played to win, but turned to some comedy routines on the court in order to appeal to all ethnic groups and were an immediate sensation. Most Americans became familiar with their red, white and blue uniforms and their tricky ball handling performed to the tune of *Sweet Georgia Brown*. A few Globtrotter stars have gone on to play in what is now known as the NBA.

The Harlem Globetrotters were barnstorming in those days as were the all black New York Renaissance. The Rens had already won the World Tournament held in Chicago in 1939. I saw the Rens play in the Memorial Coliseum where the Marion High School Giants played. The ball handling, expert shooting and trick plays were something to behold in basketball crazy Marion. The fans loved it. William "Pop" Gates was the star of the Rens.

The history of professional basketball reveals that racial tensions almost ended the chances for African-Americans to play the sport before it even got started. One report about the Rens mentioned:

> "A volcano of bigotry and hatred erupted among the white basketball community. Death threats followed the team as it traveled from town to town, particularly in Indiana and other mid-western and southern regions dominated by the Ku Klux Klan. One player recalled that team members sometime slept in jails during their mid-western tour because they wouldn't put us up in hotels. Standard equipment for us was a flint gun; we'd spray all the bedbugs before we went out to play and they'd be dead when we got back."

On the other side of the coin, "Pop" Gates told why the players mustered the courage to come to Indiana to play:

> "We looked forward to coming to Indiana to play because we knew that we'd have a good ball game in Indiana. Indiana was much like New York City in that it was a hotbed for basketball. Many of the nation's premier players were coming out of Indiana. It was one of the top basketball states in the country at the time."

I realized about the time I was in the sixth grade that part of the excitement about basketball in Indiana centered around the naming of a high school All-Star team made up of the best senior players in the state. This All-Star team began to play Kentucky's All-Stars in 1940, the same year Indiana University had won the national championship. The first game was held in Butler Fieldhouse in Indianapolis. Proceeds from the game were donated to help the blind. Records show that Indiana beat Kentucky 31 to 29 and Bill

Fowler, the first All-Star from Marion, scored two points. He later played at the Univerity of Kentucky for two years. He became the radio announcer for Marion Giant games and was well known around central Indiana.

Kentucky didn't beat Indiana in the All-Star game until 1945 when future University of Kentucky stars Ralph Beard and Wallace "Wha Wha" Jones scored over half the team's points. However, the next year, 1946, an African-American from Anderson, Indiana named "Jumping Johnny" Wilson became the first player to score 30 points in a state final game. He led his Anderson Indians to the state title, was named Mr. Basketball and scored 27 points to beat the Kentucky All-Stars in Louisville. It is a well-known fact to this day in Indiana that to be named Mr. Basketball is about the highest honor a senior boy can receive. Only slightly less in importance is to be named to this team of stars that plays Kentucky's All-Stars every summer.

The Marion Giants had played well most of the 1946-47 season and coach "Woody" Weir seemed to have the team hitting its stride as he prepared it for the state tourney. Most people in town knew the names of the players. Names like Pettiford, Gugel, Earnhart, Wickham, James and McCrosky could be heard in conversations. Art Brown was a good player and Bayard King was a sparkplug. The two best players were Dick Weagley and Ralph Ferguson.

After finishing the season with strong play against some of the best teams in the state, the Giants swept into the first round of the state tournament. In those days the first round of the tournament was called "the Sectional." The second round was known as "the Regional," the third was "the Semi-State" or "the Sweet Sixteen." The state finals was "the Final Four." Many times it was the smaller schools in a county coming in to the county seat to play. In Marion's case it hosted the Sectional every year because of the 5,500 seating capacity in Memorial Coliseum. Teams such as Jefferson Township, Swayzee, Sweetser, St. Paul, which was a Catholic school, Fairmount, Gas City and Van Buren would come into the Giants home court in Grant county and try to beat them.

It would take three wins to win the Sectional. Marion would also host the Regional in those days. Teams winning Sectionals from further away from Marion such as Wabash, Huntington or Hartford City would come in for the second round of the state tournament. It took two wins to advance to the Semi-State from the Regional.

Weagley and Ferguson played brilliantly and led Marion through the Sectional and Regional. I cannot recall seeing any tournament games in 1947.

Tickets were scarce, but the games were on the radio. I had, as a fifth grader, seen the team play several games so I listened intently to the games. The team surprised even the most devoted Marion fans by winning the Semi-State. The Giants were going to the Final Four for the first time since 1926! The celebrating the town did during the week before the finals is easy to remember. There were signs in almost every business establishment in Marion wishing the Giants good luck "down state." Names of players were plastered everywhere. People were excited about their team playing in the famed Butler Fieldhouse because many exciting professional and college games had taken place there as well as All-Star games and high school final games.

It was at this time that I remember attending drawings at the Coliseum for tickets as the Giants progressed along the tournament trail. A huge drum held the applications of basketball fans wanting to purchase the small amount of tickets left after school personnel, the Booster Club, students, the parents of players, etc. received their fair share. The drum was rolled to mix the entries and names were drawn. People actually screamed when their names were called. This type drawing was a ritual for season tickets for Marion Giant basketball games. It was impossible to walk up to the ticket window and buy a ticket. Over two thousand people would come to the Coliseum *just for the drawing*. It was not difficult to figure out, even as a youngster, that basketball was very important to people in Marion, Indiana. Marion was not the only town with ticket problems. Muncie closed ticket offices.

As for "going to the state" Marion was to play undefeated Terre Haute Garfield and Shelbyville was to play East Chicago Washington in Saturday afternoon games. The winners would play that night for the state title. Garfield featured tall and talented Clyde Lovellette who would later become a two-time All-American at the University of Kansas. He also had a great career in the NBA and is in the NBA Hall of Fame.

Giant fans who could not get tickets were glued to their radios for the finals, but victory was not to be. Terre Haute beat Marion 59-50 as the 6'10" Lovellette, a junior, scored 19 points in front of 14,983 screaming fans. Dick Weagley scored 18 for Marion and Ferguson added 15 as the Giants made a good effort to bring their second state title back to Marion. Shelbyville, in somewhat of an upset, won the state championship by beating East Chicago Washington and Terre Haute Garfield. Shelbyville had two terrific black players in Bill Garrett and Emerson Johnson.

In the spring of 1947 Bill Garrett was named Mr. Basketball and scored 21 points to help Indiana slaughter Kentucky's All-Stars 86-50. Garrett went on to play at Indiana University and was the first black player in the Big Ten conference. To the surprise of no one in Marion, Dick Weagley became the second Marion Giant in history to be named to the Indiana All-Star team. Many fans were disappointed that Ralph Ferguson didn't make the team since he did make the All-Final Four team named by an Indianapolis newspaper. Weagley made two points in the Indiana-Kentucky All-Star game and Emerson Johnson made four. Clyde Lovellette made the Indiana All-Star team the next year and led the team to a 70-47 rout of Kentucky. Ralph Ferguson went on to star at Franklin College located just outside of Indianapolis.

Although the Giants lost, the loss in no way dampened the spirits of most of us who really wanted to become players as good as the Giant players who almost gave Marion its second state title. We played all summer to get ready to make the most of our chances and those chances would become slimmer and slimmer as we progressed through school. Boys from other junior high schools would be after slots on the team in high school. Everyone knew competition would be keen. There was no choice but to practice as much as possible.

John Hubbard was the coach at Martin Boots. He was known as a man who loved to teach the fundamentals of basketball and prepare players for the high school team. Our first practices in the fifth grade consisted of drills like pivoting, passing, dribbling and defensive footwork. The coach explained we could not become good players if we did not get the fundamentals down to a point where they came like second nature to us. They had to be performed automatically in pressure situations without thinking about them.

I don't think many boys got cut in the fifth grade because we mainly just practiced. I don't remember playing many games against other schools in the fifth grade, but we knew we would be playing local schools like McCulloch, Washington and Evans in the sixth grade.

When we got to the sixth grade it was such a thrill for any boy to be told by Mr. Hubbard, "You're going to dress for the next game." I remember the excitement of getting a uniform for the first time. They were blue and white, the school colors for Horace Mann.

Anticipation was great on game days as we waited for the teacher to say, "OK, you boys playing basketball today may leave for the game now." That meant if you were going to play you had permission to leave school about an hour early to travel to the school where we would be playing. It was a treat to be able to get out of school early as others stayed behind.

We didn't practice or play over the Christmas break at that young age. My parents decided to visit my mother's sister in Clarksdale, Mississippi. The thing I recall most about this visit was my aunt raised her voice to me because I opened the door of a store for a black woman who was carrying some Christmas packages. My aunt said, "You don't do that down here." I was never told why I shouldn't do that, it was like it was some big secret or something. I was shocked since I was rather certain I had opened doors for black women back in Marion. My parents had taught me to open doors and let women go first. While in Clarksdale I remember noticing signs above water fountains and bathrooms that said "colored" or "whites only." Such signs were noticeable when we stopped to get gas.

Back in Marion I think this is when I started to become more aware of the subtle way blacks were discriminated against. As youngsters we were now old enough that parents would take us to the Paramount or Indiana theatres in downtown Marion and come back and pick us up when the movie was over. One time I remember seeing some black kids I knew sitting in the balcony of the theatre. Of course, I came to find out later that the balcony was the *only* place the blacks could sit and that bothered me. I know I began to wonder why blacks and whites could drink out of the same water fountain at Horace Mann and Martin Boots and why black and white boys could take showers together after basketball practice, but could not sit together downstairs in a theatre. I was confused about how society treated blacks in Clarksdale as compared to Marion, but both towns seemed intent on making life somewhat unpleasant for black people.

In Marion, basketball teams were built with careful planning. It was important to get little kids playing in front of people. The theory was these future players would not get nervous at the high school level when they had to play week in and week out against the best teams in the state and in front of people in the largest high school gyms in the world. At the time I lived in Marion the high school gym, known as the Marion Memorial Coliseum, held 5,500 people. Muncie Central's gym could seat over 6,500. We were told it was one of the largest high school gyms in the *world*. Anderson had about 4,400 seats in the "Wigwam" for its famous Indian teams and Kokomo wasn't far behind in seating capacity. These gyms were like temples to players and fans. Attendance at games was almost like a ritual with tickets at a premium in every town. Hoosier Hysteria had taken hold everywhere.

Each year the sixth grade teams in Marion got to play one game on the Coliseum floor. As I remember playing in my sixth grade season I was playing in and out of the line-up and was not certain I would get to play much when the big game arrived.

Friends like Gary McKillip and John Macadam seemed to be playing the best as we neared the end of the sixth grade season. I don't recall our team record. The main thing I remember was telling myself to keep working hard enough so I would get to play on the big floor. It was the dream of every boy in town just to get a few minutes on that famous floor. We would go to varsity games and stand by the edge of the floor and wait for balls to bounce over to us as the "B" team and varsity warmed up before their games and at half time. It was such a thrill to get a shot and just try to get it up to the goal. The crowd would even cheer when a seventh or eighth grader happened to be strong enough to make one from the corner. This ritual, it seems to me now, was a small part of becoming a Hoosier.

Word finally came down to us from the high school that the Horace Mann sixth grade boys would be playing between the "B" team and the varsity game and again at the half of the varsity game. Everyone knew that a sell out crowd would be in their seats at the half of the varsity game because the Giants were playing well again against the best teams in the state. Besides this, people liked to see the little kids play. You can bet long time fans would be ready with comments like, "Hey, that kid is pretty fast. His cousin was All-State in Kentucky," or, "Looks like we've got some size coming up," or, "Looks like number five has a nice touch on the ball." You can bet also that at least a few fans would say, "Looks like we are going to be pretty good in a few years when these kids are in high school." These type conversations are a big part of Hoosier basketball lore. Fans begin to talk about players coming up and those gone by on a regular basis.

I remember distinctly that the game we would be playing would start right after the "B" team game and right before the varsity game between Marion and Logansport. It would continue at the half of the varsity game. Logansport would be a conference game for Marion.This game would take place in February which was late in the season and just a few weeks before the Indiana high school state basketball tourney would begin.

I know I was rather nervous getting ready to go out on the Marion Memorial Coliseum floor. We had practiced there a few times so surroundings were not entirely new, except for the crowd of people. When we took the floor I remember some empty seats and this was due to the fact that the varsity game was still about a half-hour away. As we began to play I remember how big the floor looked as compared to Martin Boots where we usually practiced. I made a basket and heard the crowd roar. It is something I will never forget, but it even got more exciting the second half because when we returned to the floor the gym was filled to its 5,500 capacity because every Giant fan and a few from Logansport were in their seats. I made a basket in this half and cannot believe even to this day how much noise that crowd of people made. It had to be the most exciting thing that had happened to me up to that time in my life. I have no doubt that this is when I became a Hoosier or at the very least if I was not a Hoosier I was certain that I wanted to be able to call myself one.

Adding to the noise in the gym was the rather famous Booster Club made up of girls from Marion High School. This cheer block numbered eleven girls across and eleven rows deep. It was quite a thing to behold as they sat in their short-sleeved gold and purple jersey sweaters. Win or lose, these girls made certain the gym was filled with noise and for a sixth grader to hear their voices in unison only added to the excitement a basketball game in Marion could bring.

It was not a good time for some of my friends. Gary McKillip, my good friend to this day, was one of our better players and he did not make a basket, which was a dream of every kid. After the game I saw Gary sitting on the locker room floor with his hands over his face, probably in tears. I mention this just to show how important doing well in basketball is in Indiana even at such a young age. I remember Gary telling me that his dad promised to give him a quarter for every basket he made and he was disgusted with himself. Parents often put pressure on kids and sometimes it didn't help.

The year 1947 was a good one for sports around Marion and the nation. It was in April of that year that a black baseball player by the name of Jackie Robinson broke the color barrier in the major leagues by taking the field for the Brooklyn Dodgers. The taunts and insults Jackie Robinson received made it clear that America had not learned much from reports about how the great Olympian, Jesse Owens, was discriminated against while he attended Ohio State University in Columbus, Ohio.

In the 1940s and 1950s athletes in sports who were African-Americans did more than their share for America in helping to break down prejudice, bias and misinformed attitudes concerning black/white relations. These years were especially rough times for black people and the successes, the courage and outstanding personalities of Jesse Owens and Jackie Robinson helped to lay the ground work to better relations in the years ahead. Looking back, young Hoosiers of that era can now only imagine what kind of treatment basketball stars like "Jumping Johnny" Wilson, Bill Garrett and Emerson Johnson endured while playing for their schools in Indiana.

There is no question whatsoever that 1947 was a very formative year for me. The roar of the crowd I heard after making two baskets on the Coliseum floor and the Giants going to the state finals were enough to immerse any boy into Hoosier Hysteria. I was also beginning to become more aware, at the age of eleven, about the bigotry and hatred present in the culture in which I was growing up.

One other event in my life played almost as big a part as the ones just mentioned. While walking home from the house of a friend in late summer of 1947 I ran into Dick Weagley who did not live too far from me. Dick had just played in the Indiana-Kentucky All-Star game. I have no idea what we talked about as we walked, but I do remember how big a thrill it was to talk to one of the best players in the state of Indiana. I just remember how nice he was to me and thinking about what it would be like to be as good a player as Dick Weagley. I knew at that moment I had to do my best to become the best basketball player I could be. I began to dream more about playing for the Marion Giants and even being good enough to earn a college scholarship and play at a major college in Indiana. I now know that such a dream was commonplace for boys growing up in Indiana.

CHAPTER TWO
Marion Wins! Marion Wins!

"I HAD PRETTY GOOD SUCCESS PLAYING ON AND COACHING NCAA CHAMPIONSHIP TEAMS. I'VE BEEN INVOLVED IN MANY WAYS. BUT THERE'S NOTHING THAT QUITE COMPARES TO PLAYING ON AN INDIANA HIGH SCHOOL TEAM. THE FINAL FOUR IN COLLEGE BASKETBALL ... IT JUST DOESN'T COMPARE WITH THE INDIANA HIGH SCHOOL TOURNAMENT." (JOHN WOODEN)

The above quotation by John Wooden should be enough to convince most people that playing basketball in Indiana was something special. Those who never got to experience the thrills of which coach Wooden is talking about can only dream about what it was like to take part in such hysteria.

Still pursuing the thrill of playing, I moved on to the seventh grade at Martin Boots Jr. High School for the 1948-49 school year. It seems to me I played everyday in the summer. Basketball camps didn't exist back then and we didn't get much coaching. Any help we got in learning the game came from neighborhood men who had played the game. Don Gilbreath lived down the street and took an interest in me. Don had played basketball in high school. He was interested in teaching me some skills. I did all I could to get my parents to put in an asphalt court in front of our garage behind the house. My parents were not poor, but I know at times money was rather tight. An asphalt court was almost out of the question, so Mr. Gilbreath asked my dad if he could pay for it. I think they saw my intense interest in basketball and decided the best

17

way to encourage me was to build the court. It was a nice court, probably one of the best in town and friends began to show up almost every evening for games. We were all so thankful we had a friend in the community like Don Gilbreath.

It was about this time in my life when the Sutter family moved in next door to us on West 6th St. Jack and Jean became good friends with my family. Jack's family owned Sutter's Dairy in Marion. Jack stood well over six feet. He had been a good player at Marion High School and he knew the game. He would play with us, but he worked long hours at the dairy and his time to help us was limited.

Martin Boots Jr. High was different in that we did not have the same teacher all day long. We began to socialize with other students in the hallway and cafeteria. The school was integrated and black and white students got along well with each other. Of course, being in Indiana we were allowed to play basketball in the gym during lunch in the winter and played on the outdoor court in good weather. The games in the gym were known to all concerned as "the noon league." We would be placed on or form our own teams and Mr. Hubbard would make out weekly schedules and watch us play. I really think this was the first real intense competition we had. It was not difficult to figure out that a lot of boys were working hard so they might have a chance to play at Marion High School.

Everyone knew that a boy had to be good enough as a seventh grader to make the eighth grade team. At least the school team was called the "seventh and eighth grade team." I do not remember much at all about playing basketball the seventh and eighth grade year. The most exciting thing was Martin Boots played all of its games at Memorial Coliseum. The seventh and eighth grade game was held first followed by the ninth grade game. A few people, probably mostly parents and friends, would show up to watch the games. This arrangement made playing more exciting, but we did not get to play in front of the big crowd as we did in the sixth grade. However, we played big schools from Muncie and other well known basketball towns.

Gary McKillip and John Macadam were still playing and I became a friend with Ed Thurman, who was my first African-American friend. He was a good player and could run like a deer. In one-eighth grade game we were all playing in a referee called a foul on me right after someone on our team had missed a free throw. I was clear at the other end of the floor as one person had to stay back for defense. I went up to the ref and said, "Sir, that foul could not have been on me because I was at the other end of the floor." The ref must have been a local guy because he said, "Jonesie, don't learn to blame your fouls on your teammates." It was the first bad call by a ref I could remember, but it wouldn't be the last.

The thing I remember most about the eighth grade team was we got to travel. We called it "getting to go out of town." It was a big deal in junior high basketball in Indiana if someone asked, "Are you going out of town?" That meant you were on the traveling squad, a well thought of prize as boys started out in Hoosier Hysteria. We would travel by school bus. We had to pack our uniforms and the trips created fond memories because we got to eat at the Hill Top restaurant on return. It wasn't far from school and was a favorite hang out of kids. If you were in this selected group you were a source of envy and still alive as far as having a chance to fulfill dreams and play basketball at Marion High School. This process took place in almost every community in Indiana.

I was in and out of the lineup in the eighth grade. I think I got to be a starter in a few games, but I sure don't recall setting the world afire. I would make a basket once in awhile and I felt as though I was getting better, more confident with every game and took them very seriously. The next year would be my freshman year and it was nearly impossible to make the high school team if you were not a starter on a freshman team in Marion. Plus move-ins were not uncommon as families learned of the success of the Marion Giants.

In the 1949-50 season the Marion Giants were again a threat to beat any team in the state. Watching this team play was even more exciting than watching the team of 1947 that went to the Final Four. The team had great high school players. Pat Klein was the team leader and there was a sophomore sensation named Jim Barley and another good sophomore named Chet Jones who was black. Norm Edwards and Francis Fisher had established themselves as Marion players who would be remembered as did Bob Casey, who was also black. Other good players were Ed Bick, John Banter, Dean Vogel and Ronnie Montgomery filled out the roster.

I understood basketball better and could learn a great deal by watching the games. Great players on other highly ranked teams would have their names well known in Marion before ever taking the floor at the Coliseum. My friends and I were able to attend most games and became attached to the team. The Giants romped through the Sectional and Regional and won the always difficult Semi-State at the spacious Muncie Central Fieldhouse. We were going down state again and the town was delirious. As in 1947 banners were in every store. At

Martin Boots it was more exciting because students would display all forms of booster items. Anything with gold and purple would do as these colors were the colors of the high school team. It was a proud moment for those of us on a team as people expected us to be the next Giants…the next Marion team to go to Indianapolis and make the community proud.

As was customary, a drawing was held at the Coliseum for tickets to go down state. This time however, television was much more common around town and somehow the city fathers made it possible for TV sets to be set up at the Coliseum for the Saturday afternoon game pitting Marion against Madison's Cubs. An Indianapolis channel had been carrying Indiana University games and would carry the finals of the high school tournament. Madison had lost the state final game by one point to Jasper the year before and returned several good players from that team. Now known throughout the state were Spence Schnaitter and Ted Server. Madison promised to be a tough opponent for Marion just as Terre Haute Garfield had been in beating the Giants in 1947.

On the Saturday Marion Giant fans will never forget the Coliseum was jammed with mostly students as parents stayed home to watch the game on their television sets. It was a party atmosphere as the Giants took the floor. The game was close all afternoon long and finally near the end sophomore sensation Jim Barley took a shot with Marion trailing 50-49. He missed, but the referee quickly called Madison's fine center, Spence Schnaitter, with interfering with the net. The ref ruled the shot good and the score board showed Marion 51-Madison 50. The announcer screamed, Marion wins! Marion wins! Wid and I went crazy and ran out of the Coliseum to meet my dad who was to pick us up. We had to get dinner and get right back to the Coliseum for the championship game that evening.

As we got in the car my dad said, "What are you so happy about, Marion lost?" We couldn't believe it and at first thought my dad was teasing us. He explained the referees got together and changed the decision on basket tampering. Marion had, indeed, lost 50-49. This score is indelibly etched in the minds of anyone who saw the Giants go down to defeat. It is especially difficult to swallow because Madison routed Lafayette Jefferson in the final game 67-44. The Cubs were led by Schnaitter and Server, both of whom made the All-Star team.

Pat Klein scored 22 points against Madison and Norm Edwards had 13. Pat's performance was the best of all Final Four players. As things turned out Marion ended up as one of the top two or three teams in the state. Fans in that era, a great one for Indiana basketball, will always remember how close the Giants came to the coveted state title.

It was never known to a lot of people in Marion, but the two black players on the team, Chet Jones and Bob Casey, were not allowed to stay with the team in an Indianapolis hotel. These two players were forced to stay in private homes. The subtle discrimination was kept silent and in deep contrast to the publicity teams with black players received when they won. The feeling of being left out and only partially enjoying a team accomplishment is a sad memory for black players in Indiana. They suffered through racism and prejudice as they participated in Indiana basketball in what may not have been to them such a Golden Era of Indiana basketball.

In the Marion-Madison game two of the best coaches in the state went head to head. They were Woody Weir of Marion and Ray Eddy of Madison. Both coaches were very active on their benches in riding the referees and yelling at players. Many reports down through the years seem to verify that this final was one of the most colorful in Indiana history, mainly because three legendary coaches were there coaching. The other coaching legend was Marion Crawley of Lafayette Jefferson who won four state championships at two different schools. Ray Eddy became the head coach at his alma mater, Purdue University, in September of 1950. He took Indiana All-Star guard Ted Server with him.

To the victor usually belongs the spoils, but not this time. Pat Klein of Marion was awarded the coveted Arthur Trester Award. Mr. Trester was the Indiana High School Athletic Association Commissioner from 1925 to 1944 and was a very well respected figure in the state. The award was given to the player in the Final Four who displayed the best mental attitude. It is still an honor for a player to receive this award. On top of this honor Pat Klein was named Mr. Basketball in the spring of 1950. He deserved the honor after leading Marion to Indianapolis and his great performance against a fine Madison team. Pat won both of the most coveted honors a high school athlete can receive in the state of Indiana. Pat Klein would become a legend and his accomplishments helped inspire Marion boys to become as good as players as they could become.

Even after basketball season was over we continued to play indoors until it became too hot to stay inside and play noon league games. My friends and I would gobble down a hamburger and usually a chocolate milk in the school cafeteria and head for the gym. Games would not last long, but it was good practice. Everyday I went to school I would check to see who might be absent so I could take their place and maybe play two games. I would give up lunch to play two games.

There is little doubt that the success of the Marion Giants in 1947 and in 1950 created such excitement that every boy with much coordination at all at least wanted to find out if he could play the game. As a result, playing in the noon leagues, after school and in the summers was the thing to do if a boy wanted to have a chance to become a Giant.

In the summer of 1950 Pat Klein played in the Indiana-Kentucky All-Star game. Pat scored six points and helped Indiana beat Kentucky 70-57. He played against Frank Selvy from Corbin, Kentucky. Selvy made only one point in this game, but later, in 1954 he scored 100 points for Furman University which is a Division 1 record that still stands in the NCAA. Pat Klein went on to Indiana University, but never played in a varsity game. He came back and worked in Marion the rest of his life.

Pat Klein's sweep of awards in Indiana basketball solidified the identity of Marion as one of Indiana's premier basketball communities. Marion's tournament success brought increased competition among boys in junior highs throughout Marion in the summer of 1950. The next basketball season would be a very important one for those dreaming about becoming a Giant. More courts sprang up and games were easy to find, especially behind my house on West 6th Street. Al Harker, who was a player and friend on the eighth grade team didn't live far from me and he would walk over and we would play one-on-one, the game of 21 or "horse." More often than not, we would have enough to play three-on-three and this was good competition. Most scoring plays in a basketball game do not involve more than two or three players so we got in a lot of good practice.

Larry "Wid" Mathews was beginning to play again and he had a goal at his house, but it was a dirt court. Wid had been hit by a truck in the fifth grade in front of Dave's Shell Station which was owned by Gary McKillip's dad. Wid's leg was still stiff, but he could play and we spent hours together on the courts. He was tall and I had to work to get a shot off.

I used to coax two guys to play me because they could make it tough to drive or get off shots. I did this with my brother and friends of his like Larry Uptegraft, John Knipple or Jim Aldrich who lived close by. Many days I played alone trying to develop shots, working on dribbling or shooting free throws. I learned early on how to get the proper spin and arc on a shot and how to use the backboard.

As mentioned before, professional basketball had problems getting started in Indiana and around the country for that matter. Much of the delay was due to the discriminatory practices of hotel and restaurant owners. Pro ball had been mostly of the barnstorming variety or of leagues that would start up and then fold. Games were held in old armories or even dance halls. There is little doubt that the excitement about the sport created at the high school and college level in Indiana helped to solidify a place for the pros in Indiana.

During my eighth grade year, in 1949-50, I was looking to read anything I could about basketball and news centering around the development of the NBA was on Indianapolis television channels or in the newspapers. My folks had bought a TV set by then, but of course everything was in black and white as color TV was only dreamed about at that time. The NBA started playing games in three cities in Indiana in November of 1949, but not many games were televised.

I can remember talking to anyone I knew with a drivers license and a car to take me to games to see the Indianapolis Olympians, the Anderson Packers or the Ft. Wayne Zollners play. A man named Claude Rude was real good about those kinds of things. He took a lot of my friends and I to professional and college games. "Rudy" worked at Meadow Gold, a teen hang out. I saw my first NBA game in Anderson, Indiana in the winter of 1950. It is also a vivid picture for me seeing the world champion Ft. Wayne Zollner Pistons play in Ft. Wayne, but there was a story about the NBA developing in Indiana that should never be forgotten. It concerned the development of the Indianapolis Olympians NBA franchise that played at Butler Fieldhouse. The team was formed in the following way.

In the late 1940s the University of Kentucky was dominating college basketball. Coached by the famed Adolph Rupp, the Wildcats from Lexington, Kentucky zipped to a 34-2 record in 1946, but lost in the NIT finals. Names never to be forgotten by basketball fans living in the exciting basketball era of the 1940s and 1950s were on this team. They were: Ralph Beard and Wha Wha Jones who helped Kentucky beat Indiana in the Indiana vs. Kentucky high school All-Star game in 1945. Alex Groza, Cliff Barker and Joe Holland rounded out the starting five. In 1947-48 the all white team won the NCAA tournament.

NBA owners took great interest in the Kentucky stars when they won the NCAA tournament, but even more interest when they won the Olympic games in London before returning to college ball as seniors. They lost only one game their last year in college. A strange twist of fate took place when highly favored

Kentucky seemed to go stale and they lost to Loyola of Chicago in the finals of the prestigious NIT in Madison Square Garden in New York City. It was one of the biggest upsets in college basketball history.

Despite the shocking loss in the NIT the owners of the NBA teams thought the Kentucky lads were so good they offered them a chance to play as unit in the NBA. The owners, rightfully so as it turned out, thought the team would be a great drawing card around the NBA and especially in the mid-west where many teams held franchises in the NBA. The Kentucky players gratefully accepted salaries and an offer to play home games in Butler Fieldhouse in Indianapolis where they would become known as the Indianapolis Olympians. Indianapolis then became the third city in Indiana to sponsor a team in the up and coming NBA.

The Olympians were named such because of their gold medal performance in London. Their uniforms would reflect the red, white and blue colors of the American flag. The words of one historian should reflect the impact the team had on the state of Indiana and the city of Indianapolis:

> "I think the Indianapolis Olympians are one of the greatest stories of all times in professional basketball. It's like a classic American myth. Five college buddies go out and form their own team so they can stay together ... and they were incredibly successful. They really took the city of Indianapolis by surprise."

The Olympians sold out the nearly 15,000 seats in Butler Fieldhouse which was considered the best place to play in the NBA at the time. The team went 39-25 and won the Western Division of the NBA...*all as rookies*. I watched every game I could as the team beat Sheboygan in the play-offs, but lost to the Anderson Packers. The Olympians became the shot in the arm the NBA needed and professional basketball was off and running in Indiana.

As the NBA caught on, battles between teams took place for talented players. Nate "Sweetwater" Clifton was a tremendous basketball talent. He was an African-American playing for the Harlem Globetrotters. The Trotters, or Globies as some fans called them, were now a big attraction around the country. The Trotters knew if good black players were ever allowed to play in the NBA it would cost the Trotters more to sign them and make the team more difficult to maintain. The NBA owners didn't want to upset the fame the Globetrotters were bringing to pro basketball, but finally it was decided business was business. The New York Knickerbockers extended a contract offer to "Sweetwater" Clifton.

On May 25, 1950, a headline in the *New York Times* read: "Clifton, Negro Ace, Goes to Knickerbocker Five."

Actually the NBA signed three black players in 1950, but none on the Indiana teams. Besides "Sweetwater" the Boston Celtics signed 6'5" Chuck Cooper out of Duquesne and the Washington Capitols signed Earl Lloyd, a 6'6" forward from West Virginia State. Lloyd is, to this day, considered the first black to play in the NBA, but only because his team opened the season a day earlier than Clifton's and Cooper's. There wasn't the fanfare that followed Jackie Robinson when he broke the color barrier in Major League Baseball three years before. Baseball was, and still is, the national pastime so black players in the NBA sort of sneaked into the NBA so to speak. However, those black players did face hard times with the bigotry and prejudice. The following statement is borrowed from a historical account of the NBA to show how bigotry and hatred were still very much alive in America...and even more so in my home state of Indiana.

> "Clifton, Cooper and Lloyd faced the hardships of racial prejudice on their NBA trip. Even though the three owned contracts worth in the neighborhood of $10,000 each, they still could not eat in many Indiana restaurants when their teams traveled to the Hoosier state. Apparently the game advanced faster than midwestern society in 1950."

Despite the racial issues, the NBA planted roots in Indiana and the Hoosier state can take a great deal of credit for whatever excitement the NBA has brought to the sporting scene in the United States.

Although professional basketball was being promoted in Indiana to the extent that it was difficult not to follow it, I was also keeping my eye on college basketball. Just like most Hoosier boys, I had dreams of playing in college. I watched intently whenever games were on TV and then would practice any moves I saw players make.

Since both Indiana University and Kentucky were making noise in college basketball in the mid-west the newspapers published statistics about teams as well as individual players around the country. I enjoyed reading about players and their achievements. I know I read about a player named Paul Arizin. He played at Villanova University in Philadelphia. I had read where on Feb. 12, 1949 he made 85 points in one game. He was 6'3" and made first team All-American in 1950 after leading the nation in scoring with a 25.3 average for 29 games. The thing that made Arizin unique is he was jumping and shooting the ball over other players. Not even NBA players were shooting jump shots at that time. Remember, Hank Luisetti had introduced the one-hand shot a few years before, but no one could jump and shoot until Paul Arizin came along.

One reporter got Arizin to tell how he never made a team before he graduated from high school. He loved the game so much he continued to not be discouraged and played in church leagues and independent leagues in Philadelphia. The reporter got Arizin to tell what happened while playing on these teams.

> It was during this time that Arizin discovered the jump shot. "It came by accident," he said, "Some of our games were played on dance floors that became quite slippery. When I tried to hook, my feet would go out from under me, so I jumped. I always was a good jumper. My feet weren't on the floor, so I didn't have to worry about slipping. The more I did it, the better I became. Before I knew it, practically all of my shots were jump shots."

Arizin didn't come into the NBA until 1950-51 which would be my freshman year at Martin Boots. I don't remember seeing him play until the 1951-52 season, but I knew he was jumping and shooting. Many of us tried the shot, but could hardly hit the rim, much less make the shot. Almost daily I experimented with the shot on my own, but could never get it off in pickup games. It was somewhat discouraging, but I kept in mind that Paul Arizin never even played in high school.

It is noteworthy that Paul Arizin played the 1951-52 season in the NBA with the Philadelphia Warriors. He was a "territorial draft pick" in those days. He then went into the military service for two years. Upon returning from the Marine Corps he led the Warriors to the NBA title. The next year he won the NBA scoring title. More about Paul Arizin later.

It seemed like a long wait over the summer to get to the basketball season. We did play some baseball and a few Major League games were televised then so we could watch.

A bunch of us went to Gordon Campbell's house right across the street from Horace Mann and Martin Boots and watched on TV the 1950 baseball All-Star game played in Comiskey Park in Chicago. I think it was the first All-Star game ever televised and it was a thrill for my friends and I to see the players we had only listened to on the radio or read about in the newspapers. In that famous game the St. Louis Cardinal's second baseman, Red Schoendienst, hit a home run in the 14th inning and won the game for the National League by a 4-3 score. Schoendienst had sat out the first ten innings because Jackie Robinson had been voted in as the All-Star second baseman. Jackie had overcome many of the jeers and taunts and insulting remarks about his race since he came up with the Brooklyn Dodgers in 1947. However, racial tension existed in many communities.

When school started in August every boy interested in basketball knew it was to be an important year. The two best ninth grade teams would play each other on the Coliseum floor late in the season for the city championship. Woody Weir would be keeping a close eye on players and the junior high school coaches would be working their teams hard to get players ready for the high school team. When boys congregated, the talk was usually about basketball and most were playing almost everyday after school.

Basketball practice finally rolled around. I wondered and worried, since I played in and out of the line up on the eighth grade team, what my chances would be. I wondered how much I had improved over the summer. Boys came in not just from Horace Mann, but from other schools around town. I met Wynston Lynn for the first time. He had attended Evans school and lived just outside Marion. He had an option of where to go to school in Marion so he and his parents chose Martin Boots. We became immediate friends. He lived on a farm and had a basketball goal, but it was not paved so we didn't play there much. Wynston or "Wynn" as everyone called him, was left-handed so this gave me some practice guarding a left-handed person.

As the basketball season began Jim Barley was back as a junior and everyone was excited to see the boys play who were on the team when Marion lost to state champion Madison in the state finals. As freshman headed for the high school next year, we got to go to all the games. It was a busy winter following the varsity and playing our own games at Martin Boots. Some players were cut and their dreams of basketball success exploded.

Basketball became more interesting because now we were running plays. I was playing the guard position and if a pass was made to a forward I had to cut a certain way and the same if I passed to the center. There were more things to remember in freshman ball. I found I had made progress as I started some games, but still considered myself to be only in the top six or seven players. Mr. Hubbard was good about giving playing time so guys had a decent chance to develop their skills. I don't recall our team record, but we were considered the best in Marion. Playing in high school and college was still a dream.

The basketball season was going along OK as we headed for the Christmas break. We did not play or practice during this time in those years. Our family visited relatives in Dallas, Texas. We saw Tennessee beat Texas 20-14 before 68,000 fans in the Cotton Bowl game. It was a good trip for me because I saw Southern Methodist University play basketball and saw how slow and methodical basketball was in the Southwest in those days. The play was uninspiring and solidified for me the thought that I wanted to play in college in Indiana where the game seemed to move at a faster pace.

After returning to Marion my Martin Boots team beat McCulloch Junior High for the city championship on the Coliseum floor. Ed Thurman and Jim Gross helped win that game and I did get significant minutes. McCulloch was on the South Side of Marion and Washington Junior High was on the North Side with Martin Boots being on the West Side. Once again we did travel some and it was a fun season, but as it ended I was still nervous about my chances to make the Giants.

When the season ended I had a chat with Mr. Hubbard and he told me he thought I had a good chance to make the high school team. He said, "I think they are going to like your passing over there." I was surprised and told my dad what Mr. Hubbard had said. My dad said, "I wonder why you didn't play more this year if that is the case?" Three or four players did get more playing time than I did, but nevertheless Mr. Hubbard's comment encouraged me. I knew once again that in the summer months I must improve my skills to have a chance to play at Marion High School. Making the Marion Giant "B" team became the goal. It was, for certain, the goal of many boys in Marion.

As school was about to let out for the summer I remember Mr. Hubbard talking to us in gym class. He had us all lined up and sitting against the gym wall and was going down the line asking each of us what we wanted to do for a job. When he came to me my response was not unlike many Hoosier boys then and now. I said, "I want to play in the NBA."

Somehow that summer two friends of mine, Ed Wilkinson and Jack Caldwell began talking about going to a baseball camp in Salem, Missouri. It was called the Ozark Baseball Camp and the three week camp was run by former Major League ball players. I had turned fifteen years old in June and the camp was to be for boys sixteen years and younger and a separate camp for those over sixteen. I was a little apprehensive about going because I knew this would take away from my time to play basketball and I needed the time to get better. One thing I wanted to know was…did the camp have basketball courts? It did and I was told I would have free time in camp to play. I doubt I would have gone if the camp didn't have basketball courts because I knew I would have to beat out a lot of guys just to make the B team at Marion High School.

I kept thinking it was a mistake to go to the camp and lose practice time, but I also thought that if I didn't make the basketball team I could turn to baseball and maybe do something in that sport. My chances for basketball success were borderline at the time, especially since I was not near being the best player at Martin Boots.

I went to the camp and was able to play basketball at night as the basketball court was lighted and the baseball diamonds were not. I found some competition and thought that I wasn't getting too far behind.

No one can ever know the feelings that went through me when at the end of camp I was told I had made the camp All-Star team for boys sixteen and under. There were over two hundred boys there from thirty-four states and Canada. I was still in shock when I was told that I was to call my folks in Indiana and tell them that I was going to be playing in an All-Star game in Sportman's Park in St. Louis two days after the camp was to end. The camp team of sixteen-year-olds and under would be playing an All-Star team from St. Louis and I would be starting in left field. The game would take place between a St. Louis Browns-Chicago White Sox twi-night doubleheader. I just couldn't believe it. I guess for a few brief moments basketball left my thought processes.

It was unfortunate that my folks were to come and pick us up at the camp. My dad had to get back to Indiana for important work and my brother had to be picked up at a camp in Indiana. I didn't get to play in Sportsman's Park in St. Louis. It was one of the biggest disappointments of my life while growing up in Indiana, but my thoughts turned back quickly to basketball.

On return to Marion I worked hard on basketball, played very little baseball, went swimming at Matter Park pool, did some running and did whatever I could to get in shape. I was getting anxious about the time I would attend my first class and try out for the team at Marion High School. It was getting close to the time where the decision would be made for me regarding what sport would be best for me to follow. I wanted to play basketball for the Marion Giants!

CHAPTER THREE
Not So Tall Giants

*YOU ARE NOT A HOOSIER UNLESS YOU
CAN STAND IN YOUR YARD AND SEE AT
LEAST TWO BASKETBALL HOOPS.*

One of the first things any boy wanting to participate in sports at Marion High School had to learn was that he must sign up for "athletic study hall" the last period of the day. The reason for this was that practice sites were so far away it took a lot of time to get there from the school on the near North Side of Marion. During the season the athlete participated in he would head out for practice instead of going to study hall. The huge Memorial Coliseum was about a fifteen minute walk from the school. I found out I had to make a decision between taking my second year of Spanish or the athletic study hall. I didn't have trouble making the decision, but was concerned that not going on in Spanish could hurt my chances of getting into college and, hopefully, play basketball.

Bob France had moved to my West Side neighborhood from Washington Jr. High School on the North Side and was a year behind me in school as a freshman. Bob seemed a little more dedicated to basketball than some of my other friends so we hit it off right away. We played a lot of one-on-one. Don Gilbreath was helping us learn about basketball. Bob did not make the seventh grade team, but, since he too wanted to become a Giant, he worked hard and came back to play in the eighth grade.

On a sad note, the elderly lady next door to us complained to the police that we were making too much noise on the basketball court and we had to curtail big crowds and late evening games somewhat. When Wid Mathews found out what the lady had done it made him mad. He proceeded to dribble a basketball real loud on her porch when she was sleeping. In Wid's view, disrupting boys from playing basketball was just not acceptable.

Basketball tryouts began in mid-October. Bob "Stormy" Pfohl, who had played for the Baltimore Colts, was the new football coach. He was to be Woody's assistant and would coach the Marion "B" basketball team. Stormy lived about six houses to the west of us and I got to know him a little bit. He became a friend of our neighbors, Jack and Jean Sutter. I was hoping Stormy would see me shooting as he passed by our house and relay the message to Woody Weir that I was working hard at the game.

Tryouts were nervous times to say the least. It seemed like every boy in a high school of some 900 students was trying to make the team. Woody would cut guys real fast who he knew would never be able to play for Marion. The "B" squad was to be cut to about fifteen boys, but only twelve would dress for games. One week before the first game coach Pfohl, maybe accidentally, told the Sutter's that I was going to dress for the first game and they told our family. I was so happy that my practice had paid off and I had made at least the reserve squad of the Marion Giants. As things turned out only five sophomores from Marion's junior high schools made the "B"team. To the surprise of many, Ed Thurman got cut. He had been instrumental in Martin Boots winning the city ninth grade championship. Seven juniors were kept in hopes they could provide some senior experience next year as ten players would be graduating off of the good varsity team. Many boys in Indiana still talk about the day they got cut from school teams.

I know I was filled with pride as we ran a lay-up drill to open the season against Eastern High School which was a little school near Kokomo. Just getting to wear a uniform that said "Giants" across the front gave me a sense of accomplishment. Jim Gross and John Macadam from Martin Boots also made the team.

I don't remember much about the "B" team games as I again played in and out of the line-up. The juniors were getting most of the playing time. The big deal for me was to be in practice everyday and watch the big Giants practice and sometimes even get in scrimmages and play against them. It was exciting being on the same floor with seniors Jim Barley and Chet Jones, who had played in the Indiana state finals as sophomores.

The "B" team traveled everywhere the varsity did and played before the varsity games. We either went in cars or a school bus. We played in many towns in central and north central Indiana. Our conference was named the North Central Conference and was considered by far the toughest in the state. It was comprised of the following schools: Indianapolis Tech, Muncie Central, Anderson, Lafayette, Logansport, Kokomo, New Castle, Frankfort and Richmond.

While on the way to Ft. Wayne to play we ran into a bad snowstorm. There was a bad accident and traffic was tied up. Woody told us to get out of the cars and stretch our legs while the accident was being cleared from the highway. While walking around I saw several really tall guys. I asked if they were basketball players and they said they were traveling with the Philadelphia Warriors of the NBA. They were on their way to play the Ft. Wayne Zollner Pistons. When I asked them their names I was shocked when one player stuck out his hand and said, "I'm Paul Arizin." He then introduced me to Ed Mikan who was the brother of the famous George Mikan. He stood 6'9". I told them how I listened to games on the radio and mentioned to Arizin how I was working on the jump shot and having trouble perfecting it. He said, "Keep working, it will come around."

It was so neat meeting some professional players. I followed Arizin's career to the end. His second year he led the NBA in scoring with a 25 point average and was MVP in the league All-Star game. The next two years he went into the Marine Corps, but on return he led the NBA in scoring and helped the Warriors win a NBA championship. He was one of the all time great players in NBA history as he averaged 22 points a game for his career. Paul Arizin was a good role model for getting the point across to young players to never give up on their dreams. Remember, Arizin never made a team until he got out of high school. To become skilled enough to lead the NBA in scoring was quite an accomplishment. He should have been born in Indiana! I kept his desire to play in the back of my mind as I tried to improve as a player...and accomplish my dream.

Our "B" team, also known as "The Little Giants" was so-so and the varsity, playing one of the toughest schedules in the state, finished 10-10 and in eighth place in North Central Conference. In this 1951-52 season, Jim Barley broke every record at Marion High School. He scored 30 points in one game. Fellow Giant Mickey Barton told me after that game, "If you're hungry, sit beside Jim at the restaurant because he won't eat much." Jim played so hard during his career he couldn't eat after games. He scored 490 points in his senior season and 1015 for three years. He also set a North Central Conference scoring record of 221 points in his senior year. In one classic confrontation, he went head to head with Joe Sexson at Indianapolis Tech. Sexson was to become Mr.

Basketball, but Jim was not awed by him. While holding the ball on his hip as Tech stalled out a lead, Sexson smiled at Barley as if to taunt him. Sexson knew Jim was leading the conference in scoring with only three conference games to go. As Tech stalled out the lead to beat Marion, Jim flipped Sexson the bird and our fans went crazy.

During a scrimmage a day or so before the Sectional opened, I sneaked in behind Chet Jones of the varsity and, as luck would have it, a rebound came right to me near the basket and I put it in without coming down. Woody chewed out Chet saying to him, "How can you let a little guy like that do that to you." I'll never forget that moment. I was pleased that at least I had shown Woody I was not afraid to get in there with the bigger guys. I was only about 5'8" at the time and weighed just a little over a hundred pounds. I thought to myself, "If Chet doesn't kill me after practice, I might be able to play for the Marion Giants someday."

The Giant varsity got better real quick and provided tournament thrills for Marion fans as Jim Barley and Chet Jones led the team through the Sectional and Regional. Help came by Phil Linville, Bob Casey, Bob Gowin, Mickey Barton, Andy Wycoff, Don Weber, Eddie Hacker, Tom Archey, Roger Rix and Norm Carter. They lost to Kokomo in the Sweet Sixteen at Muncie Fieldhouse. Muncie Central beat Kokomo 62-60 and went on to win the state championship for the second year in a row. Marion finished the season with a 15-11 record. The Giants once again ended the season making a good run at the state title. The school was gaining state-wide respect for its basketball.

I ended the season thinking I had progressed quite a bit as a player as I got in most of the games and many scrimmages. I thought my chances looked good to make the varsity for my junior season, but I knew I would have to get better in the summer months if I was to get significant playing time. I knew I would have to get better on my own as it was against the rules for coaches to offer any help before the next season started.

Even though the school year went well in our integrated school every once in awhile I would hear about racial issues that would be confusing to me. While growing up in Marion I know I learned that black kids often walked to school in the alleys because white people would put their dogs in front of their houses and make them bark at the black kids as they walked by each day. Once in awhile there would be rumors that some black kids were going to try to get in Marion's well known Matter Park swimming pool and they were told they would not be served in restaurants. For some of us who were friends with the black kids, it was hard to understand what was behind keeping them out of the pool and restaurants, especially since we ate lunches together during the school year in the high school cafeteria. It was a rather well known fact around central Indiana that black kids could go to the famous Tee Pee drive-in restaurant in Indianapolis...but only as long as they stayed in the cars.

Near the end of the school year, Jim Barley was named to the Indiana All-Star team and would be playing against Kentucky in Indianapolis in June. Leading the North Central Conference in scoring would be good enough most years to land a player on the All-Star team. In fact, of the twelve players named to the squad in 1952, five were from North Central Conference schools. Fans in Marion, which was nearly everyone, were excited about Jim playing in the All-Star game as it was a source of community pride.

Jim caught some bad luck just before the game. He had his appendix removed in Marion General Hospital and it looked doubtful for a time if he could play. It would be a crushing blow for Jim, or any Hoosier player for that matter, to miss the game most boys in Indiana can only dream about. I went to the hospital to see Jim as a bunch of us had plans to go to Indianapolis to see him play. He told me, "Don't worry, I'll be out there." Even though he was limited on practice time and was a little weak, Jim played and scored four points to help Indiana beat the Kentucky All-Stars 86-82 in what was to be the first overtime game in the classic series. In an oddity in the game coaches were given unlimited time outs because of the heat. The Kentucky coach, Ed Diddle of Western Kentucky University, called thirteen time outs to make it a rather long game. Madison's Maurice Lorenz scored 25 points and was named Star-of-Stars.

Jim Barley received a scholarship to play basketball at Indiana University. Marion basketball fans were excited about Jim playing for the Hoosiers. His success served to motivate me to play in college. Jim is enshrined in the Indiana Basketball Hall of Fame.

During my first year at Marion High School, especially during the cold weather, I stayed home nights to study and listen to professional and college games. In most of the games either the Ft. Wayne Zollners, the Indianapolis Olympians or Indiana University would be playing. Television was still in its infant stages. We could get good reception form the Indianapolis channel, but Bloomington TV was usually fuzzy.

During this basketball season the Anderson Packers had financial problems and had to drop out of the NBA. Indiana still had two teams in the league and my friends and I attended games when we could. In the early part of the 1951-52 NBA season most of the Olympians took a side trip to watch the upcoming Rochester Royals of the NBA play a college All-Star team in the Chicago Stadium on Oct. 19th. After the game, detectives arrested Ralph Beard, Alex Groza and two other Olympians and took them to the Cook County Courthouse for questioning about fixing games while they were playing on the great teams at Kentucky. Beard and Groza were asked about the 1949 first round NIT tournament game against Loyola at Madison Square Garden in New York. As readers recall, this was one of the biggest upsets in college basketball history.

Ralph Beard and Alex Groza were the type players who could control a game and it was proven that gamblers approached them to fix the big NIT game. In the end, gamblers testified they paid the players large sums of money to keep the spread of the Kentucky-Loyola game under eleven points. Beard and Groza denied they did anything in the game to alter the score. Rumors of the two players fixing outcomes of other Kentucky games surfaced and they did admit they took money from the gamblers. Those in basketball who had to make the decisions about what to do with the two famous Olympians decided that their taking the money was unjustified. Years later, in a public television interview, Ralph Beard stated:

> "As long as I live, I will never forget October 19, 1951. The whole thing was so confusing to me at the time. But I told all those policemen the truth, which was that I never did anything to adversely influence the score of a basketball game. As God is my witness, I can tell you that. Yes, I took the money. But I never shaved points or did anything like that. I just couldn't. I wanted to win too much. I know some people may call me a liar, and I guess God and I will only know the truth. But the money meant nothing to me. I would not, and could not, shave points in that Loyola game."

To this day the story of the two famous Olympians is one of the most controversial in sports history. Ralph Beard and Alex Groza were banned from the NBA for life...at the ripe age of twenty-three.

The betting scandal helped to start the decline of the Indianapolis Olympians. The team signed a terrific scorer out of Butler University by the name of Ralph "Buckshot" O'Brien in an attempt to bolster local interest. The league did all it could to help supply players to the team. It wasn't enough as the team decided to call it quits at the end of the 1952-53 season. Now the state of Indiana had only one team in the NBA... the Ft.Wayne Zollner Pistons.

After watching Jim Barley in the All-Star game, the rest of the summer was spent playing with sophomore to be Bob France and friends as we worked hard to get ourselves in position to play basketball in the 1952-53 season. When school began there were some unfamiliar faces in the halls of Marion High School and rumors circulated that some good players had moved to Marion. Also, there were some good sophomores. I began to sweat a little bit if my longed for position on the varsity was going to be there or not.

Practice began in mid-October, but it was mainly running for returning players to get in shape. If anyone had any ambitions of making the team it was wise to do some running before school started. We had to report to the Coliseum everyday after school. Woody had set up a five-mile route for us to run from the Coliseum, across the Mississinewa River at the Washington Street bridge, out River Road to near Matter Park, cross a river bridge again and take Washington Street back to the Coliseum. Training was going well until one-day word circulated around school that Woody had caught two players smoking at the Meadow Gold, which was a hangout like Hill Top for kids on the West Side of town. Woody let it be known he didn't want any smoking even out of season. Coaches sought every way they could to get an advantage on opponents.

When we went to practice that day Woody was not looking very happy. It wasn't hard to tell when he was upset about something. He named the two players who were smoking and they were there on this foggy and somewhat chilly day. He shocked everyone when he told the two he was going to drive his car the route he had set up for us to run. The two smokers were to *run in front of his car between the headlights.* The rest of the team was told to keep up by running behind the car.

I was a little intimidated watching and listening to Woody yell at the two in front of his car and telling them if they didn't run fast enough he would run over them. He did this all the way out to the turn back point which was probably about two and a half miles. When he got the two boys back to the Coliseum he kicked them off of the team. If a coach did something like that today he would probably be accused of harassment and hauled into court. Woody had built up a winning program in Marion and his word was gospel. He could get away with such strong discipline methods and many parents supported such authoritarian actions.

I went home and told my dad about what happened. He said, "What does that tell you?" I said, "It tells me that if I want to play basketball I better never smoke." I don't think I even went close to Meadow Gold for two weeks after Woody's tirade. Also, I never smoked a cigarette in my life. Years later my wife and I attended a wedding in Marion and Woody was there. When he walked into the church I said to my wife, "There is the reason I don't smoke."

Woody decided to keep four seniors, only two of whom had played on the varsity the year before. Those two were Bobby Gowin, a good all-around athlete and an African-American named Tom Archey. Tom was more known for his cross-country and track ability than basketball. A good athlete by the name of Jim Gross and I were the only juniors. Six sophomores rounded out the team. We were going to be very inexperienced and would have to grow up quickly to compete in the North Central Conference.

The basketball season began a lot better than it ended up as we beat a little school, Eastern of Howard County, 53-39. We did not get too far into the season when Woody began to have problems with a couple of senior boys. One game Woody inserted three sophomores into the line-up and took out the seniors. A father of one of the senior players came to the bench area and started arguing with Woody. A fight broke out involving the player, his dad and Woody. It was a mess as people had to break them up. I think the incident shows just how important playing time in Hoosier Hysteria was to some people. Many parents overrated the ability of their sons and took it out on the coach when the boys didn't get to play. I suspect such scenes were not limited to Marion basketball.

The player involved in the melee either was kicked off the team or quit. A couple of seniors got caught drinking. It was almost unheard of for seniors to play on the "B" team, but Woody played a couple of them there just to give them a chance. Woody knew he would need senior leadership to be able to compete with a tough Mississinewa team come Sectional time. His experiment didn't work out as the players just didn't care about basketball. Most students at the high school knew a couple of the seniors were staying out late, not training and generally not interested in basketball. The attitude problems affected the team and a long losing streak took place before Christmas.

Adding to Hoosier Hysteria in this era, the Ft. Wayne Zollner Pistons were winning consistently and a new arena opened for them in September of 1952. We were to play in the arena in a four team New Years Day tourney at what was later named the Ft. Wayne Allen County War Memorial Coliseum. Everyone on the team was excited about getting to play on the same floor where the NBA Zollner Pistons played. In this tourney the two top ranked teams in the state were to play. We were to play the No #1 ranked Muncie Central

Bearcats and Ft. Wayne South Side was to play the No #2 ranked Richmond Red Devils.

In what had to be one of the most embarrassing games for a Marion team, Muncie beat us 91-38. Do the math, that's a fifty-three point differential! Muncie had won the Indiana state championship the previous two years and was favored to make it three in a row. I played in the game some, but mostly sat on the bench and watched the slaughter. General Custer had a better chance against the Indians than we had against Muncie. I distinctly remember one of our forwards coming off the defensive board with the ball. He took one dribble and All-Star guard to be Charlie Hodson of Muncie stole the ball and laid it in the basket. In fact both of Muncie's guards, Hodson and Jerry Lounsbury, would later be named to the Indiana All-Star team that beat Kentucky 71-66 in June

This holiday tourney was played all in one day on January 1st before the football bowl games became popular on TV. We played Muncie in the afternoon and Richmond easily defeated Ft. Wayne South Side. We lost to Ft. Wayne that night in the consolation game and Muncie was to take on Richmond in the title game. The beautiful arena, with a big, brightly lighted scoreboard hanging overhead, seated about 10,000 and it was sold out for both sessions and two thousand more fans were outside trying to get in. Muncie beat Richmond that night to maintain their No #1 ranking and remained there most of the year.

Although the Indiana University Hurryn' Hoosiers were the talk of the state, the NBA was causing excitement in this magical era of basketball in Indiana. The state of Indiana was once again going to participate in basketball history as the annual NBA All-Star game was to be played in the Ft. Wayne Memorial Coliseum. It was the first NBA game to be broadcast from coast to coast by radio. Two well known NBA announcers broadcast the game. One was the play by play man for the New York Knicks, Marty Glickman. The other was the well-respected Hilliard Gates, who broadcast games for the Ft. Wayne Zollner Pistons.

It is interesting to note that an article appeared in the *Ft. Wayne Journal-Gazette* before the NBA All-Star game and it told about how the crowd would be close to 10,000, the largest ever in Ft. Wayne. The governor of Indiana declared the week of the All-Star game in Ft. Wayne as Indiana Basketball Week and reporters flocked to the city. Evidently the Ft. Wayne reporters didn't remember the Muncie Central-Richmond high school game which was played in the Coliseum on January 1, 1953, just twelve days before the NBA

All-Star game was to take place. Having played in the Coliseum at that time, I know I was told that over two thousand fans stood outdoors in the cold trying to get tickets to the classic match-up of the #1 and #2 ranked high school teams in the state. Everyone knew that high school basketball was still king in Indiana.

By the 1952-53 season the Minneapolis Lakers, named for the cargo shippers on the Great Lakes, had acquired the contract of George Mikan and were running roughshod over their NBA opponents. The league even changed the rules and widened the lane in an attempt to slow down the powerful Mikan.

I followed intently as the Ft. Wayne Zollner Pistons added to the glory days of Indiana basketball because they became thorns in the sides of the mighty Lakers. In 1953 they met in the playoffs. In hard fought battles, the Lakers still managed to beat the Pistons and then beat the New York Knicks to win the NBA title. Professional basketball was making its mark in Indiana and the new Ft. Wayne Coliseum added a great deal of excitement for the hysterical basketball fans in the state. The early 50s were truly great years for Indiana basketball and I'm positive this helped to fuel my interest in playing.

When the regular high school season resumed in mid-January Muncie beat Richmond again, but Richmond got even in the state tourney by upsetting Muncie to advance to the Final Four. The Richmond team featured a black player named Lamar Lundy who later became a member of the Fearsome Foursome of the Los Angeles Rams football team after an All-American career at Purdue. Wayne Van Sickle was a good shooter for Richmond and later became a star at Ball State University. Lundy joined Hodson and Lounsbury on the Indiana All-Star team in June.

One of the things that made this season not so memorable was that we had to play Muncie and Richmond again. I don't remember much about the Muncie game. In the Richmond game in Marion late in the season Woody put me in the game. I lined up right beside the 6'7" Lundy on a free throw attempt. When the ball came off of the rim Lamar got it and dunked it. Dunks were rare then. I had not seen a dunk in a high school game and seldom if ever in college. It is a moment I will never forget as it stunned me a little.

The Giant season moved into February and Bob France and I were getting to play more because the seniors, except for Gowin and Archey, were just not getting the job done. Even at that, Woody stuck with them far longer than most people thought he should have. It even became embarrassing for the

GROWING UP IN INDIANA
41

players after awhile. Fans and maybe even the Booster Club organized a yell that would try to coax Woody to put a player in the game that they thought should be playing. It was a simple yell: "We want Jones! We want Jones! We want Jones!" or, "We want France! We want France!" One of my teammates who didn't get to play much said to me, "They're yelling your name." It was embarrassing for the players, mainly because we all knew Woody would play who he wanted to play. The winning climate built up over the last few years took a beating during this season.

In this, my junior season, I came in off of the bench and made the most of my chances. I scored in double figures a couple of games, but was still in and out of the line- up. One time Woody told me I would be starting the next game against Columbus on a Friday night. It just so happened one of my uncles was going to be in Indianapolis and my mom called him to see if he wanted to come to the game. He had been a good college player, having scored 33 points in a Junior College game in Mississippi and then played a year at Memphis State. He came to the game and the five starters played the entire game...but I wasn't one of them. Of course, I didn't say anything to Woody and was thankful my mom didn't either.

In another crazy incident with Woody, we were playing at Lafayette and did manage to pick up our second win in overtime. It would be our last win until the Sectional tourney. Woody was well known around the state for being active around the bench, a very rambunctious sort. He took me out of the game and was giving me some instructions when all of a sudden a referee made a call that really upset him. He had taken off his coat and spread it over the bench. He grabbed his coat and ran out on the court swinging it around. He then came running back, jumped over the bench and swept the coat over my face hitting me in my left eye with a button. My eye became watery and I couldn't see out of it. Of course, Woody then put me in the game and I was running around on the court with one eye nearly closed. I got through the game by turning down shots and passing off a lot.

After playing at Lafayette we spent the night at the Purdue University Student Union. All of us thought we might get to go swimming in the nice pool at Purdue. Woody told us we wouldn't be going swimming as it might soften up our muscles and we would be vulnerable to injuries. Coaches were so protective of players because in Indiana high school basketball winning was everything. Or perhaps they were protective of the black players we had on the team who might not have been allowed to go in the pool because disgraceful racial tensions still existed behind the scenes in most parts of Indiana.

I suspect that we stayed at Purdue because it was a state-supported institution instead of a privately owned hotel. It might have been difficult to find a hotel that would accommodate our African-American players. Former Muncie Central player Phil Raisor verified such racism when he wrote in his memoir, "When we traveled during the season I kept my eyes open. I found that we could only stay in certain hotels or eat at certain restaurants when we went to South Bend or Marion because we had black players."

The 1952-53 basketball season in Marion may have been one of the worst ever for the Giants. Problems with attitudes, poor shooting and not having the poise to win close games made the winter colder than most. We won our first game in the state tourney over little Jefferson Township, but only by a point. That wasn't a sign of good things to come. Mississinewa, located in Gas City, Indiana had developed quickly into a central Indiana powerhouse. They were led by 6'5" Larry Hedden, Martin Burdette and Dick Smith. We met them in the Saturday afternoon game of the Sectional in Marion and they ran us right out of our own Memorial Coliseum. The score was an embarrassing 61-34.

As the season ended, I was confident I could be a starter the next season. I had made all of 75 points during the season, but knew with some senior maturity that I had a chance to meet the goal I had set since the sixth grade when I had made baskets in front of 5,500 people. Somehow I sensed that I would never become a full-fledged Hoosier if I didn't have some success on the basketball court as a varsity player. It would be absolutely imperative that I play all summer and try to get better if I was to become good enough as a senior to be considered for basketball scholarships.

Woody gave Bob France and I each a basketball to use during the summer and told us to, "Wear it out." I felt sorry for Woody during that season because he had some players taking up playing time who were not dedicated. He had underclassmen who could use the playing time and were not getting much. Woody had been very successful in Marion up to this lousy season. He knew the next two years were going to be very important to him. Bob France and I vowed to do our best to help Marion get back on top.

Our season ended well before the college season ended. The 1952-53 season was a great one for Indiana University. They won the Big Ten championship with legendary stars Don Schlundt, a 6'10" center, and guard Bobby "Slick" Leonard. Since Jim Barley was now playing at Indiana, I began to listen to the Hoosier games. Coach Branch McCracken rounded out a good first five with Burke Scott, Dick Farley and Charley Kraak. This Hoosier team went on to

Kansas City for the NCAA finals where Leonard made a free throw late in the game that won the national championship against Kansas University, 69-68. Things were buzzing at Indiana University and around the state since Schlundt and Leonard would both be returning for the 1953-54 season for the team now ranked number #1 in college basketball.

Right at the end of our season Woody told me he wanted me to go out for track and run the mile. He thought it would be good for me when basketball came around next season. I didn't want to do it because it would take up time playing basketball, but I felt as though I better do what the coach was asking me to do. Bob France also ran track so I joined the team. My buddies teased me about my best mile time being "only about one minute off of the world record," but they all knew I was out there because Woody wanted me there. We were all aware that no one had broken the four-minute mile up to that time as it was a track record considered difficult to break for humans.

As summer vacation arrived, Bob Custer opened up a drive-in restaurant on the North Side of Marion and named it Custer's Last Stand. It was one of those places where they had *teletray* service. It became a very popular place to go after playing pick-up games around Marion. To order we needed to just press a button, talk over a micro-speaker and food would be brought out to the car. A hamburger was twenty-five cents, as was a milk shake. Popular breaded tenderloins were thirty cents. Chicken-in-a-box with fries, a salad and a hot roll was only a dollar and sixty cents. It was an ideal hang out for young people. Friends Gary McKillip, Bill Allen and Larry Hickman had cars and Wid, Wynn and Don Melnik and I often chipped in for gas, which was 22 cents a gallon.

One night at Custer's my dedication to basketball almost got me in trouble. Wid Mathews and another friend and I sat in a car and talked with Jim Barley until four o' clock in the morning. We were fascinated with his stories about Indiana University and Big Ten basketball. When I got home my dad was waiting for me and asked where I had been. When I told him I had been talking basketball with Jim Barley at Custer's he said, "Oh, OK," and went back to bed. As far as people in Marion were concerned, if you were with Jim Barley you were not headed for trouble. Great players were held in such high regard it was like they could cast a spell over people.

Bob France hurt his knee in track and had to have surgery in July. He didn't have the money so Woody got some business men to pay for the operation. Once again, the people in most any town in Indiana would do whatever it took to help the high school have a good basketball team. Basketball was so important it was like a certain group of men took care of everything that a coach or player might need. The expensive operation was going to cause Bob to get off to a slow start come basketball season. Woody giving each of us a ball was a rather good indication to me that we were going to be in the fold for the next year. Bob and I didn't want to just make the team, we wanted to win and help restore some pride to the Marion Giant program. It looked to me as though with Bob missing early practice and possibly even playing time, it would be tough to win.

I tried to be realistic about my chances to become a good basketball player in Indiana and what my odds were to play in college. Players who achieved such goals down through the years seemed to have much more success than I had my first two years in high school. I thought it wise, with the success I had at the Missouri baseball camp, to not rule out baseball as a sport to play if the more competitive world of basketball didn't work out for me in the years ahead. It was this thinking that caused me to stay close to baseball. I was thrilled when a friend invited me to attend the Major League All-Star game at Crosley Field in Cincinnati. My friend Larry Hickman drove his car and Wynston Lynn, Larry Mathews and I saw the National League win 5 to 1.

To fill out the rest of the summer, my dad put me to work as his business of installing popular Youngstown kitchens was doing well. A new product called Formica was replacing the steel tops in most kitchens. I picked up some spending money, but didn't like the work. I was often too tired to shoot baskets after work. I spent most of one day on my back under a house with spiders walking on my face and spider webs getting tangled up on my body. I told my dad I didn't like that and he said, "Get an education and you won't have to do that." This incident in my life I have not forgotten and I believe it inspired me even more to work hard at basketball and possibly earn a college scholarship.

There is no question in my mind that the great excitement about basketball in this special time and special place ignited my interest to the point that I just had to see for myself how far I could go with the idea of becoming a respectable player.

CHAPTER FOUR
Senior Moments

"IF YOU'RE NOT PRACTICING, JUST
REMEMBER ... SOMEONE, SOMEWHERE,
IS PRACTICING, AND WHEN YOU TWO
MEET, GIVEN ROUGHLY EQUAL ABILITY,
HE WILL WIN." (SENATOR BILL BRADLEY
AND FORMER NEW YORK KNICK)

I wish I had heard Senator Bradley's profound words when I was in high school, but I think I followed the advice the words gave rather closely during the summer of 1953. Bob France and I both knew we were going to have to improve a great deal to have a chance to compete in the North Central Conference and beat Mississinewa and cut down the Sectional nets. After the surgery all Bob could do was shoot free throws.

We had learned before school started that Ralph Ferguson was returning to Marion High School to become Woody's assistant. "Fergie," as the players called him, had been instrumental in leading Marion's 1947 team to the state finals and had played four years at Franklin College. I recall watching Fergie play in college because a small college tourney was held at the Marion Memorial Coliseum and he played a few games. I remember clearly how the college players shoes squeaked when they made quick cuts. My cousin, Don Gilbert, who was playing at Tri-State College from northern Indiana also played in the tourney so it was quite a thrill for me. Don, who was from Battle Creek, was a good ball handler and a good defender and could score some.

As I worked myself into my senior year it seemed to me that most of the students got along well with each other. In retrospect, I don't think many of the white students, including me, had a good understanding of the sources of the racial tensions still present in Indiana and many of the southern states at the time. As mentioned, African-American Tom Archey and I were teammates my junior year. Tom and his younger brother, Oatess, were well respected in Marion. They lived in an all white neighborhood on Marion's North Side and attended Washington Jr. High before entering Marion High. The likable boys had many white friends. "Odie" was the nickname they gave Oatess and they sat with him in the balcony when they went to the movies together. During my senior year, Oatess would be a junior, a teammate and a friend on the Giant basketball team.

Racial division, prejudice and discrimination showed its ugliness when blacks in Marion had to go somewhere else when their white friends went to the YMCA or Matter Park pool or to a restaurant that only served whites. As far as I knew at the time there had not been any racial conflicts at Marion High School the first two years I attended. The thought of such evil hardly, if ever, occurred to me in my time there.

Oatess was to become an outstanding athlete and both he and his brother were respected not only for their athletic accomplishments, but also for the class and dignity in which they handled themselves. It wasn't easy for them. Oatess, as will be seen, returned to Marion in his later years. He was even mentioned in a book written about the lynchings in Marion. In the book Oatess described how he and his African-American friends felt about living in Marion and about the tension they felt at Marion High. Author James Madison, in discussing Oatess, stated:

> "Adults didn't need to explain to him what the tree on the square and the massive jail represented. He knew they were signs "to stay in your place." He knew he had to be especially careful with the white girls when they were overly friendly to him, a handsome black male athlete: He said, "We knew there could be serious trouble" even if the teenage white girls were too innocent to understand."

The culture in which I grew up in Indiana had to have a different view from the standpoint of Odie, Tom, Ed Thurman and another Giant teammate to be, Tommy Nukes. I'm sure the tension they felt was not felt by the white people around them as such cultural differences were kept quiet by those helping to create such tension.

A few weeks before basketball practice started I noticed a girl in the hallway who I had not remembered seeing before. She certainly wasn't from Martin Boots as I knew all of the girls with whom I had attended school with for years there. Each day I went to school I would look for the girl and her pretty face and black hair. I don't remember how I met Sharon Secrest, but I suspect it was through the usual way of finding a girl I knew who knew her and have that girl introduce us. When I did meet her I think my heart skipped a few beats. I thought she was gorgeous.

Somehow Sharon and I began to date and she let me know she had been going with a fellow named Jim Riddle who graduated one year ahead of us. One of the concepts adults preached in those days was to "date other people." I did see girls dating different guys and vice-versa, but for the most part if couples really liked each other they went "steady" in those days. Since Jim wasn't around Marion High School it was, at least in the beginning, easy for me to dismiss the idea that Sharon had someone else in her life. The fact is, I didn't have much money, seldom could use my dad's car and Sharon and I saw each other mainly at school.

Limited somewhat in my options to make an impression on her, Sharon and I still struck up a good relationship before basketball season got started. That is not to say that we didn't go to Custer's or go to lovers' lane once in awhile when I did have access to a car. I approached the season happy that I had a pretty, congenial girl friend and confident I would be playing a lot of basketball. I gave little thought as to what effect Sharon Secrest might have on me as I tried hard to fulfill my dreams of playing basketball.

I think it struck me that it was time to get real serious about the basketball season as calls to organize the Booster Club were made. My pals Wynston Lynn and Joe McIntosh along with a girl named Sue Stewart had been named cheerleaders in the spring. I knew Sharon was going to be in the Booster Club. Little did I know however she would be sitting in the first row right on the Coliseum floor and along side Bettie Riddle, the sister of her boyfriend.

As a team, we were short on experience as Jim Gross, Dave Bunce, who had moved in the year before, and I were the only seniors. Senior classmate Al Harker had played some before, but chose to study more because he wanted to become a lawyer. We had Bob France and African-American players Oatess Archey and Tommy Nukes, who were juniors, along with Jim Aldrich, Larry Bricker, John Knipple and Phil Yeakle. We had two sophomores in David

Pettiford, who was also black, and Bill Wampner. Senior classmate and friend Ed Wilkinson was the student manager.

We opened our season with a 59-43 loss to tough Ft. Wayne Central, but came right back with a win against Auburn, 49 to 48, as Bob France hit a shot late in the game. This game was played at the Ft. Wayne War Memorial Coliseum. It was a thrill to play again where the Ft. Wayne Zollner Pistons played their home games. The close game ended with me dribbling the ball at center court to stall out the time. Late in the game I got chewed out because Woody signaled to me to call time out as I dribbled near the bench, but I first passed the ball to a forward and then called time out. He said, "What did you pass the ball for?" All a player had to do was hold the ball and ask the referee for a time out. Woody was upset that I didn't do that because the pass could have been intercepted and we would not have been able to get the important time out. I learned.

When we got to the parking lot after the game everyone was happy after winning on the Pistons court and the site of the NBA All-Star game… and on the road. It was the best win we had accomplished in over a year. When Woody opened the trunk of his car to put some equipment in it I saw a case of beer bottles. I said, "Hey, let's have a party." Woody said, "Jones, the way you played you don't deserve a party." Woody may have been embarrassed that some of the players saw the beer bottles, but I knew he was right, I had not played well.

We lost to Muncie Burris 62-54 and highly regarded Anderson, 60-37, but again came back to beat Hartford City. I made two free throws in the last few seconds to win that one in overtime. It took awhile, but I was finally out of Woody's doghouse. We were missing Bob France, who could only play about a half, and lost our next four games. One was a 46-42 heart breaker to the Anderson team that had mauled us just a few weeks before. We did show improvement. Highly ranked Kokomo ran over us and I remember thinking to myself that most of their guys looked a lot older.

We were to play the tall Huntington Vikings, a 7-3 team, just before the Christmas break in the Marion Coliseum. Woody had told me he wanted me to take about eighteen shots a game and I would run two laps for every shot under eighteen I took in the next game. Against Huntington I played well, making 15 points. Bob France made 16, but we lost 60-46. I made seven out of seventeen, which is a .412 percentage. This was a very good percentage in the 1950s, but I still had to run two laps in the next practice. I didn't like having on my mind the idea that I needed to take eighteen shots and I guess my body language delivered the message to Woody. He never said anymore about it, but he got his message across that I needed to shoot more.

Being a little discouraged, I had not even started keeping a scrapbook before the Huntington game as most families with boys on a team did in Indiana because we were not a very good team. I didn't think I was contributing that much and my dreams of even becoming a decent player were fading. I recall the Huntington game gave me some confidence because Woody was telling me to shoot more. Bob France, who was healing fast, and I enjoyed reading what the *Marion Chronicle* had to say about us in that game:

> "The Vikings made one bad mistake, though, when they maintained a zone defense against the Giants letting sharpshooters like Bob France and Norm Jones get shots off from mid-court. The two scrappy little Giant guards paced the Giants throughout the game. Jones snapped the nets for seven field goals and added a free throw while France canned four buckets and added eight free throws."

The publicity was nice, but winning would have been better. Write ups like this one could help catch the eye of college coaches or possibly alumni on the lookout for players to go to their schools and play basketball. I knew I would need more good games to even come close to having a chance to play in college. It was also important to play on a winning team to get noticed. It would also help a player to stay in the state tourney as long as possible.

The Huntington game was also the game where I went to Sharon's house the next day and her dad said to me, "You played a good game." Later on he told me how I had cost him the pool he was in at his work when I made a shot right at the end of the game. Sharon's parents were very nice to me. I regarded them as good, solid family type people. Sharon had been to my house a few times. My mom made us peanut butter and banana sandwiches, which Sharon liked. We had been dating about three months now and I was enjoying this dating business a great deal. Sharon had a good sense of humor and kept me laughing. It was a nice departure from Woody's strict discipline. My dad even commented on me being with Sharon. He said, "It relaxes you doesn't it?" I nodded yes. My mom caught us kissing once in the front room of our house, but she just smiled.

Neither the team nor I played well in the New Year's Tourney held in the big fieldhouse at Muncie Central, which was jammed with 6,500 fans. We lost to Muncie 50-34 and then to Richmond 54-38. Surprisingly, Muncie Central lost the tourney to Ft. Wayne South Side. (This is the Muncie team that would play little Milan in the state final game later in March. It would be the game that was used as a story line to make the film *Hoosiers*.) We were 2 and 9 at the Christmas break and Mississinewa was undefeated. We had to get better...and, with France at full strength, we had a chance.

Indiana did not need a boost for Hoosier Hysteria in this Golden Era of basketball, but it got one...from Ohio. Early in the season I learned that a player named Bevo Francis was going to play against Butler University in the Butler Fieldhouse in Indianapolis. Bevo was the nickname given to a 6'9" player from Rio Grande College in Ohio by the name of Clarence Francis. Bevo had been sensational in 1952-53 when he led tiny Rio Grande to a 39-0 record. It is a record that still stands for most wins in a season by any college team in America. Bevo averaged an amazing 50.1 points per game. He could shoot from anywhere and once scored 116 points in a game.

In Bevo's second year, Newt Oliver, the Rio Grande coach was so confident in his team that he scheduled teams like Wake Forest, Creighton, Arizona State and Butler so Bevo could display his talent. Bevo's unheard of 116 points was against Ashland Junior College. Since Ashland was a junior college the NCAA did not recognize Bevo's feat as a record. However, in 1954 he scored 113 points against Hillsdale College of Michigan and that total still stands as the college record for all divisions. Bevo and Rio Grande were like a traveling road show that was drawing big crowds.

As was my penchant for wanting to see basketball at its best, I started angling for a way to get to the "Bevo" game. Sure enough Rudy said he would take three other guys and me. On the way down we decided to put some money in a pot and the guy who came the closest to predicting how many points Bevo would make against Butler would win the money. I guessed 48 points and remember rooting for Bevo. He made exactly 48 points in a 81-68 Rio Grande win and broke the fieldhouse record. He got a standing ovation from the sold out crowd. I went home thinking what a thrill it would be to play at Butler.

I was pleased I had won some money because that probably meant I could treat Sharon to something more than a peanut butter and banana sandwich... maybe even something at Custer's. My folks did give me some money to date girls in high school, but during basketball season Woody watched over us pretty close and I stayed home a lot.

We had nine games left before the state tourney would start in late February and all nine would be with teams from the rugged North Central Conference. As luck would have it I jammed both thumbs in practice just before we had to go to Richmond, a team that had defeated us by 14 points earlier. I didn't tell Woody about the injury and thought I could play if I limited my shots. I was concerned about not shooting because of what Woody had told me about shooting more. I always tried to do what he told me to do.

At Richmond I mainly tried to distribute the ball and Tommy Nukes, Jim Gross, Don Pettiford and Oatess Archey all scored between 7 and 11 points. France made 12 and we upset Richmond on their court by a 53-47 count. The newspaper the next day reported "the Giants flashed their best form of the season." I only made 3 points, but Woody didn't say anything to me about not shooting as he was real happy with the way we played. I'll never forget the Richmond coach, Art Beckner, opened the door to our locker room and shook his fist at Woody and yelled, "I'll get you next year Woody." Those two were great competitors and helped make Indiana high school basketball what it is today. Fans would say Beckner's tirade was typical of Hoosier Hysteria.

The next game was at home with Newcastle. This school had won the state championship in 1932 and was, like Marion, basketball crazy. (As of this writing the gym that exists there now has the largest seating capacity of any high school gym in the *world* at 9,325. Indiana has **31** high school gyms that seat more than 5,000 people).

During practice that week Woody told the players, "Move around and Norm will hit you." I appreciated his comment because I think he noticed that we upset Richmond without me having to take eighteen shots. I do recall at this time my junior high coach, John Hubbard, telling me, "I think they will like your passing at the high school." I was young, but even then I knew basketball was a team sport and everyone had to work together to improve. I began to realize I could do two things well on a basketball court and they were shoot and pass. I wanted to parlay them into a college scholarship.

In the Newcastle game Bob France put on a spectacular display of shooting. He made nine field goals and eight free throws for 26 points to lead us to a 64-55 win over the Trojans. Sophomore Dave Pettiford and I added 10 each and Tommy Nukes had 7 points and several rebounds.

Now we had to hit the road to play arch-rival Wabash. They were 9 and 3 at the time. We won again by the close score of 54-51 as Bob France made 16 points, the improving Tommy Nukes had 14 and Jim Gross and Oatess

Archey were all over the floor on defense in a game described by the *Marion Chronicle* this way:

> "Marion's fast charging Giants used North Central Conference savvy here tonight to spoil a four game Wabash winning streak by dropping the Apaches, 54-51, in a thrill-packed, foul-filled high school basketball game."

I only made 4 points, but we had won our third straight game and the newspapers and the fans were noticing our improvement. Oatess Archey later revealed to me that he heard racial taunts while we visited Wabash. It seemed to me that people who came out with the taunting always seemed to hide it from everyone except the black players. It was like these prejudice people were not proud enough of what they were doing to let the white teammates of the black players know they were doing it. Perhaps these people taunted blacks in such a way to get it done and not cause fights at games. More taunting of black players went on than white players knew about at the time.

I know it was about this time that I was getting to see Sharon more as my parents trusted me with the family car. It was also becoming difficult for me to not notice her pretty face right in the front row of the Booster Club, but for the most part I was able to concentrate on playing. To me, to not look her way once in awhile would be like being in a room with movie stars at the time Liz Taylor or Natalie Wood and not looking at them. I thought the world of Sharon, but some people didn't. A female classmate sat next to me in Mr. Bolander's typing class. One day she said something to me that got my attention. It centered on the idea that Sharon didn't like me as much as I would like to think and I should get rid of her. I liked Sharon too much to let her go. It was common for people to speak out on things they thought affected the performance of players or the team. It was simply a part of Indiana high school basketball.

Just to show how crazy Indiana basketball was in that era, consider this example. Mr. Bolander was a good typing teacher, a basketball nut and…a smoker. He would come by my desk even while I was taking a typing test and say, "Jonesie, come with me to the boiler room and talk some basketball, I need a smoke." I would say, "How about my test?" He answered, "You are going to get a C anyway." It seems to me I spent almost as much time in the boiler room as typing class. I'm sure my classmates were not impressed, but what could I do when a teacher wanted to do such a thing? I was a little concerned that Woody would smell the smoke on my clothes and who knows what would happen then? I got a C, but Mr. Bolander knew all season long what was going on with the basketball team. Team success was important to almost everyone in town.

We had a tough assignment in our next game. The Lafayette Broncos were coming to town. I think it was the Wednesday night before the game on Friday that Sharon had invited me to go ice skating with her and Bettie Riddle. I had never even tried to ice skate, didn't have any skates, but was sure fired up to be out with Sharon. I was able to get my dad's car on this cold mid-winter night and picked up the two girls right after dinner. We knew we should not get home late on a school night.

After Sharon and Bettie had tried to teach me how to skate on some small pond close to Marion we started home. It was misting and cold. Although I had not taken driver training I knew enough to be careful driving in those conditions. I was going to take Bettie home first, kiss Sharon good night a few times and head home. As I approached a stop sign near where the girls lived in South Marion I noticed a glare on the street. I was not going fast at all. I hit the brake real lightly to stop, but the car skidded through the intersection. I saw a car parked on my left and, luckily avoided it. The car swerved out of control, turned completely around and we hit a tree almost head on. I was stunned for a few seconds and when I became aware of what happened I saw Sharon sitting in the street behind the car with her hands on her face. I don't recall where Bettie was, but she had also been thrown out of the car.

I asked Sharon if she was hurt and she said her neck hurt, but she was OK. Bettie was shaken, but OK. About that time some fellow came up to the car and he said to me, "You been drinking?" I said, "No." He said, "I smell alcohol." We figured out the radiator was busted and the anti-freeze was leaking so drinking wasn't going to be a problem. I called my dad and he took a cab out to get me. We got the girls home and the car towed. There was a lot of damage to the front end of the car. I was just thankful no one was badly hurt. My dad was real nice about the entire incident and told me even the cab driver had trouble getting from West Marion to South Marion. My dad was very encouraging when I had trouble later on getting behind the steering wheel of our car.

I laid awake most of the night thinking about what could have happened that night and how my dreams of playing could have been shattered. The newspaper the next morning reported how bad the storm was in Marion. In fact, there were thirteen accidents in Marion that night, the most ever in one night. That didn't make me feel much better after hurting Sharon and scaring both girls half out of their wits. I felt as though I was a victim of circumstances.

Of course, bad news travels fast so I began getting quizzed as soon as I arrived at school. Fergie, Woody's assistant, came and got me out of study hall. Woody taught Physical Education courses ("Gym" in those days) at the Coliseum so he was not in the high school building except for assemblies or some special occasions. Fergie asked me if I had been in an accident and after telling him I began to think, "This is not going to be good." He asked me if I was OK and if I had any injuries that would keep me from playing against Lafayette? I assured him I was OK. He quizzed me a little bit about whom I was with and what time I got home and the usual investigative techniques parents and teachers used. He said, "See you in practice."

Figuring Woody had been clued in by Fergie about the accident, I went to practice a little nervous. Little did I expect what took place and I will never forget it. After warming up Woody called the squad together at center court. That usually meant we were in for a lecture or something we had not seen before. He told the team we needed to learn to get the ball into the center position more frequently. He wanted us to get the ball in and back out and move it around as he thought this would open up the offense even more.

I was shocked when he said, "Jones I want you to guard me and I will demonstrate to the team how to get position at the center position." I thought this was a little weird since I played guard and never guarded a center. He showed everyone how to throw the ball into the center by looking at the player guarding the center and then throwing the ball to the side furthest away from the defender. This would help our offensive center to know where the defense was and possibly make a move to the basket.

I got behind Woody and assumed a defensive position. Someone threw the ball into him and he hooked his right leg around me to go to the basket. Woody played three years at Indiana and was All-Big Ten so he knew how to play. He planted his elbow right in my gut as he laid the ball in the basket and yelled, "Guard me." He again got the ball, faked, and charged right into me. Another time he stepped on my toe, elbowed me again and nearly knocked me down a couple of times. I was getting the picture. Woody was not happy that I was out with two girls on a bad night two nights before we were going to play for our fourth straight win against a tough North Central Conference opponent.

We then began a normal practice going over a game plan for Lafayette. Woody didn't say another word to me the rest of practice, but I didn't practice with the starting five. He had me nervous. I knew I was in Woody's doghouse again! He told us the Lafayette game was going to be Marion High School's first attempt to film a game. Films were unheard of in those days for high school basketball, but every coach could see the importance. I was concerned that I wouldn't even play and be on the film. (The films didn't turn out).

It is not a fond memory, but one etched in my mind forever. I can see myself sitting on the bench in the locker room in front of the blackboard. Woody is getting ready to go over things before we took the floor against Lafayette. He always wrote the names of those starting the game on the blackboard one at a time and would say a few words to each player. All season long he had been putting France and Jones first. On this night, however, he listed the names in this order...France-Gross-Nukes-Pettiford. When he got to the last slot for a name he said to me, "Jones do you think you can concentrate on playing basketball tonight?" I don't remember what I said, if anything, as Woody wrote my name on the board. I could see my starting position as well as all my dreams going down the drain. I felt stupid and embarrassed in front of my teammates and had a big lump in my throat when we took the court. I knew I was skating on thin ice.

Despite the harassment from Woody I tried to tell myself that he was just trying to make me a better player and help me grow up. I played what I think was the best game I had played in high school up to that time. I hustled on defense, made good passes and don't remember making a mistake...or even looking at Sharon. Lafayette had two of the best guards in the conference in Steve Martin and Eddie Becker. Bob France had 19 points and I had 13 and we outplayed Martin and Becker as we outscored them 32 to 22. We lost 67-56 in a well-played game, but we were badly out rebounded. I think I grew up a lot the night we played Lafayette. It was, at times, tough growing up in Indiana. It helped when, walking down the hallway to the locker room after the game, Woody placed his hand on my shoulder and said, "Norm, you played a real good game tonight."

Our next game would be at highly ranked Indianapolis Tech. Tech had started the season ranked #1 in the state and their record was 13 and 2. There was an incident just a few weeks before where a Tech guard by the name of Dave Huff was threatened. He was told if he played in Tech's game against Indianapolis Crispus Attucks he would be harmed. The threat story hit newspapers all around the state and probably every basketball fan knew about it. It seems three men jumped Huff on his way home from practice and told him if he made even one point they would "cut him wide open." Oscar Robertson, who was not yet the legend he would become, was a sophomore at Crispus Attucks. He reported how he was also threatened. A caller said he would be shot. He said, "I didn't think much about it." Huff, his family and coach decided to hold him out.

The Indianapolis Tech-Crispus Attucks game in Dec. of 1953, was perhaps the most publicized game in Indiana high school basketball history.

Five players were threatened, police guarded the dressing rooms and even escorted players to the court. FBI agents were roaming around and taking notes. About 10,000 fans saw the game in Butler Fieldhouse which was then a record for a regular season game in Indianapolis. The threats were attributed to gamblers. Indianapolis was not immune to stories about gamblers fixing basketball games especially after the Olympians folded.

Woody told the team about the threats and how it would be a different atmosphere playing in Indianapolis. He told the story about Dave Huff and then teased me a little by saying, "Jonesie, we will put you on Huff, but no closer than you get to your man on defense there is no chance you will get shot." Everyone laughed, it was a good joke...I think.

We came within two points of pulling off one of the biggest upsets in the state that year when Tech beat us 51-49. The newspaper noted the game was played before a capacity crowd of 4,600 in Tech's gym. Also reported was how both Bob France and I stole passes in the last seconds and scored to nearly pull off the upset. Dave Huff and I both made 10 points and France made 18. In this game John Knipple and Jim Aldrich contributed and that was a good sign because they had been up and down to the "B" team and back to the varsity all season. I vividly recall guarding Dave Huff in this game and wondering a couple of times if someone would try to shoot him while I was guarding him. It is difficult to forget those kind of stories coming out of Hoosier Hysteria.

The day after the Tech game I went to Sharon's and after being there for only a few minutes, her dad said, "Come on and go to the store with me." I really didn't want to go because I wanted to spend time with Sharon, but thought it polite to accept his offer. On the way, Sharon's dad told me that he was counting on me to use good judgment with his daughter. I knew what he meant and I let him know that I wanted to be able to play ball and go to college and not start a family at such a young age. He said, "Those are good goals, stick to them." That was about it...Mr. Secrest got his point across and I was pleased we got that agreement between us. I was also pleased that maybe Sharon was letting her parents know that she really liked me and that I had a chance with her.

Not long after that visit to Sharon's house I got a call from her boyfriend. He let me know that he didn't like me going out with his girlfriend and he might do something about it. He didn't scare me any as I thought maybe I was winning Sharon's heart and she would one day drop him.

We had four games left before the state tourney would start. Mississinewa was still undefeated, but they had to know we were getting better after winning three games in a row and nearly upsetting ranked Indianapolis Tech. Our next game would be at home against Frankfort's Hot Dogs. Frankfort had won the state championship four times in 1925-1929-1936 and 1939 and was known as a rabid basketball town. The Hot Dogs were 10 and 7 coming to play us. They had a 6'7" center and a good shooter named Jim Ulm. The results of the game were described this way by the *Marion Chronicle* the next day.

> "Norm Jones is Mr. Basketball in Marion today since he flipped in a field goal with five seconds left to give Marion's Giants a 58-57 win over Frankfort here Friday night in a thrilling North Central Conference game."

Large bold print above the article read, "Jones' Shot Gives Giants 58-57 Win." As the game ended I heard the band playing a recent hit tune titled *The Whole Town's Talking About The Jones Boy* as a bunch of friends and fans shuttled me off toward the locker room. My brother came bursting into the locker room and said to Woody, "Where's Norm?" Woody said, "He's over there, go tell him he could play better than he did." It really can't get much better for a player in Indiana to hit a game winning shot like I did against Frankfort. Woody was right about the way I played and such a night rings a little hollow when you have not played well and are playing on a losing team in a town that is used to winning. Nevertheless, I was proud I helped my team pull out the victory. I will never forget that moment as long as I live. Most Indiana boys live their lives dreaming about making a last second shot like that and I was lucky to have it happen to me. In all of the days of practice I couldn't count how many times I had called out, "Five seconds to go, Jones shoots from the right side...that's all brother?" Dreams come true!

The Frankfort game saw our team have four players in double figures. Our 6' 3" plus center, big John Knipple, had by far his best game of the year scoring 14 points and Tommy Nukes contributed 12. France and I each scored 10 and, according to the newspaper, junior Jim Aldrich rebounded well. The game was, again, a confidence builder as the state tourney was only three weeks off.

It is ironic that Frankfort finished near the bottom of the North Central Conference because during the course of this 1954 season they beat Muncie Central and Milan. These are the two teams that played in the famous state final game that inspired the movie *Hoosiers*. (The film is still popular and was once used to motivate the New York Yankees in the American League playoffs).

I could not use my dad's car the next morning to go to Sharon's house in South Marion so I walked and ran along a railroad track. I was now thinking more clearly to watch my step and not sprain an ankle or something and get back in Woody's doghouse. I was becoming more responsible for my actions. I know I wanted to see Sharon while I was basking in some glory because I sensed she was not real impressed with me smashing up my dad's car and scaring her out of her wits. I also reminded her that the Sectional was just around the corner and I was going to stay rather close to home and not take any chances of getting in trouble with Woody. I wanted to focus on playing well in the Sectional.

I figured I had only a few more days to be with Sharon as we approached the last three games of the season so I made arrangements to go to Sharon's house one night right after practice. During this practice for the upcoming big weekend games with Logansport and Kokomo I made another mistake. I didn't see it as a big mistake, but it was with Woody. Woody hollered at the team, "Make ten free throws and get a shower." Anxious to get to Sharon's, I stepped to the free throw line real quick. Bob France fed me real fast and I zipped in ten straight and took off for the locker room. Woody yelled at me, "Jonesie, where you going?" I said, "In." Woody said, "Take twenty-laps!" I swear, this man had a transmitter on my heart! He seemed to know if it was beating for basketball or Sharon. At any rate, I was the last one out of the locker room and I think it hit me that maybe I was girl crazy.

We still had three tough basketball teams to play. Logansport at 11 and 7 and Kokomo at 12 and 7 were coming to Marion Friday and Saturday night. Following those games we had to go to conference leader and state ranked Muncie Central. We led Logansport for three-quarters as Bob France scored 21, Nukes had 12 and I played well again making 13 points. We lost to a good team 59-54. It was about this time I remember noticing that almost every team we played had a winning record. I was hoping that playing such competition would pay off in the Sectional. We had played some good games. There was no question that Woody had helped us improve from mid-season.

Kokomo ran over us in front of over 5,000 fans at home as we turned the ball over far too many times. Muncie Central, which had righted the ship by bringing up sophomore guards Jimmy Barnes and Phil Raisor, won the North Central Conference with an 8 and 2 record by beating us 70 to 48 in the season finale in Muncie.

I won't forget Woody using me as an example as we approached the end of the season. Before practice started one day he told me to get down on all fours, which I did. Then he told me to shake my right leg like a dog, then waggle my tail like a dog and shake the other leg, which I did. The players were laughing and one said, "What does this have to do with basketball?" Woody told me, "Now, bark like a dog," which I did. At this point, with all the trouble I had been in with Woody, I didn't really believe I had a choice except to do what Woody told me to do. Woody surprised me by saying, "Now, if the rest of you guys would do like you are told like Norm does, we might have a better team." Growing up in Indiana basketball was sometimes strange, but lessons were learned in many different ways.

Woody spent most of the last week and a half of the season going over plans for Mississinewa as it seemed likely we would meet them in the Sectional. I thought it was time well spent as it was unlikely we could beat the likes of Kokomo and Muncie Central.

In discussing our season the *Marion Chronicle* stated that despite our 6 and 14 record, we "had come quite a way since the early portion of the campaign." The newspaper pointed out that we would not be the favorites in our own Sectional as Mississinewa was highly rated and had completed the season with a 21-0 record. In bold print on the sports page the paper reported:

GIANTS' TOUGHER SCHEDULE MAY PROVE HELP IN SECTIONAL TOURNEY OPENING THURSDAY

Under the above notation an article mentioned that our "caliber of a schedule" made us a threat in the tourney. It also said that, "Marion actually played only two poor games (Kokomo and Muncie Central) in its last nine and, at one point, had three wins in a row on the books." Statistics about players were given and pictures of the team were shown. It was mentioned that we had drawn Jefferson Township in the Sectional and would play Friday night at 7:00pm. The random drawing of Sectional parings, done in downtown Indianapolis, was a big deal throughout Indiana and often broadcast on the radio and later on television.

At this point in my high school career I thought I had grown up quite a bit and gave Woody Weir credit for teaching me how to focus on basketball. I wanted to show people that I had improved as a player. It was going to be important for me to play well in the Sectional and prove to people that Sharon was not affecting my play to any measurable degree. Also, a friend of mine, Harold "Whitey" Sherick, who was about three years older than me, told me that coach Claude Wolfe from Manchester College was going to try and see me play in the Sectional. I never did find out if he did come to a game. Whitey had played at Manchester after playing a year at the United States Naval Academy. He took an interest in me and thought Manchester might be a good place for me to play college ball.

We routed Jefferson Township 72-44, out scoring them 42 to 20 the second half. Bob France got in foul trouble early and only scored 6 points. Woody put in Larry Bricker who had not played much all year. He filled in well with two baskets and hustling defense. I had my best scoring game in high school with 21 points which came on eight field goals and five free throws. Dave Pettiford added 11 and Tommy Nukes had 10.

The same night we won our first game in the Sectional a friend, Dick McAvoy, was playing against Fairmount for St. Paul, the Catholic school in Marion. Dick was dating a senior girl from Marion High School named Connie Leckie. She lived down the street from me on West 6th Street. During the summer my friends and I had tried to talk Dick into coming to Marion to play basketball. Woody Weir visited with Dick also, but Dick stayed loyal to St. Paul. He was a good player and scored 12 points for St. Paul as they lost. (Movie star James Dean played for Fairmount in the late 1940s. He starred in *Rebel Without A Cause, Giant* and *East of Eden.* I saw him play. He was a good player).

Mississinewa easily beat Van Buren so now we would play Fairmount and Mississinewa would play Swayzee on Saturday afternoon with the winners meeting that night. With good games from France and Nukes we beat Fairmount 61-46. I was taken out of the game early for rest since I had played the entire game against Jefferson Township. Most basketball fans agreed it was grueling to play a game on Friday night and then two games on Saturday and I would find that to be true. Mississinewa's Indians beat Swayzee 50 to 29 to set up the game anticipated state wide between Marion and undefeated and state ranked Mississinewa.

Woody told the team it should be focusing on nothing but basketball while we were still in the tourney and I agreed. Woody was so intense about keeping us in line that between games on Saturday the team stayed at his house. No one went home. Woody lived right across the street from the high school. We were to stretch out and relax, tend to any minor injuries and then we would eat an early meal in the school cafeteria. It was here that Woody whispered to me, "I'm going to need 15 points out of you tonight."

During the week before the Sectional, Woody devised a game plan to stop Mississinewa's great player, 6' 5" Larry Hedden. Woody and Fergie had noticed throughout Mississinewa's season that Hedden shot only about fifty percent from the free throw line. Woody figured that if we could keep Hedden shooting free throws we could get the ball since he would be away from the basket after he missed. If Hedden, who shot free throws under handed, hit his usual fifty percent we should be in good shape if we shot the ball well. Also, Woody instructed our centers, John Knipple, Dave Pettiford and Bill Wampner to foul Hedden whenever he looked like he was going to make a move to the basket. This would cut down on his field goals and keep him at the free throw line.

The atmosphere come game time was, to me, electric, and I was never more fired up, more determined for a game. At least it was equal to the feeling I had after the accident when I had played so well against Lafayette.

The newspaper reported that a full house of 5,500 spectators watched the Indians move out to an eight point lead by half time. Coming back out on the floor Woody reminded me, "Where are those 15 points?" I said, "I'll get'em this half." We pulled within five points with 5:57 to go in the game. I hit a drive in shot with less than three minutes to go to bring us to within four points. All players were playing the game Woody had visualized, except we did not shoot real well. Bob France and I were not getting many shots. Hedden went to the free throw line often as our centers used ten fouls on him. As great players do, he adjusted to our strategy and made fifteen out of seventeen free throws, which was well above his .500 average. Had he made eight, as Woody figured, we would have been right there. I thought Woody had a great game plan and it gave us a chance to win, but we lost 55 to 47 as the Indians went to 24 and 0.

Martin Burdette was a very good player for Mississinewa. In fact, I know I was told later on that he would have been the twelfth player picked on the Indiana All-Star team that summer, but I never verified that fact. This was one of the years that only ten players were selected. Larry Hedden was selected as the fourth best player in the state. Our defensive standout, Jim Gross, held Burdette to zero and Jim's performance helped keep us in the game. I didn't get the 15 points Woody said he needed. I made 8 and Bob France made 9. No one for us scored in double figures. Mississinewa got the early lead and slowed the game down to preserve the win.

We had held Hedden to three field goals and pretty much carried out our game plan, but it wasn't enough. Dick Smith of the Indians made some

shots from way out on the court that hurt us. I saw Woody cover his face
and lean up against the wall in the locker room after the game. I know
he and all of the players thought we could beat Mississinewa. It was a lot
better effort than the year before, but still not a good way to end a season
in Marion.

Phil Raisor's dad may have put it best. Phil's dad told Phil as he was getting
ready to play for Muncie Central in the state championship, "Losin' tonight,
son, will hurt you all your life." It is no different at the Sectional level, especially
when you are a member of a North Central Conference team and hosting the
Sectional. Adding to that disappointment, is the fact that Marion just didn't
lose that much over the years. We expected to win our own Sectional.

Although worn out and about as sad as I had been in my short life I
showered and got ready to get on with my life. Bob France and I had agreed
that it might be good for us to hang out together after the game and he
had a car. There was to be a party for Marion High students at Emily's
restaurant in Marion. We decided to calm down a little before attending
the party and probably not real anxious to meet our friends after not
winning the game the entire town was so excited about. I didn't know what
Sharon was going to be doing and was not looking forward to seeing her
in my discouraged state.

Driving around, Bob and I agreed that everyone played great, but we
just couldn't get enough shots to help the team. Why I don't know, but we
decided to go to the Mississinewa gym where they would be celebrating.
We had become friends with Larry Hedden during the summer. We used
to drink root beer with him at Bud Ritter's A &W root beer stand not far
from Bob's house. Larry was a great guy and you could tell he was a winner.
Bud Ritter was then the head coach at Peru, Indiana High School, not far
from Marion.

When we got to the Mississinewa gym there was a big crowd there. The
administrator in charge of the celebration saw me come in and asked the crowd
if they would like to hear a few words from Norm Jones. I wasn't expecting the
invitation, but the crowd got excited and I went to the microphone. I told them
I didn't want to say much because this was their celebration for their players
and coaches. I just said, and I think these words are fairly accurate, "I played
against Hartford City and Huntington, the teams we now know you will be
playing against next Saturday in the Regional. Mississinewa is the best team
in the Regional and I will predict that you will be playing in the Semi-State in

Ft.Wayne in two weeks." The place went wild and I figured I had said enough and walked out.

My prediction came true as Mississinewa romped through the Regional and played Muncie Central in the finals of the Ft. Wayne Semi-State. They lost to Muncie to end the best season any team (other than Marion) in Grant County has ever had. (Just a few years ago this Mississinewa team that went 27-1 in 1954 was voted the best team other than Marion to come from Grant County in a *100* years!)

Bob and I decided to go to the party and of course a lot of people came up to us and tried to tell us we played a good game and Mississinewa was really good and all that stuff, but it really didn't help much being from a basketball crazy town like Marion.

A crazy thing did happen during the party. There was a drawing for prizes that people had registered for as they came in. Some of them were nice prizes so everyone got real quiet. The last prize to be given away was a gray flannel suit to be tailor made and fitted by a clothing store in downtown Marion. My name was drawn and everyone applauded. Later, some of my friends like Wid Mathews, Jim Fletcher, John Roush and Gary McKillip teased me about the drawing being fixed. I suspect many people there thought it was fixed just to make me feel better after the devastating loss. I didn't know about any fix. I could have won twenty suits and I would not have felt much better. In a few days I went with my mom to the clothing store and got measured for the suit. I had the suit for years, but one problem was, every time I wore the suit it brought up memories of Larry Hedden making all those free throws and us losing the Sectional.

After the party I was to spend the night at the home of my friend Wid Mathews. I couldn't wait to get there and get my shoes off. I had blisters on both feet. On my right big toe was a blister filled with blood. I popped it and blood spewed out like the geyser at Yellowstone National Park. Wid just cringed. I had played three games inside the time line of 7:00pm on Friday to about 10:00pm on Saturday. Not even the Ft. Wayne Pistons or the Indiana University Hoosiers had to play two games in one day and those players would be better able to take such a grueling schedule.

Wid and I talked into the night. I told him it was too bad he got hit by the truck and was not available to play on the Giants. He later played for the Marion YMCA and proved that he could play the game. I told Wid if he had been able to play and if Dick McAvoy had come over from St. Paul our chances would have been much better. I went to sleep thinking about how I had performed in the Sectional, graduating and what I would do about my dream to play in college.

I suspect the morning after losing the championship game of the Sectional in Indiana high school basketball has to be one of the most difficult mornings for a young basketball player to get out of bed. I was in no mood to read about how Mississinewa beat us, but somehow most of us humans muster enough courage to get difficult times behind us. I knew it would be discouraging to face schoolmates who had counted on us to do what most Marion teams had done in the past.

Bob Lee was a good sports reporter for the *Marion Chronicle* and he often wrote a column titled The Morning After. In the article about the Mississinewa-Marion game he quoted Indian coach John Fredenberger who said, "I thought Marion played a good game against us." Mr. Lee wrote that, "The final game didn't follow the pattern we had anticipated." Evidently we surprised people because, "It was the Giants who fast-broke whenever the opportunity arose, while the Indians took their time, refusing to waste shots." Mr. Lee added, "The Giants stuck closer to the pace than we expected. With a little more accuracy in their shooting, they could have made it closer still." We took 53 shots and made 16 for a .302 percentage. The Indians were 18 of 43 for a .419 clip. Free throw shooting was about even. They turned the ball over 11 times and we had 7.

As a team we led the Sectional in important categories like field goals made, percentage, free throw attempts and total points. As for me, I made the All-Sectional team as I was tied for fourth in scoring with 36 points for a 12.0 average per game. (Hedden led with 51) Showing good concentration I had the highest field goal percentage for those players who took more than ten shots. It was .438, which is still good by today's standards over fifty years later and was close to NBA leaders at the time. I do not believe I could have played much better even if I had never met Sharon Secrest. I set out to prove any critics I had wrong and take some misplaced blame off of Sharon. I think I accomplished that goal. The only thing missing was that we did not win against a great team that had more experience than we did and a great player in Larry Hedden.

In Bob Lee's column the next day he wrote words that help explain how important winning is in Indiana high school basketball. He wrote:

> "Unfortunately, an interesting, well-played final game had to
> be marred by the hoodlumism of some irresponsible fans when

the Indians were exercising the winners' privilege of cutting down the nets. Here was the disgraceful scene: Some young punks stood alongside the playing court pelting the Indians with coins and other objects. And despite a plea over the public address system, the barrage continued. And two men in blue-who apparently had adopted a see-nothing, hear-nothing, do-nothing policy-stood not too far away."

Bob Lee mentioned that it might be better to bar spectators from the games and that it could happen that Marion would one day not host the Sectional and Regional. To lose the right to host the Sectional and Regional and the home floor advantage would be a real jolt to Marion Giant fans. The Marion-Mississinewa game of 1954 will go down in Indiana high school basketball history as one of those games where the little school beat the big school and helped to keep alive the term Hoosier Hysteria.

CHAPTER FIVE
Life Goes On

POTENTIAL MEANS YOU AIN'T THERE YET.

Shortly after the discouraging Sectional loss Jim Barley got word to me that he wanted me to come down to Indiana University and watch the Big Ten championship game between Indiana and Illinois. Indiana still had All-Americans Don Schlundt and Bobby Leonard and Illinois was led by big John "Red" Kerr. Somehow I finagled a ride and Jim gave me his university ID to get into the student section.

The big crowd was exciting and I thought to myself how thrilling it must be to play college basketball. I know this game only added to my desire to play in college. I sort of think that is partly why Jim invited me. It helped, at least a little, to overcome the loss to Mississinewa and to look forward to better things.

Bobby Leonard made clutch free throws and Don Schlundt shot the lights out as Indiana beat Illinois 67-64 for the title. After the game Jim invited me into the locker room. It was a scene still etched in my mind. It was Hoosier Hysteria at its best. Flash bulbs were going off everywhere, but mostly around Bobby Leonard. Barley took me over to meet Don Schlundt near his locker. Schlundt didn't seem to like the reporters and all the glitter like Leonard did. He took me by the elbow and said, "Come over here and talk to me." He got Jim and I and a couple of other guys between him and the reporters and struck up a conversation with us. Finally, the reporters nudged their way in and began interviewing Schlundt. Jim then introduced me to Bobby Leonard, but that was a quick, "Nice to meet you, you played a great game," from me and a fast, "Thanks," from Leonard.

I appreciated Jim Barley getting me in a big game like that and firmly believe the excitement at Indiana University that night helped to motivate me to become the best player I could possibly become. Incidentally, Indiana was upset in the second round of the NCAA tournament that year and was replaced by LaSalle as national champions.

Making for what would become a great year in Indiana basketball, the Hoosier state added to its Big Ten championship good success from the Ft. Wayne Pistons. The NBA was going strong in Indiana in my senior year in high school, 1953-54. Perhaps the most significant thing to happen in the NBA in 1954 was the addition of the 24-second shot clock that still exists today. The clock was implemented to prevent stall tactics. It was brought about by two stall games that fans did not enjoy. These games took place in the 1950-51 season. In one now famous game in Minneapolis the Ft.Wayne Pistons held the ball and the score at the half was 13 to 11. The 7,000 fans did not pay good money to watch Laker star George Mikan stand around. I listened to this game on the radio. The Pistons won 19 to 18 and the fans chased the teams to their dressing rooms. Still, it took the NBA three years to make the change that mandated a team must attempt a shot within twenty-four seconds of gaining possession.

Another experiment took place in the NBA in my senior year. All of basketball, including the college ranks, became concerned about the big men dominating the game as Mikan had done at DePaul and with the champion Minneapolis Lakers. The NBA decided to play an official league game with 12-foot high baskets. The game was to be in Minneapolis between the Lakers and the Milwaukee Hawks. The Lakers won 65-63 and most observers agreed the higher basket didn't accomplish much. Mikan was quoted as saying, "It just makes the big man bigger."

It is ironic, but the town of Muncie, Indiana was doing just the opposite of the NBA. The elementary schools in this hoops crazy town lowered the baskets to nine feet hoping that this move would help youngsters in Muncie develop into good shooters. The town hardly needed help as it had won the state championship in 1951 and again in 1952.

Our well liked, popular and respected Dean of Students, Bernie Carmin, asked me to stop by his office during study hall shortly after the Sectional. He showed me a letter from the principal at Fairmount High School. The principal happened to be in the crowd when I was asked to speak at Mississinewa's Sectional celebration. The letter stated that the principal regarded my talk to the Mississinewa fans as "one of the finest displays of sportsmanship he had seen in a high school student." Bernie told me he was proud of how I had represented Marion High School and that I should be proud of myself. It was a nice moment for me and one no athlete could forget.

About the same time Mr. Carmin showed me the letter, which cost 3 cents in those days, Woody ran me down in study hall and showed me another letter. This one was from Texas Christian University. The basketball coaches there were trying to find players from Indiana to play for the Horned Frogs. Woody told me he thought I could play there and would contact the coaches and recommend me for a basketball scholarship. I never heard of Texas Christian and the name Horned Frogs didn't thrill me. I thought back to how SMU basketball did not impress me and I told Woody thanks, but I was sure I wanted to stay close to home and play at a college in Indiana.

It is understandable, at least for Hoosiers, that colleges were seeking out Indiana players in those days. One story exemplifies the reputation Indiana basketball enjoyed in the 1950s. My junior year we had a senior player by the name of Larry Duckwall on the Giants. "Duck" was a better golfer than basketball player, but he was good fundamentally and had some shooting skills. Shortly after high school Duck joined the Army and was sent to Ft. Leonard Wood in Missouri. One day on the parade ground the drill sergeant told all of the boys from Indiana to step forward. Duck stepped forward, wondering what was going on. Then the drill sergeant said, "If anyone else wants to try out for the base basketball team, please step forward." It was just assumed that if you were from Indiana that you knew how to play basketball.

In what turned out to be the most famous high school basketball game in the history of Indiana, powerhouse Muncie Central from our conference was to meet little Milan for the state title. I was among the 14,983 fans in Butler Fieldhouse in Indianapolis. Milan stalled and kept the score low and close until the final seconds. In a shot many Hoosiers say was heard around the world, Milan star Bobby Plump hit a jump shot with the score tied as time ran out and Milan upset Muncie 32-30. I remember a woman passed out right in front of me and she wasn't the only one who fainted that night. The fabled game put a thrilling end to what was perhaps the most exciting year in Indiana basketball history.

Watching this famous game and wondering what a thrill it would be to play in Butler Fieldhouse in front of a lot of people, it became a goal for me to play there. I had seen Bevo Francis make 48 points against Butler earlier in the winter and recall seeing the NBA Indianapolis Olympians play a game or two on that majestic floor. In my view no Hoosier boy could watch a game at Butler and not want to play there, especially after becoming aware of all the nostalgia and history that took place there.

It seems to me a lot happened in the last two and one half months of my senior year in high school. On the saddest of notes for me it was early in April when Sharon told me, and I remember her exact words, "I think it best you find someone else." I can't say what she said was a total surprise to me since she had been going with Jim Riddle for quite awhile before I even met her, but I liked her so much it hurt. I don't remember ever having an argument with her. She had told me I had treated her with respect. It would hurt any senior boy in Indiana to lose his "first love" and the Sectional so close together.

Of course, I caught some flack from people who said Sharon was only going with me because I was on the basketball team. Only Sharon will ever know the truth. I saw it a little differently. I think she wanted to date a boy in her class while in high school and to also find out if maybe her boyfriend was the right one for her. It never made sense to me that a girl would go with a boy just because he was on the basketball team, especially a losing basketball team. Nevertheless, some said the timing of our dating proved them right. We dated from about the start of the basketball season to until just after it was over. I saw Sharon as being understanding and she wanted to give me plenty of time to find a date to take to the prom. Our relationship ended amicably as far as I was concerned.

I was lucky because a really good-looking girl by the name of Nancee Carson had moved to Marion from Libertyville, Illinois the summer before our senior year. She sat right beside me in History class. I decided the best thing for me to do when Sharon let me know the bad news was to take her advice and find another girlfriend. I was coming out of my doldrums when Nancee came to the house to meet my parents. My neighbor, Jack Sutter, saw Nancee and told my mom, "Norm sure knows how to pick'em." I took that as a compliment to both Sharon and Nancee, the only two girls in my life up to that time.

Cheerleader Wynston Lynn, who was also an outstanding wrestler, and I were awarded Kiwanis Achievement Awards for our respective sports. During an all school assembly we were called to the stage together to accept the nice trophies. To receive an award from a nationally known organization like the

Kiwanis Club took at least a little out of the sting of losing the Sectional and Sharon.

Just a few days after receiving the Kiwanis award, Woody sent me a note and asked me to make an appointment with a Mr. Mason who had an office in downtown Marion. I was told Mr. Mason liked to talk to the graduating basketball players and usually gave some good advice. My dad told me to go and, "See what you might find out." I think he knew Mr. Mason.

My time with Mr. Mason was well spent. He gave an interesting little talk about how to succeed in life, meet goals and become a responsible person. I still remember something he probably told everyone he talked to. He said to try to remember this when you get in difficult situations in life:

"Do the best you can;
With whatever you have;
Wherever you are."

He told me if you follow what is behind those words that it won't make any difference what type situation you are in, you will have a good chance to come out on top. You will know you have done your best and won't feel as bad as you might if you had not made your best effort. Mr. Mason asked me what I was going to do. I told him all I knew was I wanted to get an education and I wanted to play college basketball. If I wasn't good enough to play on scholarship then I planned to play AAU ball and be a coach. He told me he thought I was going to do just fine and wished me the best. I thanked him for his advice and left his office wondering how I might have applied his little motto had I known it during my senior year. I think I came rather close, except maybe I could have studied a little harder…and stayed out of Woody's dog house.

In May I took Nancee to the prom and she was really a fun date with a great laugh and a bubbling personality. Still, it was tough getting over Sharon as she was a nice girl and wasn't the burden to me that some rabid basketball fans thought she was. Nancee and I dated into the summer until I went off to college. Nancee smoked and was talking about marriage. I told her I could not marry a girl who smoked. Maybe I should have called Woody and asked him to run Nancee in front of his car so she would learn not to smoke!

It was also in May, in fact it was May 6th, 1954 when I was at the home of Terry Cox, who was a friend in our senior class. Several classmates were there and we all noticed a report on TV that Roger Bannister had broken the four-minute mile in Oxford, England. Of course, I caught some friendly teasing from friends that I was only about a minute off of the world record with my time in the mile. It was just a few months later in August that the first copy of *Sports Illustrated* magazine became available.

About a week before we graduated Bernie Carmin called me back into his office and introduced me to a representative from Butler University. The rep emphasized that he was not there to offer me a basketball scholarship to play for legendary coach Tony Hinkle. Rather he did say that if I wanted to walk on and could make the team that I would then be granted a scholarship. I was beginning to think that maybe my play late in the season and making All-Sectional caught some attention from coaches. I knew I had become more confident and was sure I was on my way to improving by leaps and bounds over the summer and into my freshman year in college. It was a difficult decision to turn away from going to Butler because I had at least caught the eye of Tony Hinkle.

I already knew that Bobby Plump had decided to go to Butler and his running mate, Ray Craft, was too. Plump had just been named Mr. Basketball in Indiana and Ray Craft was named the #6 player on the Indiana All-Stars. Larry Hedden had been named #4. He chose to play college ball at Michigan State. Ray Craft was the leading scorer for Milan in the victory over Muncie Central. I thought my chances to play would be slim with he and Plump going to Butler together. I declined the offer and told the man from Butler that I had pretty much made up my mind to go to Manchester College where I thought I could play. I really wanted to play at a bigger school than Manchester, but most of all I just wanted to chase my dream and continue to play basketball.

I'll never forget sitting with my cap and gown on and listening to the speeches at the graduation on my 18th birthday. I reminded myself that I was a young senior and that I actually would be eligible to play another year if I came back to Marion High School. On the other hand, I began to think that I would also be a young college player and wondered how much it would come into play that teammates would be a little more mature than I would be. Six months of development makes a big difference at that age.

During the summer Woody and Fergie took me up to Manchester College which is located not far from Marion in North Manchester, Indiana. We met coach Claude Wolfe and looked around the campus and went into a boys' dorm. Woody said, "I think this will be a good place for you." Fergie had played at Franklin College which was in the same Hoosier College Conference as Manchester. He too thought I could play at Manchester. I was to have a job working in the gym doing odd jobs like washing towels. It would pay me $35.00

per month, but my folks and I would have to pay for my room, board and tuition. I felt a little guilty about not trying to walk on at Butler or accepting a scholarship at Texas Christian so my folks would not have to pay. I wanted to go to a school close to home where I had a chance to play.

My dad told me he would get the money somehow and I could go to Manchester. I did visit St. Joseph College in Rensselaer with my friend Bill Abdon. Bill was an Honorable Mention All-State center in football at Marion High School and we had talked about going to college together. He was going to accept a football scholarship at St. Joseph and they had excellent small college success under coach Bob Jauron. Basketball coach Dick Scharf liked what I told him about me playing at Marion and offered me essentially the same full scholarship Bill Abdon received.

I guess, after talking more with Whitey Sherick, that I found Manchester more to my liking. I decided after the visit to St. Joseph to attend Manchester...without the scholarship I had dreamed about. At that time St. Joseph was a member of the Indiana Collegiate Conference (ICC) and played bigger schools than Manchester like Ball State, Indiana State, Butler and Evansville. The chance to play without a scholarship was more important to me than sitting on the bench with a scholarship. My goal was to play and get an education. I thought playing would motivate me to study and get an education.

Woody Weir had a profound influence on me, but perhaps the life that touched me more than anyone I knew around Marion was that of my African-American teammate, Oatess Archey. He married Barbara Casey, who was in my class. Tommy Nukes married another member of my class of 1954, Sandra Perkins who was a friend of Oatess and Barb. Through my eyes, Marion was a great place to grow up. Through the eyes of Oatess Archey and my other African-American friends the experience of living in Marion was quite different than mine. I knew at the time we were growing up it had to be a nervous time for them. In retrospect, I now believe I was raised in a secret culture, a culture of deceit, bigotry and hatred. The racial issues were seldom discussed with white kids and therefore somewhat hidden.

As pointed out earlier, Oatess reiterated that African-Americans in Marion didn't have to be reminded to "stay in their place." The maple trees on the town square where the lynchings took place in 1930 and the restaurants where only whites were welcome were vivid reminders that bigotry and hatred were still part of the culture in Indiana. From 1930 to 1954 Marion was relative calm regarding racial tensions as compared to the violence staged by segregation backers in the south and around the nation when civil rights activists came into their communities.

One of the prime sources of irritation for blacks in Marion was the fact they were not allowed to use the public swimming pool at Matter Park and the YMCA pool was off limits. The park pool was city owned and operated and all families, black or white, paid taxes for its upkeep. When black people were refused the right to swim there it had to cause past racial tensions to flicker in their minds. One trumped up reason for local authorities to keep blacks out was stated in a book about the Marion lynchings:

> "In the 1940s and 1950s many whites thought "colored people" were "dirty," they didn't want to be polluted by their "blackness."

Oatess and his black friends tried to find ways to cope with the bigotry. He and his friends had to board a bus and travel thirty miles to Anderson to swim in a pool. They would often just swim in the Mississinewa river. Oatess, Tommy and I did not pal around together, but we became friends as teammates on the Marion Giant basketball team. My African-American friend Ed Thurman was in my house once and I went to the Archey home once where I recall seeing the many ribbons that Oatess and his brother, Tom, had won in track events. Tommy Nukes, who lived in South Marion, always had a smile on his face and seemed happy. He told me once, when we talked about the discrimination in our hometown, that he just tried to roll with the punches and get on with his life. Tommy and Ed seemed to have similar attitudes about the discrimination.

Oatess was different. He seemed very serious and gave the impression he was always on the watch for fear of doing something that might provoke racial tension. He was observant to the point that he tried to understand what was behind the discrimination and what, if anything, could be done to make things better in Marion.

The residents of Marion were divided as to whether or not they should do something about the racial injustices that still lingered around town after the lynchings. Some white people seemed to want to bury Marion's ugly history while those more sympathetic to the cause thought it best to get the issues out in the open and deal with them. The decision was more or less made for everyone in early May of 1954 which was about a month before my class graduated from Marion High School. The United States Supreme Court handed down the decision that many believe was the most important in the twentieth century. In the now famous case, **Brown v. Board of Education,** the Court ruled that segregated schools violated the Constitution's guarantee of equal protection under the law. Segregated schools could not be, according to the ruling, separate, but equal.

Few people could recall that Indiana beat the United States Supreme Court to the punch as far back as 1885. The Indiana Civil Rights Act promised all Hoosiers, regardless of color or race, the right to use restaurants, public transportation, hotels, theaters, and other public places. However, laws on the books meant little when officials didn't act to enforce them.

Like a silently ticking time bomb, the racial issues in Marion were ever present and could explode at anytime. The **Brown v. Board of Education** decision, which started in Topeka, Kansas, caused immediate problems throughout the country. Part of the problem was the ruling was interpreted by segregationists to mean that *only* public schools had to be integrated. That wasn't a problem in Marion as the schools were integrated, even though there were not any black teachers in the Marion system.

Prejudice owners of businesses declared it was their right to keep blacks out if they so desired because the **Brown v. Board of Education** decision only applied to public schools. Even people who managed public lunch counters, restrooms, bus terminals and beaches and park districts thought they now had the right to determine who could avail themselves of their services. Blacks, on the other hand, interpreted **Brown** to mean that *all* public facilities should be open to all Americans. The culture in Marion at the time was such that local officials winked at the law and racial tension continued to fester.

Organizations such as the NAACP and the Urban League had kept a close watch on Marion since the lynchings. It was decided after the **Brown** decision to use the Matter Park Pool to see if freedom for blacks had, indeed, been legalized. Rumors became rampant in my hometown that blacks would attempt to integrate the popular pool. The local media reported that things got so far out of hand that, "The president of the park board had warned that any black person who entered the pool might be shot."

On June 20, 1954 seven orderly and polite black men were refused admission to the Matter Park Pool. The denial made news all across the midwest, but that wasn't the end of the quest for racial equality. In what would now be regarded as a quickly expedited ruling the NAACP won a decision in the United States District Court of Northern Indiana on July 30th that held:

"All persons shall be entitled to the full and equal enjoyment of the Matter Park swimming pool and all other park facilities, regardless of race or Color…in accordance with the Fourteenth Amendment to the Constitution of the United States."

I remember watching the first black person dive into the Matter Park Pool and at the young age of eighteen the event left indelible marks on my mind about what segregation and integration meant to some people. I know it meant to Oatess and Tommy and Ed they would not have to take bus trips to Anderson to swim in a nice pool. To some of the older people in town the event probably reminded them of how the armed Indiana National Guard patrolled the downtown streets of Marion on August 9, 1930. To others there was little doubt in them that with the integration of the pool that Marion would once again become the center of racial controversy. They didn't want pictures of ugly racial confrontations printed on post cards and in American newspapers as they were in the 1930s after the lynchings. People were afraid such bad publicity would put limitations on attracting businesses to the community. Such fears never came to being regarding the integration of the Matter Park Pool as the people in my hometown avoided violence that was so common in the south.

To my way of thinking, Oatess Archey showed a great deal of courage as he swam in Matter Park Pool. Many white people never returned to swim in the pool, but for the most part, the blacks gained support from sympathetic whites and Marion tried to move forward. It is clear that the events of discrimination that Oatess Archey had to endure made him resolve to himself that the progress Marion had made during our time of growing up together would not take steps backward. As Oatess left Marion I am sure it did not rest well with him that the town did not have any black teachers or coaches. Before Oatess left Marion he was named All-State in football and also won the Indiana track championship in high hurdles. He ran and played with the heart of a champion and it would pay off for him.

Oatess Archey attended Grambling State University in Louisiana on a track scholarship. He was offered scholarships to Indiana University, Drake, Tennessee State, Clark College and Houston Tilloston College. After graduation he came back to Marion and applied for a teaching and coaching position. He was hired…as a janitor, but a year later he became the first African-American to teach in the city of Marion. During his time back in Marion Oatess had to be somewhat disappointed in that which he learned about the progress our hometown had made in terms of easing racial tension.

In the early 1960s, when Oatess was back in Marion, blacks were still being denied service in restaurants. Black sections of the local cemetery had swastikas painted on tombstones. The police force had few black officers. One historical account noted that, "The summer of 1969 was one of the worst in Marion's history, as it was for many American cities. Arson, looting, marches and protests, verbal and violent confrontations between blacks and whites sent anger and shock across the nation." Fire bombings took place in Marion, police brutality was charged, and racist activity in the workplace was charged and shootings took place.

There was no question that the civil rights movement of the 1950s and 1960s was alive and well in Marion and there was no question that many people there were going to fight racial equality. The integration of the Matter Park Pool by a federal court order was not enough to convince prejudice local people it was important for a democratic nation to follow the sound decisions of its leaders.

After enduring some of the terrifying racial events, Oatess Archey left Marion High School again in 1969. He was an assistant track coach at Ball State University for a short time. He would, however, over a twenty-year period, become a very respected agent in the FBI as he became interested in law enforcement. Perhaps, just perhaps, Oatess saw so many laws not enforced when he was a kid growing up in Indiana that he became interested in a career that would allow him authority to enforce the laws of our nation. His sense of duty and integrity moved him so far along in the FBI that he was one of the agents who examined the wallet of John Hinckley, Jr. after he shot President Ronald Reagan. Oatess sent out leads to other agents to interview people whose names were found in the billfold.

Oatess retired from the FBI and moved to California, but he thought often about his hometown in Indiana. He knew he had established many friends there through his teaching, athletic accomplishments and likable personality. He made calls to friends and asked them to advise him about his chances of winning an election to become sheriff. He would return to Marion and in 1998 he was elected and became the first black sheriff in the state of Indiana. My friend Oatess had come full circle as he moved from being dreadfully discriminated against as a youngster to a position whereby he would not allow such evil to take place in the town in which he grew up.

The passing of the *Brown* decision, the integration of the Matter Park Pool and other civil rights uprisings helped pave the way for the more stringent Civil

Rights Act of 1964. This time Congress passed legislation that made it clear that integration was not to take place just in public schools, but in all public accommodations and employment. Freedoms that Oatess Archey and his brother Tom and Ed Thurman and Tommy Nukes were denied have become more commonplace. When Oatess took office in 1998 he said he was pleased to see, "How far Grant County has come." The 1964 Civil Rights Act and other laws since established have given Indiana's first black sheriff the means to help his hometown once again become a proud community.

Near the end of his book, *A Lynching in the Heartland*, author James Madison pointed out that Marion's racial history would not and should not be forgotten. He wrote. "While it may have been an ordinary place, Marion experienced fundamental changes in the twentieth century. The color line that had seemed so natural at the beginning of the century had faded." As for me, the color line never seemed natural, but that is the culture in which I was raised. I gradually learned that the lines of color faded only because courageous people spoke out against racism. Understanding patriots helped to pass laws so people like my teammate Oatess Archey can help unite communities where no American citizens will ever have to "stay in their place" because the color of their skin.

CHAPTER SIX
A Spartan Debut

DISCIPLINE YOURSELF AND OTHERS
WON'T HAVE TO! (JOHN WOODEN)

After the eventful summer I was ready to head out to college. I realized that Woody Weir had taught me a great deal. A lot of what he taught me was not about basketball, but disciplining myself to be as good a person as I could be. I never gave up trying to improve my basketball skills and played a lot of basketball the summer before enrolling at Manchester College. I thought that since I was a young senior that I would do some maturing physically as well as mentally and that seemed to happen from March of my senior year until November of 1954.

While playing in out door tournaments in the summer with some ex-Giants and against good competition my jump shot seemed to come around as Paul Arizin said it would. I had grown about an inch to 5' 10" and picked up some needed weight. I could now get the jump shot off in a game and was making it with a good degree of accuracy. The town of Logansport held a well-run tournament at their Riverside Park location, which featured a nice lighted court and bleachers. The Lions Club sponsored the games and many Indiana stars showed up. High school players were not eligible. We played against the legendary Jumping Johnny Wilson from Anderson and good players from Kokomo. I had a couple 20 point games and former Giant Mickey Barton played well. I don't recall Jim Barley playing this summer. Whitey Sherick, former Navy player, contributed. We played two or three games in this tourney before we lost and I really could feel I was getting stronger and more confident. I was anxious to try to fulfill my dream of playing in college.

During the summer, Wynn Lynn decided to attend Manchester and we were happy because we would be roommates. There wasn't any wrestling so Wynn was going to play football and I would try to play basketball. We were glad to be on our own.

Manchester was just a short ride from Ft. Wayne. It was a Church of the Brethren school and Wynn and I knew we would have to attend chapel three times a week and be careful what we did with our new found freedom. Wynn didn't have to worry about eligibility because football would be over before grades came out, but I knew I had to study to be eligible to play basketball. Wynn had been dating fellow Giant Dave Bunce's sister, Susie, who was a freshman in junior high when we were seniors in high school. My friends and I accused Wynn often of "robbing the cradle" but he didn't seem to care.

We stayed in a boys dorm named Ulrey Hall and met a lot of great guys there. We became friends with Donnie Butts who was one of the best players on the varsity basketball team and freshman player, Dick Juillerat. Donnie had a car and he was very generous loaning it out for dates or going to see the Ft. Wayne Pistons play. It seemed to me Wynn was around quite often during football season and I went to the games. He was like a ghost right after football as he was spending a lot of time in Marion with Susie and not studying much at all. That short amount of time ended as Wynn became manager for the basketball team. We would both be making out of town trips with the basketball team.

Since I didn't have a girlfriend at the time, I began playing a lot on the college court to get used to it before practice started. I was shocked the first time I stood at the end of the college court because it was longer than a high school court. I remember telling myself, I am really going to have to get in shape to play at this level.

The Manchester College Spartans had won the Hoosier College Conference the year before and coach Wolfe was named Coach of the Year in the conference. The conference was made up of all Indiana colleges. They were: Indiana Central (Indianapolis), Hanover, Earlham, Anderson, Taylor (near Marion) and Franklin.

The varsity returned several quality players from the championship team. It didn't look like much playing time was going to come my way. Plus coach Wolfe had brought in a very good freshman group. Dick Juillerat, who was 6'3", broke scoring records at Larwill High School and was so good many people thought he should have been on the 1954 Indiana All-Stars. Ron Stork, who stood 6'6" and clever passing guard Mike Yoder were starters on the Elkhart High School team that made it to the Final Four. They were beaten by the Muncie Central team that played Milan in the famous *Hoosiers* game. Troy Ingram from Hebron High School and 6'6" Dick Whistler from Union City, Indiana and myself rounded out the freshman who were expected to play some varsity ball during the 1954-55 season.

Added to the talented frosh group were varsity returnees, Donnie Butts, Bud Lantz and Tom Miller. Butts was only 5'8", but was so quick that guarding him was like trying to guard a mosquito. He and Bud Lantz were scorers and Tom Miller was a steadying influence on the team. Other players were Wayne Yager, Kent Moore and Jim Robbins.

I thought it was neat that we just sort of started practice and didn't really have to try out for the team. Once practice began I was extremely happy to be playing with such good ball players. Even though the gym only held about 1,700 people, the town and school supported the championship team the year before. Games were played on the gym floor on a stage setting and the fans mostly sat in an auditorium like setting. There were a few bleacher seats behind the players bench on the main floor.

When uniforms were passed out, I remember I chose #7 because that was the number worn by one of my favorite baseball players at the time, Mickey Mantle of the New York Yankees. I really didn't care about numbers, all I was wanting to do was play. The uniforms were white and black at home and gold and black, the school colors, on the road. No cut lists were posted, we were given schedules and practice began late October.

Life on campus at Manchester suited Wynn and I just fine. We spent a lot of time at The Oaks which was really a house made into sort of a student center. Guys could take dates there for food and drink and students could play cards, watch TV or just talk.

Wynn and I had one class together. It was Biology and it met for a lab at 7:30 in the morning. As winter approached we would go to class in the dark. The building smelled a little and Wynn and I were not real fond of the class. It was a lot harder than Biology at Marion High School. My other classes were going along OK, but I knew I had to spend more time studying than I did in high school. I do remember one cold day Wynn and I wanted to get coffee at The Oaks instead of looking at frogs or leaves in what was to be a two-hour Biology lab. The lab was in an old house and the professor had to go from one room to another to monitor students. There was a lot of snow on the ground and a window was wide open for fresh air. Wynn and I timed it so when the professor left our room we dove through the window and into a pile of snow. We got our coffee.

As fate would have it, I began to notice a girl in the Biology class. She had the sexiest eyes I had ever seen. Day by day it became increasingly difficult for me to look at the frogs and leaves under our lab microscopes instead of her. She was, like Sharon, drop dead gorgeous. I learned her name was Carolyn Castleman and her friends called her Ginger. Snooping around, I found out she had a boyfriend and Woody Weir flashed through my mind. I thought it best not to get involved with a girl, especially one who had a long time boyfriend. I survived such an arrangement in high s school, but thought it would be nice to have a girlfriend all my own.

My infatuation with Ginger was just awful, especially since I was looking for a girl to date. Most of the guys in the dorm, including Wynn, Donnie "Buttsie" Butts and Dick "Jewels" Juillerat had girlfriends. I had to get busy and find a girl to have some fun with.

Dick Juillerat would do anything this side of staying out of jail. The team ate together in the dining hall where most students had meals. Ginger was there often and sat with her friends near our table. I kept telling Jewels things about Ginger like, "Sexiest woman I have ever seen in my life." Or, "What bedroom eyes she has." One evening Jewels says, "Damn it Norm, why don't you take her out." He jumped up from the table and went to Ginger's table and said, "See that guy over there, he wants to go out with you." We were so close I could hear what Jewels said, but didn't get the answer. He told me she said, "Tell him to let me know where to meet him." I sent word through Jewels for her to "Meet me in front of the student mailboxes at 10:00am tomorrow morning." Ginger said she would be there …and she was.

Ginger and I started seeing a lot of each other. I learned she was from Rochester, Indiana which was only a short distance west from North Manchester. I figured when she agreed to meet me that quite possibly she wasn't so fond of the guy she was going with and I wasn't going to worry about that being a problem. We hit it off real good. Ginger had an infectious laugh. I thought she was so pretty I had to get control of myself to focus on playing basketball.

Ginger lived in a private home with several other girls very close to The Oaks and just across the street from campus. I went there often to pick her up and got to know some of the girls, especially Ginger's good friend, Joyce Ketcham from Canton, Ilinois. I was so happy when the basketball season started. Once again I had a beautiful girlfriend and I was playing basketball. Practice didn't go so well for me early on as I found the system coach Wolfe ran to be complicated.

Our first game was at Western Michigan University in Kalamazoo, Michigan. They played in a little tougher conference than we did so it was going to be difficult to pick up a win. My folks informed our relatives in Battle Creek that I would be at Kalamazoo, but everyone knew I would not play much. Nevertheless, I was hoping a couple of my uncles or a cousin or two would be there.

I'll always remember my first college game. We lost 74-69, but for some reason coach Wolfe put me in with about two minutes to go. I was so excited as Western Michigan's regulars were still in. They had a good player named Stacey and I guarded him. He came down the floor and attempted a jump shot and I blocked it and got the ball. I don't remember ever blocking a shot, but I was so excited I surprised even myself. My good fortune ended quickly. Near the end of the game I got the ball in the right hand corner and was wide open. I shot it and as far as I know it is still in the air. It was so wild a player on the far side of the basket caught it. I thought to myself... I have got a long way to go to score in a college game.

As I was walking off the court, I heard someone yelling my name. I figured it was a relative and began looking around the rather large field house. The voice came from a girl named Gariselda Pefley whom I had known at Marion High School. I waved at her, but was disappointed my relatives didn't show up. I don't think Gariselda was impressed with my errant jump shot.

The next game was with Huntington College and it was a foul fest at home. I was a star in this game, although in an odd way. There were so many fouls coach Wolfe had to put me in near the end of the game. Excited again, I jumped up and accidentally mooned the group of girls sitting behind the bench. Our pants were held up mostly by an elastic waistband and I accidentally slipped down both my warm up pants *and* my game pants. I heard a group laugh as I was standing there in my supporter. Yes, Ginger was in the group, but I can't recall if we talked about the incident.

I learned that Bill Abdon was not going back to St. Joseph to play football. It seemed to me that I had made a good decision not to go to St. Joseph as Bill would be gone by second semester. By this time I had learned that Ginger's boyfriend was a couple years older. Nelson Hunter was his name and he drove a yellow convertible. Once again I began to think my chances to win the heart of a beautiful girl was going to be slim. I just never seemed to have the resources to compete with older guys.

The team next visited highly regarded Illinois Normal, now Illinois State University, seeking our first win. I recall they were one of the highest scoring teams in the nation, mostly black players and very fast. They beat us 87 to 71, but I did get out front on a fast break near the end of the game and made my first basket in college. It was a lay-up that just barely rolled in.

Our first conference game a few days later was at home with tough Indiana Central. The team played well and upset the Greyhounds 91-77. I don't think I played, but I did keep my pants on. Bailey Robertson of Central made well over 20 points. He was the older brother of Oscar Robertson who was beginning to make basketball news in Indianapolis for all black Crispus Attucks High School. I will never forget the class act Bailey was. He came into our locker room and shook the hand of every player and coach Wolfe. Bailey was underrated as a player and set an Indiana collegiate career scoring record before leaving Indiana Central.

Christmas break came around so fast. We lost a heart breaker to conference foe Hanover College just two days before going home for Christmas. We had to be back on campus right after Christmas to practice. We were going to Chicago to play highly ranked DePaul on Dec. 30th and then on to a small college, three day New Years tournament at North Central College in Naperville, Illinois just outside of Chicago.

When I got to Marion for Christmas I found out when the Giants would be practicing. I wanted to see Woody and former teammates and get a workout. Woody put me in a scrimmage and I recall how much easier it was to get a shot off with the jump shot. I know I thought about what it would be like to still be playing for Marion because I would be eligible. I impressed Woody and Fergie with my shooting and they told me to keep working.

On returning to Manchester I found teammates excited as we knew we were about to play in the big time. DePaul was ranked in the top twenty-five in the country. We were getting out rebounded rather soundly and I knew DePaul would be a tough one. I was hoping to just get in the game. We were to spend four nights in the Chicago area and play every night. With only twelve players dressed I figured I would get in a game or two.

The first thing anyone saw when entering the DePaul gym was a near life size picture of the famed George Mikan. If that didn't get the attention of players, other things soon did. For example, it seemed like a mile through caverns to our locker room. When we ran out on the floor I vividly remember passing a table full of paper cups filled with Pabst Blue Ribbon beer. During warm-ups I noticed a smoky haze high above the floor. Mafia looking characters were sitting in the front row smoking cigars and laughing. I suspect they had their bets down. I was getting a little nervous with the big time environment and the seedy looking gambler types looking on.

We lost to DePaul 103-74, but stayed with them for about thirty minutes. Donnie Butts was magnificent to the point that the first thing legendary coach Ray Meyer did after the game was shake Donnie's hand. I had watched a lot of basketball, but Donnie's play that night was unbelievable. He would get the ball and fake those big guys and drive to the basket. They would knock him down and he would smile and get up and make two free throws. I do not have a box score, but I think Buttsie made around 30 points that night and I think over twenty of them were free throws. For a 5'8" player to do what he did was incredible and I will never forget it.

Coach Wolfe put me in the game and I was a little scared. I thought about guarding Dave Huff of Indianapolis Tech in a dangerous situation. Chicago was scary. I know I wound up guarding future NBA player Ron Sobiesczyk. He got the ball and faked me out of position so bad I sprained my ankle trying to keep up with him. I had to come out of the game that I had just entered.

The very next night we played North Central of Naperville on their home court. Coach Wolfe taped my ankle so well I was feeling little pain. We lost 84-74. One of the things that stands out in my memory about this game was the shooting of a player named Bill Warden. He was sensational. To this day he is still in the NCAA record book. He had the highest average in the country in 1955 at 34.7 per game. However, the record book shows that he only played thirteen games and I don't know why.

The next night became a very exciting one for me. Coach Wolfe told me while taping my ankle that the team we were playing from a small college in Iowa liked to run, run, run and everyone had to be ready. He asked me if I thought I could play and I said, "I'm ready." His tape jobs were solid and I wasn't about to tell him my ankle was sore. Warming up I remember how the floor seemed to have more spring in it than most floors and my ankle felt good.

Sure enough it was an up and down game without much defense going on and guys got tired and in foul trouble. Coach put me in early in the second half. I zipped in two jumpers real quick and was so tired after about six minutes that coach Wolfe took me out. I knew why. I was barely alive. It was the most I had played in a varsity game. Players know that there is a difference in being in good shape and being in game shape. I suspect the tension of a game drains strength fast, but I found out this night there is a difference.

Coach Wolfe had me sit beside him and surprised me by putting an ammonia capsule under my nose. It helped revive me. He said, "Take some deep breaths. I'm going to put you back in and I want you to keep shooting." Feeling a lot better, I went back in and quickly made two more jumpers. The score was approaching a 100 points for both teams. We were ahead something like 96-94 with about five minutes to go. During a free throw I went up to Bud Lantz, our standout senior work horse and said, "If we keep hustling we are going to make a 100." Bud said, "If we don't keep hustling we are going to get beat." That taught me a lesson as a young freshman…hustle until the game is over.

My biggest thrill of my freshman year came on my next shot. I hit a jumper from the right side of the foul lane for our 100th point. It was also my 10th point. We won the game 107 to 102. It was the wildest game I ever played in. I had scored in double figures for the first time in college and helped my team win. I know my ankle hurt after the game, but the pain was minimized after such a big night for me.

We lost our next tournament game to Wartburg College of Iowa, 103-96. Headed home, most of us agreed we better get to work on defense. Everyone was disappointed with our start, but we were 1-1 in the conference race. The goal was to win the conference and qualify for the NAIA (National Association of Intercollegiate Athletics) tourney in Kansas City. For small colleges this was the goal every year. It was considered a big tourney and is still operating as this is written.

Some of the trips in college were longer than high school and I did a lot of thinking on the bus. Of course, I thought a lot about Ginger because I had grown to like her in the few weeks we had been dating. She had such a pleasant personality and we had several romantic sessions during which I could have used another ammonia capsule to clear my head. There was just no question, Ginger had my number and it was probably on a bus trip when I decided I would give it my best shot to win her heart. I had learned in high school, at least near the end of playing as a senior, how to focus on basketball at the right time and not let girls interfere.

I didn't have people saying things to me about girls like I did in high school. Basketball at Marion High School was far more serious for people in town than it was for people at Manchester. I was, however, a little disappointed in that type atmosphere because the roar of a crowd in Indiana high school basketball is something not to be forgotten. I had learned that as early as the sixth grade!

I wasn't much for studying on the bus trips and had to work at things to do to keep my mind off of Ginger. I would look for basketball hoops on barns or try to sleep. One thing that was fun to do was read the Burma Shave signs. They were small red signs with white letters posted along side the roads. Five signs, about a hundred feet apart would give a slogan and then say Burma Shave. They were great advertisements and went something like this:

Passing school zone	Don't lose your head
Take it slow	To gain a minute
Let our little	You need your head
Shavers grow	Your brains are in it
Burma Shave	Burma Shave

After the Chicago trip I remember how thrilled I was to see Ginger because it had been over two weeks. I always had that fear in the back of my mind that she would one day tell me, "I think it best you find someone else." I figured she had been with her "other" boyfriend for most of the Christmas vacation since they both lived in Rochester. My fears seemed groundless as Ginger seemed happy to see me, even affectionate.

I can't remember going to movies or doing much of anything as far as dates were concerned. The $35 per month I earned washing towels for a few hours a week seemed to go a long away. Our dates seemed to be getting a bite to eat, walks near the campus or going to lovers' lane if I could use Buttsie's car. Ginger never complained and there really wasn't much to do around the small town of North Manchester, Indiana.

Our next three games were conference games at home and we won two of them. We then went on the road and got beat at Franklin. All were high scoring games. We were now 3 and 3 in the conference and trailing a couple of teams in the standings. I saw limited action and coach Wolfe became concerned that four of us freshman were not getting enough floor time. We had a college

"B" squad and they were to play a very good independent team called the Buttermilk Bobs. Coach wanted the four of us to play.

The Bobs consisted of former college players. One was Carl McNulty who was a great player at Purdue and had played for the NBA Milwaukee Hawks. Another was Bill Schroer from Valparaiso, who, as a sophomore in 1949, led the nation in free throw percentage for Division 1 at 86.8. Other good players were Phil McCarter, Paul Buzzard, John Nelson and Jack Macy. Many of these players were high school coaches in the area. Macy would become the father of Kyle Macy who became Mr. Basketball in Indiana and then played at Purdue, Kentucky and in the NBA.

I won't forget the Bobs game because the North Manchester newspaper gave it a big write up. Troy Ingram, Dick Whistler, Mike Yoder and I played most of the game. We lost 105 to 83, but it wasn't a bad effort for a bunch of college freshman going up against experienced men. McNulty had 20 points, Schroer 16 and McCarter 18 for the Bobs, but Troy, Dick and I stayed close to their totals. I had 19 points, Troy 16 and Dick 13. Mike added 8. The Bobs were a good AAU team. They ran their record to 11-1. The AAU (Amateur Athletic Union) was good basketball in those days. Teams would compete in state competition throughout the country and winners could add players and go on to Bartlesville, Oklahoma for the national AAU championships.

I think I learned a lot in this AAU game. Jack Macy covered me most of the game and tried to keep the ball away from me after I hit a couple early on. He was a little guy and I figured if I could move without the ball and get open I could shoot over him. It worked for eight field goals. I was hoping to get to play more on the varsity after that performance, but I continued to play just a few minutes a game. Late in the season our varsity came back to beat the Bobs, who were from Ginger's home town of Rochester, 92-85 as Donnie Butts scored 23 points and Bud Lantz tallied 18. I made one free throw. All in all, I never forgot learning to move better without the ball to get open.

One of the strangest things that ever happened to me took place right in the middle of the basketball season at Manchester. Wynn and I woke up one morning and Wynn said, "Look, Norm." He held back the curtain in our room so we could see the dorm parking lot. Written in either shaving cream, whipped cream or something similar, on a windshield of a car were the words, I Love Norm Jones.

When something like this happens it boggles the mind. I figured Wid Mathews could do such a thing and get me in trouble. Dick Juillerat could pull such a prank. I even wondered if Sharon had changed her mind and was now ready to take me back.

The only thing a person can do in a situation like that is wait and see what happens. It must be like waiting for a kidnap note so the ransom can be delivered. Finally, word came to me that a girl from North Manchester High School wrote the message. She had seen some games and players pictures were in one program. I received her phone number. Somehow I found out a little bit about her before I called. She was good looking so I took her out a couple of times. I finally decided that I didn't have time to date two girls and I knew Ginger had my heart all wrapped up.

As the season continued coach Wolfe told the squad that Dick Piper would be joining the team as he had completed his tour of duty in the service. Dick had been a good player for Manchester before the service interrupted his career and he fit in quickly.

I was excited about our next game because it would be against Ball State in Muncie. I knew a lot of kids going to school there and had played in Muncie a few times in high school. Ball State was a larger school and played in a tougher conference, but the Cardinals were not doing so well this season. We had a chance to win if we played well. Unfortunately our senior standout, Bud Lantz, would be benched for a training violation and that, to me, dimmed our chances.

We made 42 out of 49 free throws and upset Ball State 82-80 in a game I will never forget. For some reason I was on the floor in the closing minutes of this close encounter. One of our players was shooting a free throw with about four seconds left on the clock and the score 82-80. I was lined up on the free throw lane next to Ball State's big center, Stan Davis. As the ball came off of the rim, I saw a chance to get it and stall out the game. I got it, but came down with both knees in the middle of Davis' back. He pulled a good play and ducked down low and let me fall right into him. The ref was right there and whistled me for the foul. Coaches at that time didn't think about taking players off of the free throw line or telling them not to jump to avoid any chance of a foul.

It was embarrassing to walk to the other end of the floor knowing I could be the goat of the game if Davis could make the two free throws awarded in the last three minutes during that particular season. He had already made six free shots. I was feeling stupid. Lucky for me and the team he missed both shots. It was a nice win, but a tough lesson for me to learn.

All ten players who played in the Ball State game scored as Dick Piper made 17, Butts 14, Juillerat 14 and Wayne Yager made 14 filling in for Lantz. Six of our last eight games would be conference games and we would need to win all of them to have a chance to win the conference. We reversed an earlier conference loss to Hanover by beating them by a 72-70 margin. We then went to Detroit to play Lawrence Tech and on the way back from the 76 to 63 loss the bus broke down out in the middle of no where. We were late getting back to campus and worn out. It was unfortunate we had to go to Indianapolis to again play Indiana Central three days later.

Bailey Robertson and his Indiana Central crew beat us 72-59 in a hard fought game in Indianapolis to take us out of the conference race. I had one other game I remember during this season and that was at Anderson College. Coach Wolfe told me to play a half in a "B" team game and still have a half left for the varsity game. I made 15 points the first half of the "B" team game and really felt improvement in this game. I played sparingly in the varsity game which we lost 69-65. I thought I could have helped in the varsity game and became a little discouraged after that loss.

I was looking forward to the next game at Taylor University. I had talked to the great coach there by the name of Don Odle. He tried to interest me in playing for him just before I enrolled at Manchester. Coach Odle took teams to the Orient on a Christian mission they called a Venture for Victory. He was highly successful and well thought of in Indiana basketball. Taylor is located in Upland, Indiana which is just outside of Marion.

Ginger and I set it up so she would go to the game with Joyce Ketcham and another friend. Ginger would stay at my house in Marion after the game, but I don't recall where everyone else stayed. I got permission to visit my folks and not go back to school on the team bus. We beat Taylor 73-72 and my friends went to my house after the game. Bill Abdon came over and Ginger and I introduced him to Joyce. We had a nice week-end and I was happy Ginger made a good impression on my folks. As it turned out Bill made a good impression on Joyce.

We finished the season on Feb. 19th with an 83-70 win over Indiana Tech in Ft. Wayne. Our record was a disappointing 10 and 12 and, with a 6 and 6 conference record, we finished in fourth place in the Hoosier College Conference. Still, I believed I had learned a great deal, was developing as a pretty good shooter and passer and would return next year. We would lose Bud Lantz to graduation, but Buttsie, Jewels and Ron Stork would be back along with friends Mike Yoder and Troy Ingram so I remained excited about basketball and our title chances.

Our season ended in time for me to get back to Marion and watch the Giants play in the Sectional. The team had not had a good season, but was the choice to win the Sectional. It was sad for all of Marion to see little Fairmount upset Marion in the Sectional final on a last second shot by a player named Stroup. It was Woody's third straight year to lose a Sectional. Bob France, Tommy Nukes and Oatess Archey, like me, never got to cut down Sectional nets at Marion. I had also just lost out on cutting down conference championship nets in college. I felt the pain of my former teammates and Woody.

As was his custom, Woody had the Giant players rest at his house across from the high school between games on Saturday. The boys knew they were going to be told to stretch out and rest. Surprisingly, Woody told the three African-Americans on the team to come with him upstairs to the attic part of the house. The black boys would stay there together away from their white teammates. Tommy Nukes had already paired off with one of the white boys and they were going to share a bed together. This move by Woody was just one of the many times around Marion that the black kids were treated differently than the white kids. Oatess, Tommy Nukes and Dave Pettiford just wanted to be treated like everyone else on the team, but that wasn't possible at the time, or so it seemed.

Who could figure what was going through the mind of Woody Weir when he separated the black players from the white players? Was he afraid some parents might object if they found out their son was allowed to bunk down with a black person? Was Woody afraid of school board members who might get after him for allowing blacks and whites to rest together on the same bed? This situation developed after Oatess and his friends, with a federal court order, helped to integrate the Matter Park Pool so it had to be a particularly hard time for Oatess to understand why the discrimination against his race continued. I firmly believe that incidents such as this were motivational factors that brought Oatess back to Marion to become the first black sheriff in the state of Indiana.

Woody Weir may not have known at the time the feelings he created within the black players. Such actions were commonplace in Marion and around the nation in the 1950s and 1960s. The culture was such that whites who didn't want to discriminate did so because they were raised in a culture of secrecy and deceit. The blacks recognized discrimination every time as Oatess did when assigned to the attic, but whites often made discriminatory moves and thought nothing of them because they didn't have to "stay in their place" like the black people did.

While I was at Manchester Oscar Robertson was inching ever closer to the legendary status he finally achieved in Indiana basketball. As a junior, he led his all black Crispus Attucks team from Indianapolis to the first state championship for the city. The team went 31 and 1 and beat Gary Roosevelt 97 to 74 in the state final game before 14,983 fans in Butler Fieldhouse. I was at the game and it was fun to watch. I again found Butler Fieldhouse an exciting place and it made me miss the larger crowds we didn't get at Manchester. A player for Roosevelt by the name of Wilson Eison outscored Oscar in the closely watched last four games, 97 to 95. Oscar made 30 points in the final game and Eison made 31. The teams set game scoring totals for the Indiana finals. Eison was named Mr. Basketball.

The closest game Attucks had in the tourney was a historic 71-70 win over Muncie Central. Evidence was witnessed in this game that the **Brown vs. Topeka Board of Education** decision didn't seem to register with some Hoosiers. Racial unrest was still lurking behind the scenes in Indiana. Muncie Central star, Phil Raisor, in writing about Indiana basketball, mentions that as his Bearcats left the floor at halftime of the Attucks game someone put a tight squeeze on his arm and said, "Get them niggers, Phil."

When a town won the Indiana state championship the team was expected to take a few trips around the town square in fire trucks or convertibles and stop to celebrate. By their actions, Indianapolis officials made it clear they were wary of Attucks players and their followers regarding a celebration. Although the mayor led the parade with players on a fire truck and other vehicles following, the parade was stopped briefly downtown at the Monument Circle. The mayor presented the key to the city to Coach Crowe and the parade quickly moved on to the black section of town. Oscar Robertson noted that, "When Milan won the state...they got a ride around all the squares in Indy." The fact is the monument is a shrine to the Soldiers and Sailors of America who fought gallantly to preserve freedoms for *all* Americans.

Oscar went home and said, "Dad, they don't like us do they?"

One thing I really liked about being at Manchester was its closeness to Ft. Wayne. I once hitchhiked to a game when it was snowing just to see Paul Arizin play against the Pistons. I wanted to learn all I could about the jump shot and I think watching him helped me develop my shot. Having played on the Coliseum floor made it a little more exciting for me, but seeing Paul Arizin in person again was a thrill not to be forgotten.

It was in the early spring of 1955 and right after my first season of college ball that the Ft. Wayne Pistons were in hot pursuit of the NBA title. George Mikan had retired from the Minneapolis Lakers and Ft.Wayne had replaced them as division champs. The Pistons had made a bold move and hired an NBA referee by the name of Charlie Eckman to coach the team. Eckman did not have any coaching experience at all. Some games had been televised and I saw several of them. In fact the first nationally televised regular-season NBA game in history had taken place in Ft. Wayne on Nov. 6, 1954. The Pistons defeated the New York Knicks 90-83. Only about 1,000 fans showed up because everyone stayed home to watch it on television.

I had become a big fan of the Pistons. Well-known players at the time and favorites of mine were George Yardley, Mel Hutchins, Larry Foust, Andy Phillip and Frankie Brian. The Lakers were still a good basketball team with players like Jim Pollard, Vern Mikkelsen, Slater Martin and Indiana bred Clyde Lovellette. The Pistons met the Lakers in the playoffs and beat them three games to one. This win put the Indiana town of Ft.Wayne in position to play for the world championship against the Syracuse Nationals. The success of the Ft.Wayne Pistons and the Crispus Attucks teams added greatly to the history that helped the era of the 1950s to become known as the Golden Era of Indiana basketball and continue the tradition of Hoosier Hysteria.

It was a sad day for everyone remotely cheering for the Pistons when it was learned the American Bowling Congress had a contract to use the Ft. Wayne War Memorial Coliseum for seventy-three days for its mid-west tournament. The Pistons had to play "home" games in Indianapolis and lost to Syracuse in hard fought battles for the world title. I was able to attend one game in this famous series. It went seven games and Ft. Wayne lost the final game in Syracuse 92-91. It was as close to the world title the Ft.Wayne team and the state of Indiana would ever get.

It was in the spring when my friend Bill Abdon began making frequent trips to Manchester to see Joyce Ketcham. I liked the arrangement because Bill had a car and Ginger and I double dated with Bill and Joyce. It was a fun time. One night while parked in lovers' lane Bill and Joyce announced they were going to get married. Ginger and I were surprised, but happy for them. I know I thought how great it would be if I asked Ginger to marry me and she would say yes, but I wasn't even nineteen yet. I knew I had to get rid of such thinking if my dream of playing college basketball and getting an education would become reality. In fact, Ginger and I had never said, "I love you," to each other although I was having feelings that seemed to be telling me I should.

Near the end of school the college yearbook came out and people were signing them for each other. When Gin wrote in my book she said some nice things about me like how I "had been so kind and nice to her" and that she "thought the world of me." I waited anxiously for her to finish what she was writing hoping that she would sign it, Love, Gin. Instead she signed it, As ever, Gin. I don't know if I had signed her book or what the situation was, but I remember being a little disappointed she didn't sign it, Love, Gin. I wanted to make sure she did, indeed, "think the world of me" and quickly asked if we would be able to see each other in the summer? She rejuvenated my spirits by saying, "Yes, but you will probably have to come to Rochester and get me." I figured I could work that out and left school happy to go home for the summer.

It wasn't long until Ginger and I received word that Bill and Joyce would be married in Canton, Illinois on Sept. 2nd. Ginger was to be the maid-of-honor for Joyce and I was to be an usher for Bill.

My dad had informed me in the spring that I was to contact the Marion City Recreation Director, Mutt Chambers about a job. Mutt had played basketball for the University of Kentucky and knew of my interest in continuing to play basketball. During an interview with him he said he needed an Assistant City Recreation Director and wondered if I would fill the position. He said there were basketball goals in parks all around Marion and I would have duties some days, but plenty of free time to shoot and get in some practice. It was the perfect job for me and I graciously accepted and started work as soon as I got home from college. I was to keep the parks in good shape. I painted shuffle board courts, kept up the softball diamonds and readied them for games in the evening and week-ends and did whatever Mutt wanted done…and shot baskets.

Ginger and I exchanged letters and I played in outdoor basketball tournaments and fast-pitch softball with the good Hawkins Ford Mailers team from Marion to pass the summer hours. The older guys on the Mailers bought Bill Abdon and I beer after games. Twenty-one was the drinking age in Indiana, but it was easy in those days for those just approaching the legal age to get beer. I figured it helped me put on some needed pounds as I was still rather skinny.

I was stunned when I received a letter from Manchester College telling me I was not eligible to return. I thought I had studied hard enough to maintain the C average to remain in school and play ball. My dad read the letter and he could not understand why I couldn't go back because, as he put it, "You didn't fail anything." My dad never attended college and didn't know the rules. I must have earned three Cs and a D the last semester and it made me ineligible. My dad said he wanted to make an appointment with the president of the college so he could understand better what it took to get a college education. He wasn't that concerned about me playing basketball.

On the way to Manchester to see the president I had all sorts of things running through my mind. I wanted to go back and play ball and I wanted to be with Ginger. Somehow my dad struck a deal with the president. I let them know early on in the negotiations that I wasn't going back if I couldn't get eligible to play. We all three made a deal that if I came back I would have to get two Bs and two Cs in order to be eligible. We were to open the season in a sixteen team Thanksgiving Holiday Tourney at Earlham College in Richmond, Indiana. The president told us I would not be able to get grades from my instructors until the first night of the tournament which was Thanksgiving.

My dad and I left North Manchester and I got my second lecture of the day. The president of the college had pointed out to my dad that they kept close tabs on students and that my behavior was not as responsible as it should be. I suspect the dorm directors reported late night activities. Many of the guys carried on with newfound freedom from parents and Wynn and I were not void of some of that mischief.

By late summer I was pretty happy with a good job and knowing I could return to Manchester. Ginger and I were looking forward to the wedding which would take place right before school started. Considering all of these circumstances that happened to me in the summer of 1955 I would have to say it was an important period for me growing up in Indiana. My folks did mention that they were considering a move to Muncie and were looking for a house there.

It is known in Indiana if the corn is knee high or better by July 4th, farmers would have a good crop. The corn was well above knee high when Ginger agreed to come and spend two nights with me at my house. I was just so happy. I had not seen her for almost two months. I had told her I was dating a girl by the name of Sandy Southwick who I had struck up a conversation with at the Marion YMCA. It was a new YMCA and a great place for young people to go. I explained to Ginger that Sandy was only a sophomore at Marion High School and that I was not real interested in getting serious about anyone but her. I did not tell Sandy my heart was hung up in Rochester, Indiana.

During Ginger's stay I was supposed to play on Saturday night for the Hawkins Ford Mailers, but I sprained my ankle and could not play. Sandy usually came to the games, but I told her I would not be able to play. I figured she wouldn't come to the game. Ginger and I decided to go see a few innings and as fate would have it ...Sandy walked right past us. She gave Ginger a once over and I said, "Sandy, I would like for you to meet my cousin Gin from Michigan." Ginger knew what I was doing and I was able to cut the conversation short. I dated Sandy a few times after that and she never caught on, but once again I didn't want two girlfriends at the same time. Sandy did come to Manchester to see me early the next year, but, as will be seen, Ginger was on my mind.

The per chance meeting of Sandy and Ginger may have paid off for me. I had to take Ginger back to Rochester on Sunday evening. We first went to lovers' lane near Marion and she teased me a little about Sandy. Nevertheless, Ginger got me so warmed up that night that I really thought she missed me. It was all I could do to keep myself from telling her I loved her.

After that heart pounding session we took off for Rochester as I was to take Gin to her sister's house. Her sister, named Fran, was also very pretty. On the way I told Ginger I thought I could kiss her all night long. She said, and I will never ever forget this moment, "Do you want to park again?" I answered by pulling the car into a dark country road between two cornfields. Within minutes and for the second time that night she had me so hot and bothered that I thought I was trapped in the first microwave oven. It was a hot summer night in Indiana and I knew that night for sure that Ginger would always hold a special place in my heart. I don't know if Ginger seeing Sandy helped the situation or if Ginger just missed me, but she seemed to intensify our relationship.

There was some indication the rest of the summer that maybe me dating someone else got Ginger's attention. Ginger wrote a couple letters before the wedding and always signed them, Cousin Gin.

In an odd occurrence late in the summer, I saw Ginger with Nelson Hunter at the outdoor basketball tournament in Logansport. I went up to them and Ginger introduced us. It was not difficult for me to see what she saw in Nelson. He was tall and handsome and seemed very pleasant. I left thinking I had my work cut out for me to steal her heart, but when I thought back to our session in the cornfields I figured I was making progress.

Just before Bill and Joyce's wedding one of the most racially charged incidents in American history took place in Mississippi. It was so bad it sent shock waves through Marion and the rest of the nation. It was the horrible murder of a fourteen-year-old Chicago boy named Emmett Till. He was visiting relatives in Mississippi when two white men accused Emmett of whistling at a white woman. They shot him in the head, savagely beat his face beyond recognition, tied an industrial fan with barbed wire on it around his neck and put his dead body in the Tallahatchie River. It was such a brutal act the family could only identify Emmett by a ring on his finger.

Despite overwhelming evidence, it took an all white Mississippi jury only 67 minutes to acquit the two white men. Rosa Parks said she had the memory of Emmett Till on her mind when she refused to give up her seat on the famous bus incident about three months later in Montgomery, Alabama. It was as clear here as it was with Oscar Robertson in Indianapolis and my friend Oatess in Marion that any attempt to bring people of different colors together was going to be very difficult in the south and the great mid-west. Court orders like the one that integrated the Matter Park Pool didn't seem to faze those bent on keeping the races separate. All white academies sprung up in the south so white kids would not have to attend school with blacks.

Right after all the racial tension, I was to meet Ginger in Canton, Illinois for Bill and Joyce's wedding. I was going with some friends from Marion. We ran into terrible storms and had to stop and then had a flat tire and didn't get to the wedding until right near the end. After the wedding I remember Ginger and I got into a little spat about something, but it wasn't serious. We returned to Manchester the next week and I wanted to see if I could continue to make progress with Ginger. She was as loving as ever!

I knew I was going to have to be careful about using my time to study and in dating Ginger and playing ball. Two Bs and two Cs would be the best I had ever done in the classroom, but I was determined. I remember I had an Art class and a Speech class. I figured I better do well in Art and Speech because I recall the other two as being the most difficult. Wynn did not return to school so I had a new roommate to get to know.

The work in my classes reflected my intense desire about basketball. For example, in the Speech class I had to make a speech designed to introduce someone. Of course, I introduced the new head coach of the Ft.Wayne Pistons, Charlie Eckman. The instructor liked it and I was off to a good start in that class. Again, to magnify how interested I was in basketball I made an art project that focused on basketball. We were given an assignment to make a poster using script pens. We had to learn how to write in script using these pens. I spent nights in the Art building working on this project as it would be a major part of my grade. In script I wrote the following:

"The referee is a flighty bird, he has an eagle eye;
I can't get any foul past him, no matter how hard I try,
But if my guard hangs on my neck or slaps my ears down flat,
The referee ain't lookin' or he's blind as any bat."

Practice began and it looked as though I would be playing about seventh or eighth man, but I set out to play a lot more than my freshman year. The plan in the back of my mind was to come back my last two years and be a starter and help win the conference, go to the NAIA tourney in Kansas City, graduate and start coaching and teaching. If I got real lucky, I could marry Ginger. She had told me she wanted to get married someday and have a daughter named Melody. She also asked me right after we started back to school if I thought it was possible to be in love with two people at the same time? I knew what that meant and I said no. I figured something would happen this year to either bring Ginger and I closer together or she would stay with Nelson. After seeing them together at the Logansport outdoor tourney that summer I was really beginning to wonder what was going to happen to Ginger and I. It wasn't long until something did happen.

I was looking forward to getting behind me whatever it was that was going to happen about my grades, staying in school and playing ball. Taking Mr. Mason's advice, along with that of my dad, I did the best I could in the classroom. We loaded the bus to go to Richmond to start the season on Thanksgiving night. I saw Ginger just before leaving and told her I had no idea what was going to happen with my grades, but that I would not leave Manchester without seeing her.

Believe it or not, we were actually warming up for our first game and I had not received word whether or not I was eligible to play. Just before the game started a professor on the athletic committee came to the floor and told me I had made two B's and two C's and I was eligible to play. I was so happy that I had finally taken responsibility to discipline myself and met an important goal.

I remember being disappointed that I didn't get to play until right at the end of the first game. I was coming down the floor with the ball in the middle on a fast break and my right knee gave out. I fell hard on the floor and I was in terrible pain. It was the worst pain I had ever felt in my life. I was carried to the bench and vomited, but swallowed it because my folks were there and I didn't want to scare my mom. I saw my folks move down to the front row looking very concerned. One of my teammates said, "You look pale." I was in shock.

After the game I found myself on crutches for the first time in my life and made it back to the dorm where the team was staying. My knee was killing me and I didn't sleep. I got up the next morning and was shaving to get ready to go to breakfast and I passed out right on the bed behind me. My roommate, Ron Stork, called coach Wolfe and he came over. He said all they could do was wrap the knee and try to stabilize it and get me to a doctor when we arrived back in Manchester. I was too weak to go to breakfast. The team had games yet to play so in a very discouraged state, I limped around campus until the tournament was over. I was extremely disappointed that I could not play. I don't recall how the team did in the tourney, but I do know that to work so hard to get my grades and have the knee injury happen in the very first game of the season was devastating.

When we got back to campus I told Ginger what happened. I was on crutches and struggled to get to meals and classes and even to see Ginger. Coach Wolfe made an appointment for me with a local doctor and the doctor quickly told me the injury was serious and I would have to see an orthopedic surgeon. I didn't like the way that sounded. The doctor recommended a Dr. Stauffer in Ft. Wayne. I made an appointment with Dr. Stauffer and my new roommate, who had a car, agreed to take me to see him. My dreams were fading fast and I was about as discouraged as I had ever been in my short life.

Dr. Stauffer told me I had torn several key ligaments and part of the cartilage under my kneecap had broken off and locked under the kneecap. He told me I would limp the rest of my life if I didn't have it repaired. Of course, the first thing I asked was if I would be able to play basketball again. He said I should be OK, but it would take at least six months before I would be fully recovered. I decided to get this setback behind me as soon as possible and made a date for surgery just before Christmas. I was hoping I would heal fast and be able to play in the summer and the next season.

Back on campus I called my folks, who had now moved to Muncie and told them I had to have surgery and my season was over. Coach Wolfe told me that an insurance policy at the college would cover the cost. My folks told me they would be at St. Joseph hospital in Ft.Wayne the day of the surgery.

I told Ginger the date and where I would be having surgery and that I wanted her to come see me and she said she would. Dr. Stauffer had told me

I would be in the hospital about seven days. This would give Ginger plenty of time to come and visit me since Rochester was only a short drive from Ft. Wayne. Dr. Stauffer's rule was that I would have to be able to lift my leg off of the bed and raise it above my head before I could go home. The few days before surgery were some of the worst I had spent in my life. I was scared, but knew I had to go through with it if I was ever to meet my goal of becoming an accomplished college player. I didn't want to limp the rest of my life either.

The plan was for my roommate to take me to Ft. Wayne the day before surgery and my folks would make arrangements to get me home for Christmas. I know the surgery was on a Saturday morning the day after Christmas break at Manchester was to begin. It's crazy, but I know I wanted to wake up in time on Saturday to see the Pistons play on TV that afternoon. When I did wake up my folks had the game on, but there were three or four pretty nurses in the room and I turned my attention to them. They were all giggling and I remember my mom saying, "Why don't you tell him."

It turns out I was given sodium-pentothol to put me to sleep and it was the truth serum. I was told I said and did crazy things while under the anesthetic not the least of which was trying to kiss the nurses. One of the nurses was a perky French girl with pretty dark black hair. Her last name was Tuscany and the nurses called her Tusky.

I was feeling a lot of pain and I was told on top of the shots I was getting during the day that I would get one that would help me sleep that night. Dr. Stauffer said he would be in the next day to see me. That Saturday was tough to get through because my knee hurt…and Ginger didn't show up. I thought, oh well, she knows I am going to be here for a few more days.

As it turned out Tusky was my night nurse and she told me the shot I was going to get would put me out until morning. Tusky kept checking on me to see how drowsy I was getting and we talked a little bit. She surprised me right about the time I was to fall asleep. She moved her pretty face right over mine and got her lips right above mine. I remember I said, "You are going to kiss me aren't you?" She said, "Yes I am." She did and I went to sleep thinking what a great hospital I was in.

Dr. Stauffer came in the next day and asked me a lot of questions. I told him my troubles and he listened. First of all, I just had the feeling that Ginger wasn't going to show up. I told the Dr. I thought I was in love with a beautiful gal who had been going with an older guy before I met her and I was trying to break them up. I told him I wasn't sure I was fitting into the system under coach Wolfe and that my folks had moved to Muncie and I was all messed up. The next day we talked again and he told me he and the coach at Ball State, Jim Hinga, grew up together in Ft.Wayne. He suggested I transfer to Ball State, live at home, find a new girlfriend and walk on and try to make the team at Ball State. A lot of what he said made sense and I told him I would have to think about it.

At first I was somewhat lukewarm to the advice Dr. Stauffer gave me because walk-ons seldom made teams let alone play. I would be taking a big chance of not playing on a school sponsored team. On the other hand, I had played at Ball State and liked the atmosphere. It intrigued me that I would be playing in basketball crazy Muncie and I thought playing in Marion and Muncie both would be good background. I would also have the advantage of having played in two college conferences in the state and most of the decent size towns. I would be deeply immersed in Indiana basketball.

By the fourth day in the hospital I had done a lot of thinking and made some decisions. If Ginger didn't show up I was going back to Manchester and give her a chance to tell me her reason. If it didn't rest well with me I was going to tell her we were finished. I had decided I just couldn't take anymore of this sharing her with someone else. I just didn't think it was right that I was hurt so bad and she didn't come to see me. I figured she was making time with Nelson Hunter and didn't like me as much as I thought. It was just devastating to me that she didn't come to the hospital. My heart hurt a lot worse than my knee.

I remember fighting off the shot to put me to sleep that night because I wanted out of the hospital. I worked all night the fifth night to raise my leg and by morning I had done it. When Dr. Stauffer came in I surprised him by raising my leg. He said I could leave the hospital. He told me he would write coach Hinga a letter and let him know my knee should be OK. Dr. Stauffer was a big help to me. We both knew I would have to sit out a year because NCAA rules were, like they still are today, that transfers had to sit out a year before playing again. Despite the odds against me playing at Ball State I decided at that moment it would be best for me to transfer. I would just go and not look back.

I don't recall how this situation happened, but a friend, Jerry Roberts, who my folks had rented a room to in Muncie came to the hospital to take me home for Christmas. Tusky needed a ride to her home on the way to Muncie and we dropped her off there. She told me, "When you get back on your feet, give me a call." I never saw Tusky again, but I did appreciate the way she took care of me in the hospital.

Christmas at home was nice, but I knew I had to go back to Manchester and withdraw, tell my teammates good-bye and, worse yet, tell Ginger and coach Wolfe I was transferring to Ball State. I knew at the time that it would be very difficult for me to overcome the injury and even more difficult to play basketball at Ball State, a much larger school than Manchester. My mind was made up...I would accept the challenge.

I saw coach Wolfe and he understood my decision. I will never forget talking with Ginger beside the girls' dorm across the street from the private home where she was staying. I asked her point blank, "Why didn't you come and see me in the hospital?" Her answer was, and it still lingers with me, "I didn't think you were in there." That was it for me, I looked at her sexy eyes and summoned enough courage to tell her I was going to Ball State. She started crying. My plan was to kiss her and tell her I loved her, but I didn't. I was hoping, beyond hope I guess, that I would get a letter from Ginger telling me she would drop Nelson if I would come back. I never heard from or ever saw Ginger again. I left Manchester the next day with tears in my eyes knowing that one of the nicest persons I had ever known was now out of my life. It was tough, real tough.

I went home to Muncie determined to make myself a happier life. So far I had been runner-up to Mississinewa, runner-up to Sharon and runner-up to Ginger. I thought I could improve on things by changing my environment. I set my sights on finding a new girlfriend. I promised myself that if the girl was serious about someone, I would not take her out. No more second fiddle. I also set my sights on playing basketball for the Ball State Cardinals.

MEMORIAL COLISEUM -- MARION, INDIANA

MARION WATER TOWER --
1926 STATE CHAMPS (AND BEYOND)

Marion High School Booster Club

Row One: C. Horning, B. Riddle, S. Secrest, B. Hoyt, C. Miller, J. Snyder, M. Hanthorn, M. Hartley, A. Anderson, A. Kepler, C. Carmin

Row Two: P. Shields, P. Hartzell, A. Long, B. Locke, L. Conkling, S. Perkins, B. Casey, B. Twigg, J. Wood, B. Munich, S. Sutter

Row Three: J. Weimer, J. Duncan, J. Gosset, R. Allen, G. Bowman, M. Bahr, M. Davis, S. Morris, K. Bloom, C. Jackson, S. Spence

Row Four: C. Marsh, J. Kistler, S. Davis, J. Ruby, S. Gunyon, B. Molland, J. Henry, R. Malson, N. Veach, F. Harmon, P. Strickland

Row Five: J. Danforth, M. Kesot, G. Pefley, G. Gotschall, C. Lee, P. Blinn, R. Ross, N. Speece, B. Thompson, C. Russell, J. Bobson

Row Six: N. Botkin, P. Blaugher, M. Hendey, S. Grose, C. Hendey, N. Williams, L. Newkirk, J. VanDine, C. Jones, L. Buis, P. Carter

Row Seven: C. King, J. Tucker, G. Scheerer, J. Hamilton, J. Miller, S. Miller, D. Gilbreath, S. Crooks, J. Hays, S. Woodbury, J. Usher

Row Eight: B. Abernathy, V. Wilkins, V. Nutter, R. Stevens, J. Crist, L. Denton, C. Nichols, S. Ring, B. Voss, D. Evans, A. Chochos

Row Nine: B. Sprinkle, B. Clow, S. Adams, L. Steelman, M. Houston, A. Clark, J. Dakin, F. Steelman, M. McGee, M. Naugle, M. Polsley

Row Ten: B. Steele, R. Schwaiger, L. King, A. Hays, S. Eltzroth, G. McGee, S. King, M. Clingaman, S. Bowman, C. Bloom, C. Hunter

Row Eleven: F. Blanchard, M. Talbott, G. Marks, L. Tegarden, D. Johnson, M. Britton, E. Rapp, S. Griffith, F. Harmon, P. Rader, B. Gurthrie

Photo courtesy of Marion High School

1954 MARION GIANTS

First Row: Student Manager Ed Wilkinson, Tommy Nukes,
LarryBricker, Phil Yeakle, Bob France, Norm Jones, Oatess Archey
Second Row: Jim Aldrich, Dave Bunce, John Knipple,
Bill Wampner, Jim Gross, Dave Pettiford, Coach Woody Weir

WOODY WEIR

Photos courtesy of Marion High School

OATESS ARCHEY

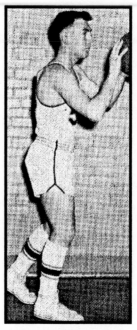

BOB FRANCE

JIM GROSS

TOMMY NUKES

Photos courtesy of Marion High School.

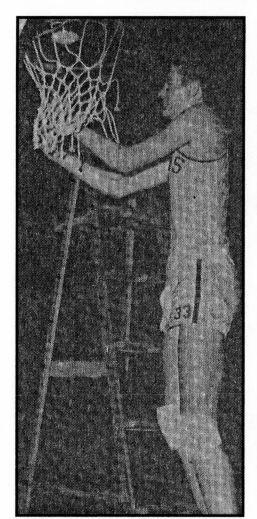

PAT KLEIN

LARRY HEDDEN ** JIM BARLEY*

In the early 1950's Marion and Grant Co. claimed three All-State basketball players. Pat Klein led Marion to the Final Four in 1950. He was named Indiana's Mr. Basketball and won the coveted Trester Award. Jim Barley, shown cutting down Marion Sectional nets, led the North Central Conference in scoring, set several Marion High records and was named to the 1952 Indiana All-Star team. He went on to play at Indiana University. Larry Hedden led Mississinewa (27-1) to the Sweet Sixteen in 1954 and was named to the 1954 Indiana All-Star team. He later played at Michigan State. Barley and Hedden have been inducted into the Indiana Basketball Hall of Fame.

Photos courtesy of Marion High School
**Photo courtesy of Marion-Chronicle Tribune*

1954-55 MANCHESTER COLLEGE SPARTANS

Standing: Mike Yoder, Donn Butts, Tom Miller, Bud Lantz, Wayne Yager, Dick Whistler, Ron Stork, Kent Moore, Jim Robbins, Troy Ingram, Dick Juillerat, Norm Jones

Kneeling: Coach Claude Wolfe

Photo Courtesy of Manchester College

1957 - 58 BALL STATE CARDINALS

Left to Right: Kenny Miller (manager), Norm Jones, Warren Harmeson, Ted Fullhart, Don Clark, Bob Crawford, Jim Sullivan, Jime Hinga (coach), Art Harman, Wilbur Davis, Dick Barkman, Larry Perry, Travis Burleson, John Lebo, Terry Schurr, George Taylor

TED FULLHART   **WILBUR DAVIS**   **JIM SULLIVAN**

Watching in street clothes from the end of the bench.

Schurr and Fullhart named to
District 21 N.A.I.A. team.

Terry Schurr
District 21 N.A.I.A. MVP

Photos courtesy of Ball State University.

CHAPTER SEVEN
Sitting Out

*"Winners don't have good attitudes
because they win, they win because
they have good attitudes."*
(Jim Tunney)

Ball State was a bigger school and Muncie a much larger town than Manchester and I remember thinking that things ought to get better for me in such surroundings. The school was known as Ball State Teachers College in those days. That meant plenty of women would be there seeking elementary teaching degrees and, for that matter, probably husbands. One of the first things I did was visit coach Jim Hinga and he had received the letter from Dr. Stauffer. He did remember the game when Manchester beat Ball State 82-80. He told me to get my knee in shape and he promised me a good look when I came out for the team. That would be over a year away and seemed like eternity to me.

The house my folks bought could sleep five guys upstairs. My brother, Wendell, was at Ball State and had begun to run around with some guys from northern Indiana. Jerry Roberts from Angola, who brought me home from the hospital, stayed at the house as did Pleasant Lake, Indiana boys Dave Waymire and John Hevel. Former Marion High classmate, Larry Dovin, stayed their for a short time. Wendell, Dave and John had decided to pledge the Kappa Sigma Kappa fraternity.

Ball State was on a quarter system and I didn't have to take any classes until about March. I got rid of the crutches after a visit to Dr. Stauffer verified my knee was healing faster than he expected. He thought I could play some in the summer and that was great news to me. In Indiana, life without basketball was like a bath without soap.

Jerry Roberts left school and Tom Weesner, a Kappa Sig, moved in for the spring quarter. My mom liked Dave Waymire and John Hevel and so did Wendell and I. Mom usually made breakfast available. I didn't find any of the courses at Ball State so difficult that I couldn't deal with them. I transferred more credit than I thought and was listed as a sophomore. I had two years of eligibility left and could tryout for the team in the fall of 1957. I saw Ball State play in February 1956. I didn't think the team looked good and this gave me some hope of fulfilling my dream and playing at Ball State. The team would have many lettermen returning and so I would have to evaluate my chances based on how well the 1956-57 team performed.

After arriving at Ball State, I decided to keep reminding myself of the decisions I made while flat on my back in the hospital. I was going to study so I never had to worry about being eligible again. I was not going to go with girls if their hearts were already taken. I was going to relax and have a good time and get in shape in time enough to try out for the basketball team. I was going to try, as hard as it was going to be, to forget Ginger. And, I would keep in mind how Paul Arizin kept chasing his dream after not playing in high school and I would not forget the motivational words of Mr. Mason. I would do the best I could, with whatever I had, wherever I was.

Needless to say, with my knee the way it was, I watched a lot of basketball on TV from the time I arrived in Muncie until the season was over. I remember how discouraging it was having surgery, not playing and leaving my friends. Having worked so hard to become eligible, then getting hurt was always on my mind. It helped that there were high school, college and NBA games on TV. Dave Waymire and my brother were basketball nuts so we watched a lot of games together.

The entire state was glued to TV sets in March of 1956 when Oscar Robertson led his Crispus Attucks team into the Indiana high school tournament undefeated. To the absolute surprise of no one the Attucks, in front of 14,983 fans in Butler Fieldhouse, won their second straight state title with a 31-0 record. They had won 45 straight games in two years. In the afternoon game Oscar distributed the ball beautifully as four teammates scored in double figures in beating Terre Haute Gerstmeyer 68-59. They beat Lafayette Jefferson of the North Central Conference 79 to 57 in the final game as Oscar scored 39 points. Crispus Attucks was the first team to win the Indiana state crown undefeated. Many regard this team as the best ever in Indiana history.

Oscar was the overwhelming choice for Mr. Basketball as he broke the final game scoring record held by Dee Monroe of Madison and set a new record of 106 points for the final four games. His coach, Ray Crowe, won back-to-back titles and was the first to win the title undefeated.

Many lawsuits had been filed in the early 1950s throughout the country to help gain freedom of movement and access to public places for African-Americans. In the two years since the U.S. Supreme Court decision, Indianapolis was still racially segregated. In fact, many Indiana towns were too slow to help African-American people gain the freedoms the law stated they had the right to. The report shown here exemplifies the racism that took place in Indianapolis as officials winked at laws:

> "Almost all restaurants and downtown stores and theaters in downtown Indianapolis were segregated. Betty Crowe, who married Ray in 1951, was allowed to walk rapidly through the L.S. Ayres department store's Tea Room to visit her father, the chief cook, in his kitchen office, but she could not sit down to eat. Once a year, on "Negro Day," black children were allowed to enter Riverside Amusement Park, but only if they presented fifty bottle caps from the Polk Milk company."

Many people believe that the victory by Crispus Attucks helped to move race relations forward a little bit in Indiana. Those who supported the team knew how bad the players were treated when they won the state title in 1954-55. They didn't want the same discriminatory after game celebration that happened after winning the first state title...but that's what they got. The Attucks delegation was shuttled right back to the black neighborhoods after another short, crisp, almost meaningless celebration at the Monument Circle. It was a sign of the times where a very gradual acceptance of blacks on teams was taking place. The Ku Klux Klan was becoming a little less noticeable.

Since Oscar had become Mr. Basketball, his presence added a great deal of interest to the Indiana-Kentucky All-Star series. The series now consisted of two games, one in Indianapolis and the other in Louisville. Indiana won both games as Oscar scored 34 points in the first game and 41 in the second. He outplayed Kentucky's Mr. Basketball, "King Kelly" Coleman who averaged 46.7 as a senior. Oscar won the coveted Star of Stars award twice for Indiana. Kentucky's Edgar Smallwood, an African-American, won the award for

Kentucky in Louisville by scoring 29 points in a losing cause in the second game.

Oscar, or "The Big O" as he was affectionately known to many Hoosiers, was given credit for moving ahead the integration of Indianapolis high schools. His performances were so impressive that white schools started allowing black athletes to attend. This also helped to overcome the powerful influence of the Ku Klux Klan which was known to campaign for school board members, judges and legislators who would see things in their racially biased ways of doing things.

People who saw Oscar play, as I did many times, could tell that he was the type player if you taunted him with racial slurs, he would just play harder. He seemed to have an inner resolve that many players didn't have. It wasn't a smart move to harass Oscar into playing harder if a team wanted any chance to beat his Tigers. Oscar is a classic example of a youngster overcoming obstacles and becoming a stronger person.

After becoming the most sought after basketball player in the nation, Oscar would leave the state of Indiana. He signed on to play college basketball at the University of Cincinnati. It was not a good time for Indiana basketball right at that point because it was being rumored that the Ft. Wayne Pistons would also be leaving Indiana. The playoff loss in 1955 hurt attendance during this, the 1955-56 season.

Back on the Ball State campus panty raids were somewhat of a rage during this era of the 1950s. Fraternity guys would break into (or be let into) girls' dorms and steal panties, bras, slips, whatever. I was sitting around the student center one warm spring evening shortly after Crispus Attucks had won the 1956 state title. I was with some Kappa Sig guys. Word came down that there was going to be a panty raid at Lucina Hall right at the time the doors were to close for women's curfew, about 10:00pm. Several Kappa Sigs had planned the raid. I wanted to see what was going to happen. The thought occurred to me to not get caught if I participated because I could get kicked out of school and destroy my dreams of playing ball at a good size college in Indiana.

I went to Lucina Hall and some guys were climbing up the vines on the outside of the building trying to get in. Girls were waving bras and panties at them, but no one could get in the dorm. When the leader, "Scottie" from Newcastle, realized this he yelled, "To the barracks." The old soldier type barracks were used to house girls further north on campus. The guys looked like a herd of buffalo stampeding through campus. I figured, wrongly, they didn't have time to make it to the barracks. As dedicated to basketball as I was, I went home and turned on the NBA playoffs.

About 11:30pm my brother and Dave Waymire came back to the house. They had plenty of undergarments and tried to put them on and prance around the upstairs part of the house. It was a scene no one could forget. News of the raid made the **New York Times.** Dave Waymire took his panty raid collection home to show his mother. She told him it was "disgusting" and "un-American." Proudly, when girls asked me where I was during the raid I could tell them I was home listening to a basketball game. Basketball kept me out of trouble more than a few times while growing up in Indiana!

I had a good spring quarter academically. My dad told me he would need my help in the summer so I was able to earn spending money as I took a break from studying. I wanted very much to get my knee back to normal as soon as possible so I started making contacts about the summer tournaments. I was pleasantly surprised when Jim Barley contacted me and invited me to play in the Logansport outdoor tournament. I still wasn't at full strength, but was lifting weights on my knee every day. Jim said we would be playing for Ft. Wayne Ideal Welding stocked with good players. I can't remember all the names, but Warren Fisher from Kokomo was one and Dick Berghoff another. Warren had played with Jim at Indiana University. Many former high school stars and good college players would make for a competitive field. I had to be one of the worst players on our team. We won our first few games and it was a real good experience for me even with the limited playing time I did get with all these good players.

This time Oscar was eligible to play because he was out of high school. The bleacher seating on the outdoor court was jammed every time Oscar's team took the court. His teammates were former Crispus Attucks stars. He was playing for a team sponsored by Dison Heating out of Indianapolis. As fate would have it we were going to play Dison Heating in the Quarter-finals. I'll never forget the night. Tournament officials decided to announce the names of players. Each player, many of whom had been All-State, got a nice hand from the crowd. I thought to myself, "What the hell am I doing out here?" Almost every player was well known. I got a little hand out of courtesy, I think.

Dison Heating, with Bailey Robertson netting 21, beat us 68 to 55. Jim and Warren Fisher fought Bailey and Oscar courageously. Jim and Oscar guarded each other. Jim scored 12 points and got Oscar in early foul trouble and held him to 15 points. Fisher led us with 14 points. Jim was considered a great defensive player at Indiana and a young Oscar had just committed to

Cincinnati. Jim got a big hand when he took himself out near the end of the game. He said, "Norm, go in and guard Oscar for a couple of minutes. He is going to be a great one." I figured I would blow out my knee again or need an ammonia capsule after Oscar got through with me." It is a moment I won't forget as long as I live. Oscar got the ball about twenty feet out on the right side. It looked like he was standing flat footed so I relaxed a little. We looked straight at each other. He then went straight up, shot the ball and it hit the back of the rim and went in without moving the net. I told Jim Barley after the game, "As far as I am concerned, Oscar is already a great one."

Since we had moved to Muncie my aunt and uncle from Clarksdale, Mississippi came to see our new place. My dad wanted to take my uncle, brother and I to a Major League Baseball game in Cincinnati. The Dodgers were playing the Reds in a night game and Don Newcombe was pitching for the Dodgers and mowing down the Reds in Crosley Field. He was to finish with a 27 win season and had his strike out ball working this night.

After Newcombe struck out several Reds, my uncle said to me, "That nigger would never strike me out." I saw that as being somewhat alarming because my uncle only had one arm! Later in the game a black lady sat down right beside my uncle. He quickly moved to another seat. As a young kid growing up in Indiana, I was beginning to understand how people would, in many different ways, let others know how they felt about integration.

A fond memory for me took place either in the late summer or early fall. The United States Olympic Basketball Team came to Butler Fieldhouse to play the national AAU champions, the Phillips 66ers from Bartelsville, Oklahoma. Bill Russell and K.C. Jones led the Olympians as they had just won their second straight NCAA title while playing for the University of San Francisco.

As previously mentioned, Butler Fieldhouse was a mecca for good basketball in the 1950s. Recall the Indianapolis Olympians played there, the famous Milan-Muncie game was held there, I saw Bevo there and Oscar with his Crispus Attucks teams. I saw many state finals and All-Star games and now the United States Olympic team came in. Seeing all these great games and names at Butler Filedhouse, to the delight of many Hoosiers, put Hoosier Hysteria at its zenith.

Somehow I went to the Olympic-66ers game, a win for the Olympians and again I had thoughts of playing on that majestic floor. During the game, I can't forget, K.C. Jones stole the ball, went full court, dunked the ball and hung on the rim. Most fans had not seen such antics before and they went wild. K.C.

and Bill Russell helped America win the gold medal in Melbourne. They then joined the Boston Celtics and they would become one of the great dynasties in sports history. I left Butler Fieldhouse itching to play again as the game gave me incentive even though I was more than a year away from becoming a walk-on at Ball State.

I was happy the way my knee was responding after playing in outdoor tournaments at Logansport, Zionzville and North Webster, Indiana. I was a little nervous about by knee, but remember running the floor well and jumping with no problem.

The summer passed and the 1956-57 school year rolled around fast. I don't remember caring much about seeing girls, but when classes started in September they were everywhere. I thought I had died and gone to heaven. The Student Center seemed to be filled every night with pretty co-eds and more so than the spring semester I had spent just the school year before.

I decided to pledge the Kappa Sigma Kappa fraternity. It would be easier now than if I made the basketball team and tried to become a pledge. Dave Waymire and John Hevel were in and I had made several good friends in that crazy group of guys. I also knew that I could play fraternity basketball. Frat ball was pretty good basketball with a lot of ex-high school players on teams. It was a fact in Indiana that if a college varsity ran short of players for some reason the fraternity teams might supply some talent.

After surviving the craziness of being a pledge, I enjoyed associating with my fraternity brothers. Our frat house was located right beside the Student Center and I liked that. My home was about two miles from campus on North Wheeling Avenue, but Dave Waymire had a car so we worked out getting to class and the frat house. We had one brother, Bob Schaffer, who was an All-Conference lineman in football. He got a draft notice from the Chicago Bears to report to St. Joseph College for a try out. Of course all of us got excited about the possibility of a brother playing for the Bears. He told us, "I'm not going up there, all they want me for is the hamburger squad. They will pay me to beat me up for a couple of weeks and send me home." We called him "chicken" and a few other choice words hoping to embarrass him into trying out, but he never went.

After a few episodes of partying with the Kappa Sigs I figured I would keep enjoying myself, but tone things down a little because those guys could really party. I certainly remembered how the president of Manchester College told my dad about the late night hours Wynn and I lived through. I figured

I needed a good woman to keep me out of trouble. I started dating again and was able to use the family car some. I took girls to football games and we would hit Orv's Drive-in and Berkies Drive-in and the Student Center or an occasional movie. I don't think I took anyone out more than twice. I began to figure out that absolutely no one was coming close to impressing me like Sharon and Ginger did. I thought about calling Tusky, but decided, since the basketball season was approaching, I better get on some teams and start playing again. Although it was a year away, I needed to get real serious and come up with a routine that would get me ready to fulfill my dream of playing college basketball in Indiana.

I was enjoying my classes and the atmosphere at Ball State. The professors, for the most part, were really super. I settled down so much I got to the point in a Geography class where it looked like I was going to get an A grade. For me to get an A was about as rare as the Chicago Cubs getting in the World Series. On October 8, 1956 I decided to cut the Geography class of Dr. Dooley and watch the New York Yankees play the Brooklyn Dodgers in the fifth game of the World Series. It had to be one of the greatest cuts ever made on a college campus. This was the day that Don Larsen of the Yankees pitched the only perfect game in World Series history. He beat Jackie Robinson, Roy Campanella, Pee Wee Reese, Duke Snider, Gil Hodges and company 2-0.

When I went to class the next day Dr. Dooley, a basketball fan, said to me, "Norm, how was the game?" I said, "Perfect." He laughed. I got the A. Roommate John Hevel had the class in the morning. I would pump him for test questions. He got a B and chased me all over campus when we got the results together at the Science building.

I happened to be in a class with a guy named Bob Collins. He asked me if I wanted to be on a team he was going to coach in the winter. He explained we would be sponsored by Jackson Street Hardware and he would get a schedule together and play some good teams in central Indiana. We would enter the state AAU tournament and would have some former Ball State players on the team. It was just what I needed. I figured with this team and the fraternity team I could begin to get myself going again. My goal was to have as many good games as I could because the box scores were always reported in the basketball crazy newspapers around Muncie. I figured coach Hinga would see them and I could keep my name on his mind.

I figured with my studies and playing on two teams I could keep busy enough that girls would fit into the picture whenever I had some time away from my more important goals. Considering the past bad luck I had with girls, I was going to be real selective.

The Industrial league/AAU teams in the area were mostly sponsored by local companies. Names like Delco Battery, Warner Gear, Kirby Wood, Muncie Parts, Newcastle Meadowgold and Mason's Oasis usually were stocked with former good players around central Indiana. During the winter I had games where I scored over 30 points several times. In one game on the Ball State floor we beat the Ball State Air Force ROTC team 94 to 84. The newspaper the next day gave me this write up which I was sure coach Hinga would notice.

> A brilliant 32-point scoring performance by Norm Jones led Jackson Street Hardware to a 94-84 victory over the Ball State AFROTC team Tuesday night.

In another game a write up read:

> Norm Jones scored 31 points on 11 fielders and 9 of 10 fouls to lead Jackson Street Hardware past the Fairmount Merchants.

We played the Ball State freshman team a couple times. Jimmy Barnes from Muncie Central, who was guarding Bobby Plump when Plump hit his famous shot, was on the team. Both were close games and I played decent as coach Hinga watched some.

In another rather interesting game three former Ball State players and I played a local team. We decided to play a zone on the small YMCA floor. We won the game 70 to 65. I was excited to see the morning paper because we had won with just four players. I had scored 26 points and former Cardinals Jack Schmeltz had 13, Norm Edwards, from Marion, had 17 and Dale Harris had 14. I wanted to see just the four of us listed in the box score. Instead, the paper listed our four names and then under Harris' name they simply put the word "blank." The newspaper either didn't want to give us credit for winning with four players or didn't want to embarrass the other team. It looked as though we had a player named blank who had the box score of 0-0-0.

My season of sitting out came down to tournament time with both the AAU team and the fraternity team I was playing on. I'm sure coach Hinga noticed when my Kappa Sigma Kappa fraternity team won their first ever Ball State campus fraternity tournament. I averaged about 20 points per game and played with some pretty good players, most of whom stayed away from the beer long enough for us to take home the trophy. To end the season of sitting out, my Jackson Street Hardware team reached the finals of the local section of the state AAU tournament as I made 19 points on the Ball State floor in a morning game and 16 later in the day to put us in the finals the next day.

In the AAU finals we had to play a Muncie team (Kirby Wood) loaded with players who had played on the great Muncie Central teams. We imported Carl McNulty, the former NBA player and Purdue standout, to play with us. We lost by a few points. Even though we fed McNulty, my friend Calvin Grim from Muncie Central limited me to two lousy points. In high school, Calvin was often said to be the best sixth man in the state when he played with the Central Bearcats. This AAU game ended the season for me and I was not happy ending on what was probably my worst game of the season. I was hoping coach Hinga would look at my entire season. I recalled he promised to give me a good look. Overall I think my plan to keep my name on his mind had worked over the season as I had several good games against decent competition.

I can't remember much more about sitting out the 1956-1957 season. I know my grades were good as I took advantage of not having to travel with a team and not being head over heels in love with some beautiful co-ed. I did play in a lot of basketball games and I did date a lot of girls, but sparks didn't fly with any of them.

Naturally I had kept an eye on the 1956-57 Ball State team. I went to many of the games and they had improved so much it was unbelievable. The squad finished the season 19-8 and represented Indiana in the NAIA tournament in Kansas City and won a game there before succumbing to tough Texas Southern. The leader of the team was Tom Dobbs who was a fraternity brother and a good friend. He set a Ball State one game scoring record when he scored 39 points against DePauw University. The Kappa Sig fraternity members never howled as loud as they did that night. I also remember being impressed with the guard play of Ball State and knowing many of these players would be returning for the 1957-58 season. I became a little uneasy about my chances to survive as a walk-on.

At this time in Ball State basketball history the team had joint affiliation with the NCAA and the NAIA. This meant that if the team was good enough it could be selected for any college tournament in the country. In those years the NIT was still the most prestigious tourney, with the NCAA next then the College Division Tournament or the NAIA. Ball State played in the Indiana Collegiate Conference with these schools: Butler, Evansville, Indiana State, Valparaiso, DePauw and St. Joseph.

The team had several impressive wins, not the least of which was one over the Quantico Marines. The Marines had big Don Lang who had been a standout at the Naval Academy during his college days and Bud Grant who later coached the Minnesota Vikings football team to the Super Bowl. He was an excellent basketball player. At one stretch the Cardinals won nine straight games and won every game at home during this season. This would be a winning streak that the next team would be expected to extend. I hoped to be a part of extending that streak.

The 1956-57 Ball State team was the best since Branch McCracken left Ball State for Indiana University fifteen years before. One of my fraternity brothers reminded me, "Norm, you are going to have to work to make that team next year." There was a big celebration on campus when the team returned from Kansas City and things looked promising for next year for Ball State basketball fortunes. Since many good players would be returning the question for me was, would I be in those fortunes?

Ball State had an exciting year, but it was disappointing for me to learn that pro basketball was still losing its luster in Indiana. The Pistons were losing their appeal in Ft.Wayne. Owner Fred Zollner needed a bigger fan base and was talking to Detroit people. The Boston Celtics won their first NBA title with a thrilling 125-123 double overtime victory over the St. Louis Hawks. I watched this game on TV and it may well be the best NBA game in history. It would set into motion the dominance of the Celtics in the years ahead.

Even without the graduated Oscar Robertson, the Indianapolis Crispus Attucks played in the final game of the Indiana high school championship. They lost 67 to 55 to an undefeated South Bend Central team.

My roommate, Dave Waymire, had announced that he was getting married on August 24, 1957. He had been dating a tall brunette named Carol Brickler from Indianapolis who was also a student at Ball State. Both planned to finish their degrees. Dave and I were about the same age and I remember telling myself I couldn't possibly afford to be married and play ball. That thought didn't linger long because I didn't even have a steady girlfriend at the time. I was still thinking clearly about my goals.

I had many summer jobs around Muncie and Ball State, but this particular summer I was fortunate to become a camp counselor and would work with young boys at the Indiana State YMCA Camp. It was named Camp Crosley and was located on popular Lake Tippecanoe near North Webster, Indiana.

Terry Schurr from Bremen, Indiana and I had become good friends. He was a crowd pleasing 5'9" guard on the Ball State team. I knew all of the players on this great team and had a good feel by the summer what it would take to even make the team, let alone play. Terry also got a job to be a counselor at the camp and we figured we could play some basketball in our free time. He was a cinch to be a starting guard for Ball State.

Dr. Stauffer had given me a weight lifting program he thought would strengthen my knee and I followed it religiously. I had a shoe weight and I lifted several hundred pounds a day. My knee seemed stable and I gave it good tests during the summer.

Terry's nickname was "Mouse" and as we began to play a lot together, I was hoping that I could be his running mate at guard the next basketball season. However, a real good player, a guard by the name of Larry Koehl from Ft.Wayne was also returning. Both were on scholarship and set to lead the team along with returnees Ted Fullhart and Wilbur Davis. I was excited about the coming season as growing up at Ball State seemed to be the right place for me. It would be frosting on the cake if I could make the team.

CHAPTER EIGHT
Glory Days

IT IS IMPOSSIBLE TO OVERACHIEVE.

The start of school in the 1957-58 school year was an exciting time. I made it a goal to play on the floor at Ball Gym as much as possible. I wanted to fall in love with the rims. I had played several games there during my period of sitting out, but was still not real comfortable with the floor. When classes weren't being held on the floor it was open for free play and not difficult to find a game. Rumor had it that between 150 and 200 guys would be trying out for the team. With seven returning lettermen and four or five good freshman on scholarship sure to move up to the varsity, I was a little down about my chances to make the team. Also, it was known that former Muncie Central star, Jim Sullivan, had transferred from Taylor University. Jim was one of the top scorers in the state while at Taylor and a cinch to make the team. This left two or three positions open for all the players coming out.

I decided to lay off booze, run and lift weights on my knee and try to find a good woman so I wouldn't have to join the dating meat market. I was going to try to find this special person and dated different girls from late summer to early fall. Dave and Carol Waymire had rented a house near campus and I would go over there after the dorms closed and both Dave and Carol would pump me to tell them if my date made a good impression on me.

The Waymire's were good friends. Frat brother and roommate, John Hevel, began to date a co-ed from Winchester, Indiana by the name of Judy Wall. All of us began to get together for small parties or weekend outings or football games. Building a float for Homecoming kept me busy with the frat

123

guys. I didn't have long before I would have to try out for basketball and was wanting to find a girl who would be a steadying influence.

I know I spent countless hours on the Ball Gym floor, some by myself just dribbling up and down and shooting trying to get as familiar with the floor and the rims as I could. When other guys played, it always seemed to be a half-court game and I was getting concerned about my full-court conditioning.

In late September I was driving my dad's car near the center of campus and saw a group of girls walking toward the Student Center. I saw a slender girl with real dark hair with a walk that for some reason just gave me a good impression. I drove around the block real quick and slowed the car to where I was just behind the group of girls. I knew right then and there I had to begin my snooping and find out who she was.

My snooping techniques helped me to discover the young lady was named Pat Walsh and she was pledging Chi Omega sorority. Somehow it was arranged for us to meet at the pep rally for Homecoming in the middle of campus. As far as I was concerned it was the first time I had seen an angel on the ground. She was gorgeous. I think our first date was to the Homecoming football game. It was the first football game at Ball State to draw over 10,000 fans. Pat was even better looking than I thought, although I was impressed when I had managed to walk by her a few times at the Student Center before we officially met. We hit it off pretty well. I learned she was from a small town named Pierceton, Indiana which was not far from North Manchester.

I was certainly happy to find out she did not have a steady boyfriend. I wanted to get to know her before basketball tryouts came around and only had about three weeks. I figured if I did get lucky and make the team, my dating time would be limited with practices and travel. I wanted to get in several dates as quickly as possible.

Coach Hinga made the call for tryouts to begin and sure enough over 150 guys showed up. Tryouts consisted mostly of scrimmages. The first week for me was just awful and I told my dad I didn't think I was going to make the team. The pressure reminded me of trying to make the team at Marion High School. One practice playing against Schurr and Koehl I looked terrible handling the ball. I couldn't hit the side of an Indiana barn, was turning the ball over and losing confidence fast. I decided the second week to concentrate on the things I could do best: shoot and pass. I would put the ball in the hands of someone else in pressure situations, get my shots and look for the open man and hustle on defense. My strategy paid off. I started shooting out of my mind and finding open players for assists. I was able to take the pressure off of myself.

After about ten days or so the cut list was down to about twenty guys and the battle for positions was getting serious. Many players cut at this time were stars in Indiana high schools and it was a sad time for them. The varsity players from the year before continued to practice as coach Hinga wanted to see how those trying out matched up against them. I recall being pleased to learn that my friend Tom Hilgendorf would become official scorer for the team and fraternity brother Earl Yestingsmeier, who would keep stats, would fill in for Tom when he could not make the trips. Norm Edwards, who scored 13 points for Marion High in the 1950 Final Four, survived. Norm had played at Ball State before and was trying to make a comeback. A good player named Larry Wagers, who was 6'6", had played varsity ball at a Florida college, was surviving as was transfer Jim McCoy. There would be one final cut. It was a nervous time for me.

Jim Sullivan was playing well. I figured my chances for the one or two spots left were slim, but a few practices before the last cut I again got hotter than a firecracker. Coach Hinga spoke to me in tryouts and said, and I will never forget his words, "I knew you could shoot, but I am impressed with your passing. Check the last cut list on Monday." It sounded like I had made the team and my name was, indeed, on the list on Monday. It was one of the happiest days of my life. To recover from the knee surgery and after having been through the grade problem, girlfriend problems and all the rest, I felt it was quite an accomplishment to just get a uniform.

Wagers and my friends Norm Edwards and Jim McCoy were all sad that they did not survive the final cut. I told my folks and Pat I had made the team. My fraternity brothers were pleasantly surprised I made the team. I had overcome the first hurdle. Now the question became: How much would I get to play?

I was to wear #22 at home and #23 on the road in our red and white uniforms. On the seventeen man roster were returning lettermen Terry Schurr, Larry Koehl, John Lebo, Ted Fullhart and African-Americans Wilbur Davis, Bob Crawford and Carl Miller. Walk-ons Jim Sullivan, also African-American, and Warren Harmeson and I made the team and sophomores Larry Perry, Dick Barkman, Travis Burleson, Art Harman, George Taylor, Don Clark and Dave Stralowski moved up from the freshman team.

As practice started in earnest, I noted that Carl Miller, we called him "Goose" because he looked like the famous Harlem Globetrotter, Goose Tatum, and Jim "Sully" Sullivan had silver rings laced tightly into each shoe. The rings were awarded them when they were standouts on Muncie Central's state championship teams in 1951 and 1952.

I had not thought much about racial issues until a news report was flashed on most television screens about the terrifying account of an incident in the south. Some black students tried to enter an all-white high school in Little Rock, Arkansas. The law of the land demanded their admission. Acting on orders from Arkansas Governor Orval Faubus, the National Guard stopped the black students from entering the school. When that happened President Dwight D. Eisenhower, in following the 1954 Supreme Court decision, ordered the National Guardsmen to escort nine black students to an all-white school. Muncie schools and Ball State were well integrated, as was the basketball team so the incident passed without any campus or city demonstrations. This incident did cause me to think back to the racism that went on in Marion during my time there.

We were to open the season with Hanover College on Dec. 2nd on their court. Returning lettermen Schurr, Koehl, Davis and Fullhart started the game, but I don't recall the fifth starter. I played about a half and was pleased that I made 7 points in my first game at Ball State, but we lost 77 to 59. Koehl was our only player in double figures with 13 points. Fourteen players saw action against this good Hanover team, led by John Jenkins with 31 points.

Four days later we played the Dayton Flyers in Dayton and the team played much better. Dayton, a real power in the 1950s, was big and had been runner-up in the NIT tournament the last two years. Terry and Wilbur made 14 and 13 respectively, but we lost, 58 to 41. I played sparingly and did not score, but this was big time basketball with a big crowd there, more like I was looking for after playing in front of big crowds at Marion High School.

Something happened a few days before the Dayton game that got my attention. Coach Hinga was talking to the squad when starting guard Larry Koehl walked into the gym in street clothes. He handed coach Hinga a slip of paper and walked out. It was a grade report telling the coach he was not eligible. Larry left school and I never saw him again. My grades were solid so I had no worries. Also, Goose Miller had been injured during the Hanover game. He decided to report for induction into the armed services. All of a sudden playing spots opened up ahead of me and I became very dedicated to play.

Our next game was to be one few people who were there could forget. It was our first home game against Eastern Michigan. While we were warming up, my brother, Wendell, who usually sat in the front row, got my attention and said, "Bud is drunk." Bud (not his real name) had not been playing much. I didn't think much about it because I was focusing on the game. With Koehl and Goose Miller now gone, I figured John Lebo would be starting at guard and with work I might be able to take over that position and play at guard with Terry Schurr. I was focused on taking advantage of whatever playing time I would get in this game. I knew the team needed shooting and thought I could do it. I didn't want to have to think about anything but the game.

After we got well into the game someone on the bench asked what time it was. Bud said, "It's about 8:15." He was wearing a watch. That got the attention of several guys on the bench because players were not allowed to wear such things in a game for fear of injuring someone. We entered the second half and we were routing Eastern Michigan. I got in the game and ran up and down a couple of times and Eastern Michigan scored. I got set to take the ball out of bounds and forward Dick Barkman, a frat brother from Elkhart, yelled at me, "Don't throw it to Bud, he's drunk." Of course, who got open for me to throw the ball to? It was Bud. He took off like a shot dribbling down court. After about three dribbles he left the ball behind him. An Eastern player picked it up and three of them came right at me and made an easy lay-up. We finally got the ball down court and here was Bud, who was little, crashing the boards like a demon. He got the rebound and fell over on his back.

After Bud made a turnover or did something silly I saw coach Hinga get up off the bench. Pockets of laughter could be heard in the crowd of about 3,000 fans as word got around that Bud was a little under the weather. Hinga called time out and I was real close to this conversation. He asked Bud if he was OK and Bud shook his head no. Coach asked Bud if he knew the color of the boundary lines around the court and Bud said no. He asked him if he knew his name and he said no. Coach said, "Bud have you been drinking?" Bud got a big smile on his face and said, "Yep." Coach said, "You know I have to dismiss you from the team." Bud said, "Yep."

We beat Eastern Michigan 92-65 and extended the Ball State home floor winning streak to 14 games. I made 10 points on three field goals and four free throws. It was my second double figure game in college. I was happy and pumped up. The next day in practice coach Hinga motioned for the team to get to the film room. This would be the first time I ever saw myself play as Manchester did not have films. We called coach Hinga "Jim." Jim wanted to go over some things, but also pointed out how comical Bud's performance was. It was like watching a comedy version of a basketball game. I was pleased I didn't let this drunken episode bother my focus on playing, but it was funny.

I noted that Lebo only made one point in the Eastern Michigan game. I figured the next game with Franklin at home would be an important one for him to perform well. I also knew that I could not afford to mess up any playing time I would get.

We extended the home floor streak to 15 games by beating Franklin College 61-49. John Lebo did not have the big game I thought he needed to guarantee his place in the starting line-up. Big Wilbur Davis and Sully took care of Franklin with 16 and 14 points respectively. I did play about a half and scored 6 points, but didn't get many chances in a game that was somewhat slow and low scoring.

The university gave us shoes and I remember I had a pair of low-cut Converse All-Stars, which was the top of the line in shoes those days. We also were supplied with practice clothing. A friend who worked in the equipment "cage" told me he knew Pat Walsh because he was from her hometown and went to school with her at Pierceton High School. I got this bright idea that I could drive Pat right to her house without her directing me. We had planned to go up there and meet her family. My friend gave me good directions and one Sunday I got my dad's car and drove her home. I told her I didn't want her to tell me how to get to her house because I had mystic powers and would drive right to it. Pat figured out how I knew where she lived and never believed I had mystic powers. We had a nice visit and I met her mother, Lorraine. Pat had a younger brother, Dave, who had played high school basketball, but he was serving his country.

I am not certain how many home basketball games Pat came to as I did not push her to attend. I was, however, trying to see her every free minute I could find and we had quite a few dates in a short span of time. Before we were too far into the season, Pat surprised me. She said she needed some breathing room and thought we ought to take a break from each other. It bothered me because I was following my plan...find a good woman, get my grades and play basketball. Since I knew if I couldn't control events I was at the mercy of those events, I agreed it might be a good idea to not see each other for awhile. Fortunately, Pat was not telling me we were breaking up. I decided I would not go out with anyone else. I don't know if she did. I concentrated on studying and basketball.

The next game against Wabash College in Crawfordsville, Indiana would be the biggest of my career. We were 2-2 and wanted to get above .500 and get in position to do well in the Indiana Collegiate Conference race and obtain a playoff bid. After arriving early Jim urged everyone to go for a walk on campus and stretch our legs. A teammate and I took off walking on campus and I ran into two guys I knew who had played a little at Manchester, Butch Ross and John Moore from Wabash, Indiana. They had transferred and were in a fraternity and wanted to show us a beer tap at their fraternity house. They offered us some, but I didn't think after what happened to Bud it would be too smart of a move. I had been through too much to make a stupid move. I know I thought about being in Woody Weir's dog house. I was living a dream and wanted to keep it going.

When we got back to the fieldhouse Jim told us he needed seven or eight guys to play a reserve game. He started pointing to guys and my heart sank. I was figuring I was now the third best guard on the team and I didn't want to play in a reserve game and use up some energy. Jim didn't even look my way and I was relieved as it meant to me…get ready for plenty of playing time tonight. It came early as John Lebo started the game, but made some mistakes. I was the first player in and we trailed at the half 32-27.

Just before half-time I remember during a free throw standing close to the big base drum right near the floor… and vomiting. Just like when I hurt my knee I swallowed it, but for a different reason. I didn't want to come out of the game. I figured if Jim saw me throw up I was out. I was not yet in "game shape" as this was the longest I had played. I managed to gather myself and made it to half time.

I started the second half. The Muncie newspaper the next morning reported that with 3:07 left "Jones caged a bucket to give the Cardinals their first lead, 59-57." Added to that was, "Jones, who led the Ball State second half comeback, had 15 points to top the Cards." It was sad that Hal Traviolia from Lafayette stole the ball from Sully in the backcourt with just seconds to go and scored the winning points. Sully had played well scoring 13 points, but fortunes turn quickly in basketball. We lost 63-61 in a game I will always remember. Many players from the North Central Conference played in this game including Traviolia, Sully and I and Benny Fellerhoff from Muncie Central who scored 10 points. He played for the Bearcats in the famous Milan game as did our own Bob Crawford.

Except for missing being with Pat and having a good woman in my life, the plan I laid out for myself in St. Joseph hospital was working. Jim told me

I would be starting our first conference game at home against rival DePauw two nights away and to "keep shooting and passing like I had been doing." I told him I would be ready…and I was. My long time dream was about to come true. I would be a starting guard on an Indiana college team…and a chance to extend the Ball State home floor streak to 16.

My folks and some of my fraternity brothers had heard the Wabash game on the radio. Morry Mannies, a fraternity brother, had become the Voice of the Cardinals a year or so before and broadcast the games back to Muncie. Morry also broadcast Muncie Central High School games.

My first starting assignment all of a sudden stirred up some interest. My folks seemingly called everyone they knew in Indiana. Our neighbors on West 6th Street in Marion, Jack and Jean Sutter, were going to be at the game. Jean was a DePauw grad and that got me fired up even more. One of the prettiest girls in my Marion High School class, Ruthanne Williamson, was a friend and she was a student at DePauw. As it turned out she was dating DePauw's best player, Tom Johnson. Ruthie was going to come to our house after the game. I had to play well to make the night the complete success I wanted it to be. Sometimes in sports a second chance doesn't come around and this is especially so at the college and professional level.

Interestingly, the Sutter's had two boys who turned out to be great basketball players, both for Marion High School and in college. John, the oldest, played at Tulane University, was twice MVP and was a Helms Foundation All-American and Honorable Mention Associated Press All-American. He was the last player cut by coach Bob "Slick" Leonard, of Indiana fame, when he tried out for the Indianapolis Pacers in the NBA.

Joe Sutter helped Marion High School to the Final Four in 1969 and won the coveted Trester Award. Marion lost to the legendary George McGinnis and company from Indianapolis Washington High School. Joe made the Indiana All-Star team and helped defeat Kentucky twice by scoring 17 points in the two games. Joe went on and played college ball at Davidson College. What are the odds of three kids from Marion living side by side on the same street earning basketball scholarships and starting positions on their college teams? It may be a record, but on the other hand amazing things happen when kids practice basketball like they do growing up in Indiana.

Just before the DePauw game an Associated Press release appeared in the Muncie newspaper. It told about how Jack Wilson of undefeated Anderson College was the leading scorer in the state with a 26.7 average. This scoring list included players from Indiana, Purdue and Notre Dame. Anderson was 8 and 0 and Wilson had scored 30 points or better in his last three games. The article also mentioned that Tom Johnson of DePauw had scored 18 points as DePauw had just beaten Indiana State to take the lead in the Indiana Collegiate Conference. It was nice to read my 15 point game at Wabash was also mentioned by the Associated Press. Things were heating up in Muncie and at Ball State and, seemingly, going my way. I recall telling Ted Fullhart, our defensive standout, about Ruthie and Tom Johnson. I said, "You gotta go after him."

There were two articles about the game in local newspapers the day after the De Pauw game. The lead ins read this way:

> Cardinals look sharp, defeat
> DePauw, 66-45.

And

> Ball State Home Wins at 16 straight

Few players can forget their first starting assignment and I never have forgotten this one. One account stated that Ball State pulled away with, "Jones bombing home his jump shots and one pretty underhand lay-up." Ted Fullhart held Tom Johnson to 3 points. Tom had a rough night, missing an easy lay-up and generally having tough luck. Everyone has a night like that once in a while and Tom survived to become one of the best players in Indiana. He later married Ruthie.

I made seven out of eleven shots for 14 points and played my best game ever as my man did not score. Ten of my points came in the second half as we iced the win with a 40 point spree. Wilbur Davis had 18 points and 18 rebounds and Sully had 10 points.

My mom told me after the game that Jack Sutter whispered some nice things to her about the way I was playing. It was nice to hear things like that after all I had been through and especially so since Jack knew about all the hours I had put in behind our houses on West 6th street in Marion and how I had struggled just to play in Marion.

In a quirk in the schedule, we would not play again for two weeks. Christmas break started right after the DePauw game. We would have some time off. Our next game would be an important conference game against Valparaiso on Jan. 4, 1958. We wanted to extend the home floor streak to 17 straight. I entered the holiday season as happy as I could be as I knew I was still in the starting line-up, my knee seemed strong and I was chasing my dream.

It was about this time that the Muncie and Indianapolis newspapers were raving about a Muncie Central sophomore sensation named Ron Bonham. When I saw the name I recalled the time in the summer just passed when I was working out alone at the well-known court at Muncie Central High School. A man came up to me and asked me what I thought of a tall blond kid shooting at the other end of the court. The kid was faking and going to the basket and working hard on moves, tipping the ball with both hands and generally following an impressive routine. I said, "He looks pretty good to me. What is his name and what grade is he in?" The man, who I took to be the father of the boy, said, "His name is Ron Bonham and he will be a sophomore at Muncie Central." Ron Bonham went on to represent basketball crazy Muncie as he became Mr. Basketball in 1960.

It was very interesting to me that during this, my junior year at Ball State, Oscar Robertson was now playing as a sophomore at the University of Cincinnati where he had enrolled in the School of Business. Oscar was also a transplanted Hoosier because he was born near Bellsburg, Tennessee on Thanksgiving Day. Most everyone knows that Oscar became, as Jim Barley said he would, a great one. Oscar played in what may have been the most difficult era for African-Americans in college basketball. The game was gaining in popularity and publicity was ever increasing for star players. Jackie Robinson never played Major League Baseball in the deep south and the southwest and some of the worst racism in the country was alive and well in big cities across that part of the country. The University of Cincinnati played in Texas and in the Carolina's. The better Oscar played, the more abuse he took. He didn't like it when the team couldn't stay together in Houston and in Raleigh-Durham. Just as two of my black friends at Marion High School had to do in 1950, black players often had to stay in private homes or at black universities.

In today's America a basketball fan could be arrested for calling out racial slurs, but not in the middle of the 20th century. Visualize, if you can, trying to make a free throw when a fan calls you a "coon" or a "cotton-picker." Coaches who chose to play black players were called "nigger lovers" when they approached their bench during warm-ups. Newspapers, especially in the south, questioned the academic preparation of black players. The federal laws governing integration were conveniently set aside.

When African-American players on teams from the north ventured into the south for their first time there they were met with "white" and "colored" water fountains and rest rooms. Interestingly, when heavyweight boxing champ at the time, Floyd Patterson, was confronted with the fountains he said, "They taste the same to me." Such occurrences for players from the north educated them as to the deceit and prejudice in America.

The officiating of games in the south and southwest, where one team didn't have any black players and the other one did, was often nauseating. Referees called far more fouls on the teams with black players. It was known that Coach Ray Crowe of Crispus Attucks often told his team to get a big lead early so when the fouls piled up it didn't matter. Teams not as talented as Attucks lost close games when players fouled out. Thanks to the courage of African-American players in the 1950s, the racial slurs, prejudice referees and other discriminatory practices have largely disappeared.

Even into the mid-1960s, as will be seen as this book closes, there were prejudice people who tried to keep alive the climate of hate, bigotry and segregation.

In the 1950s the Ku Klux Klan used sports to advance its belief of segregation. College basketball was good for that purpose because it could be found everywhere whereas big league baseball had not yet crossed the Mississippi River. The Klan was known to write threatening letters to well-known players and coaches coming south.

As a player at Manchester and Ball State in the 1950s, I now realize the effect racism had on schedules. We played either in the far north, like Michigan, Chicago, northern and central Indiana and Illinois and in Ohio. As far south as I remember traveling was Evansville, Indiana. I now suspect, since we had black players at Ball State, part of the reason we didn't travel to play in the south was to avoid the racism.

Oscar Robertson was such a good player and handled the racial incidents with such class and dignity that his play became an instrument of social change in college basketball just as it did for high school basketball around Indianapolis. There is little doubt that Oscar Robertson did a great deal, just as Jackie Robinson had done before him, to make lives of African-Americans better in America.

I'm sure the black players I played with at Ball State witnessed discrimination in some way, but it wasn't as rampant as in the south and I personally never observed any such human calamity.

The Christmas break seemed to be a happy, if not lucky time for me. Somehow Pat and I got back together and I asked if I could come and see her in Pierceton and she said yes. When I got there I was reminded that coach Hinga told the players to "stay in shape" while we were off. Pat's mom called the local high school coach, Burt Niles, with whom she had taught at the school. Coach Niles let me work out in the high school gym. He later had two boys, Mike and Ben, who made the Indiana All-Star team when they played for Warsaw High School.

I was happy as ever because I had earned a starting position and was back together with Pat. I learned a lot about her family during my stay at her house. One thing I noticed was both women smoked and that was something I didn't like.

During the break I went to the small town of Pleasant Lake, Indiana to visit roommate Dave Waymire to see his brother Don play for the local high school. Both of the Waymire's were pretty fair "country shooters" as they were called in Indiana. Don had a good game and it was good just to get back and see the craziness of Indiana high school basketball. While visiting Dave we talked basketball and even worked out with his high school coach. Dave had a great line about his playing days. I asked him if he made All-Sectional or anything like that. He said, "I was all-neighborhood in Pleasant Lake!"

During the days off I thought what a mistake it was to go so long without a game. The Valparaiso Crusaders were coming to Muncie and we were favored to beat them and remain in first place in the conference. The game was on January 4th and students were not back on campus. When we took the floor there were only about 1,500 people there and things were very quiet. We had been drawing 3,000 or better and fraternity and sorority backing was important. I didn't like the toned down atmosphere, but told myself to not let it bother my play as I was still in the starting lineup.

Not only did we have to play Valpo on Saturday, but we would have to travel to Eastern Michigan on Tuesday, play powerful Evansville at home on Thursday and then travel to Indiana State on Saturday. I was wondering who made out this brutal schedule and if the team and I could play on such little practice and rest and win.

As my luck would have it, we lost to Valpo 81 to 72. They took advantage of us not having our fans there and shot a torrid .541 for the game. They were led by Neil Reincke with 27, Topper Woelfer with 21 and Dick Schroer with 16. It ended the 16 game home floor winning streak and gave us a 1-1 record in the conference. Sully lead our team with 17 points and Terry Schurr and I each had 12, but our defense was sluggish, timing was off and to this day I believe our layoff hurt us. Still we were very much in the running for the conference race and I was playing well so my goals were still in place. Pat was back on campus and we would be seeing each other the rest of the season. My knee wasn't giving me any problems and my grades were solid...I was on a roll.

I was sky high for our next game at Eastern Michigan. We needed to right the ship and get back to 4 and 4 and get on a win streak. Since the game was on a week-night I took Pat to an early movie in downtown Muncie the day before. I think I was a team player, but the following account doesn't make it sound that way. Coming out of the movie I told her I was going out of town to play at Eastern Michigan in Ypsilanti, Michigan. In sort of a laid back comment and feeling confident, I said, "How many points do you want me to make?" She said, "How about twenty?" I thought to myself, Pat doesn't pull any punches. I also was remembering I had made 20 points in any official high school or college game just once and that was in the Marion Sectional.

In what turned out to be one of the most memorable nights of my life I made 9 out of 18 field goals and two free throws for exactly 20 points. We beat Eastern 74-63 as Sully had 15, Ted Fullhart 11, Wilbur 10 and Terry 9 in a balanced attack. It is impossible, from my viewpoint at least, to count points during a game. I knew I was riddling the Eastern Michigan zone with long jumpers and enjoying myself, but not until our official team scorer, Tom Hilgendorf, informed me on the team bus did I know my exact total. I thought it would be funny to see Pat's pretty face when she got the news. Plus, maybe, just maybe, she would be a little impressed. She was not an easy woman to impress.

Late in the game a teammate got in a skirmish with an opposing player and the referee got involved and hurt his knee breaking it up. The fans booed us and it was a bad scene. I recall Jim took me out with about two minutes to go. I had played the entire game and appreciated the small ovation I got for my shooting from the more sophisticated Eastern Michigan fans. Coach Hinga told us to shower as quickly as possible and "let's get out of town." When we came out of the gym some fans were waiting on us and started throwing snow balls at us. We hurried to get on the bus and they snowballed the bus as a squad car escorted us out of town. It was a night too hard to forget...and what player would want to forget a night like that anyway?

Coach Hinga stopped the bus to get us some sandwiches because the entire team was complaining about being hungry. We were scheduled to stay at the

Pokagon State Park lodge near Angola in northern Indiana. I will never forget this night either. Usually when the team would stay overnight somewhere, players would just pair off. On this night Jim assigned some rooms. He paired our three black players with three white players. He told big Wilbur and I to share a room. Sully and Bob Crawford, the other African-Americans on the team, shared rooms with white players. Evidently Jim thought there was some kind of a racial problem on the team. Wilbur and I went to the room and found only one bed. That didn't bother me as Wilbur was such a great guy I found no problem with the arrangement if coach Hinga thought it was that important and I don't think it bothered Wilbur either.

Once we got in the room the first thing Wilbur said to me was, "Jonesie, you were mellow out there tonight." I remember telling Wilbur I thought we played real well together as a team and he agreed. I was exhausted and laid down on the bed ready to go to sleep. Wilbur had his radio on down low listening to tunes. In about ten minutes there came a knock on the door. It was the bus driver. As things turned out Wilbur and the bus driver played cards until the wee hours of the morning. I dozed off on the bed and I think Wilbur did also late in the morning. When I awoke there was Wilbur spraying himself with deodorant after taking a shower. I remember thinking to myself, "Where do some people get the idea that blacks are dirty?" I wasn't about to take a shower as I figured I had taken one after the game and was clean enough.

I spoke to most team members about Jim assigning rooms and no one could ever come up with an answer. The team had good chemistry as far as anyone knew and so we dismissed the issue. Back on campus I remember the Ball State athletic director telling me that he had received a call telling him that, "Too many black guys are playing." Some people just never did figure out the importance of the 1954 Supreme Court ruling.

I suspect the team stayed at Pokagon State Park for the same reason my Marion High School team stayed at the Purdue University Student Union. Both were state-controlled institutions and officials in these places were not as likely to try to keep our black players out. In retrospect, I'm now sure that staying on state owned soil was easier for coaches or athletic directors to schedule rather than have to inquire about black players being welcomed at private places. It seems to me now that attempts to avoid discrimination were more abundant in Indiana than in the south, but the fact is Indiana still had plenty of racists. It made life just a little more difficult than it should have been at the time.

The request by coach Hinga for some black and white players to room together was as close as I had been to a racial situation other than seeing my African-American friends in Marion sit in the balcony at a movie theatre. I did watch as Oatess Archey and his friends went swimming in the Matter Park Pool. I never saw any of my black friends refused service in a restaurant, but then again, I don't recall them ever being present when a group of kids went into a restaurant. I suspect that, as Oatess reiterated before, the black kids "knew their place." It was like they would just disappear if they were with white friends who decided to go to a restaurant they knew they were not welcome in.

The Pokagon incident has, throughout my life, been a mystery to me because I never was given an answer. It was, in my view, part of the secret, but discriminatory culture in which my friends and I grew up.

While at Pokagon State Park I picked up a Ft.Wayne newspaper and found a nice little article about our win at Eastern Michigan. In bold black letters in the heading to the article it stated: Ex-Marion Star Hits 20 in Ball State Win. I cut it out in case I needed to prove to Pat I did what she asked. I was also pleased to see the article because I was sure some of my ex-teammates at Manchester and possibly even Ginger, would see it. I was disappointed some of my relatives from Battle Creek didn't come to the game, but I understood because it was a real bad night out. My brother, mom and dad, Dave Waymire and John Hevel heard frat brother Morry Mannies broadcast the game on the radio.

The team had to miss classes on Wednesday, but I saw Pat that night. The *Muncie Star* gave the team and I a terrific write up. It stated we shot .490 from the field and had a "balanced attack" as "Jones bombed away with a deadly jump shot for most of his nine fielders." I didn't know if Pat had heard the game on the radio or what, but when we met it became clear. She said, "So, how many points did you make?" I said, "Twenty, isn't that what you told me to make?" She said, "You did not."

I went in a barbershop near campus the next day for a hair cut and the barber, whom I did not know, said, "According to the newspaper it looks like you got a little warmed up last night." I thanked him, but was surprised. To me this shows how a player could be known in a basketball frenzied town like Muncie by people you would least expect. It was like that all over Indiana, if you had some success on the basketball court people would know about it and would let you know they knew about it. Such recognition for players was simply a part of Hoosier Hysteria.

Once my dad got word about my performance in the Eastern Michigan game he mentioned to me, "Norm, there are guys who aren't playing much who have scholarships and you don't have one. Don't you think its time to see Jim?" I agreed, but I had not thought much about a scholarship. I was just so happy to be playing with such a great bunch of guys on a pretty good team. I was having the time of my life. I knew, however, that the money could help my folks and, frankly, I told myself I had *earned* a scholarship. In two years I had come off my back in a hospital and become a starting guard at Ball State. It is the stuff of which dreams are made...especially in Indiana.

I made an appointment to see Jim Hinga. When I arrived he spoke first, "Norm, I know why you are here. I'm sorry, I've been lax in getting a scholarship together for you. You certainly deserve to be on our list." Jim said, "The next time you have to pay tuition and fees just tell the people at the administration building that you will be on the Pepsi Cola scholarship." He explained I would have to sign a green card and it would cover my tuition and fees plus an evening meal at Elliot Hall. He also said he knew I lived at home, but wanted me to give up "mom's cooking" until the season was over and eat with the team. I told him I could do that and left with tears in my eyes. It was one of the happiest moments of my life.

Following the Eastern Michigan game the most important game I was to play in up to this time in my career was the next one on the schedule. We had only one night off before the game. The Evansville Purple Aces were coming to town with a 7-1 record. Publicity for the game was stepped up as it promised to be a "barn burner" as they called them in Indiana. Evansville had already beaten Louisville, Western Kentucky, UCLA, Fresno State, Valpo and De Pauw. They were a highly regarded team after wins like that over some bigger schools. Fans on campus and around Muncie were wondering if we could trump the Aces.

The *Muncie Star* did all it could to hype the game by going overboard with statistics on both teams. Ed Smallwood, as you might recall, scored 29 points in the Indiana-Kentucky All-Star game and won the Star-of-Stars award for Kentucky. He was a terrific player for the Aces and was averaging 20 points a game and shooting .460 from the field. Ed would be voted the Outstanding Player Award in the College Division tournament at the end of this year and again in 1960. Guard Hugh Ahlering was averaging 18 points per game and shooting .479 from the field. Hugh would be voted the Outstanding Player Award in the 1959 College Division finals when the Aces won the national title. Also in the Aces starting line up would be Hal Cox from Kokomo. He was shooting .433. Hal was undercut by my Marion teammate Larry Bricker in high school and broke his wrist. He missed several games. Some folks thought the injury may have kept Hal off of the Indiana All-Star team. I thought he should have made it, he was that good. I suspected Hal would have a bad taste in his mouth about the injury or at least, since we would be guarding each other, not want a Marion Giant to get the best of him, a Kokomo Wildcat from the North Central Conference.

I was stunned when I saw a program (ten cents) for the Evansville game as my picture was the only picture in it. The program showed how I was the only player who had taken more than two shots to be shooting over .400 for Ball State. I was at .435. Terry was at .290 and I was a little surprised at that low figure for him. As box scores had indicated, Wilbur, Sully, Terry and I were the leading scorers. Statistics showed we needed to have a good night from everyone to beat Evansville.

The "barn burner" was not in the cards for me as I shot poorly the first half and we trailed by 10 points at halftime, 44-34. Something I will never forget happened at the half. The first thing coach Hinga did was write the fraction 4 over 14 (4/14) on the blackboard. He said, "Anybody know what this is?" No one knew, but I could have made a better guess than anyone else. It was my shooting percentage for the first half. Much to my surprise Jim went on to say, "What this means is we have got to let Norm keep shooting because the percentages will catch up to him." I thought it was kind of strange, but ever since high school, since Woody told me to shoot the ball, I never lost confidence. This was Jim's way of telling the team to not "get your dobbers down." It was a favorite expression of his and everyone knew what it meant. He was always telling us, if you have a good shot, take it. That was his philosophy, he didn't want to get guys discouraged about shooting. Making baskets is, eventually, the only way to win.

We came roaring back the second half. We did hit right at half of our shots the second half by nailing 15 out of 31. I only shot six times the last half and made three and two of those were near the end when Evansville almost panicked with our comeback. We lost the heartbreaker, 78 to 76. Again we had balanced scoring as Sully played a great game with 22 points, I had 16 and Wilbur had 14. Reserve guard Larry Perry played a great game, making 8 free throws. He helped to foul out Ed Smallwood with drives right at him. Terry chipped in 9 points. Smallwood had 19 points, but fouled out with 4:22 left in the game, giving us a chance. Ahlering had 23 points and Hal Cox had one less point than I did at 15. It was a great game before over 3,000 fans.

I was pleasantly surprised when after the game Woody Weir and Ralph Ferguson, my high school coaches, visited me in the locker room. I was down and didn't feel like talking much. I recall Woody saying, "They are letting you shoot more aren't they?" I told him I pretty much had a green light to shoot, but that, "I didn't hit so well tonight." I had only made 7 out of 20, not my usual percentage. They tried to cheer me up. I was happy someone from Marion came to see me play and thanked them for coming.

We were now at 1 and 2 in the conference and were faced with two tough ICC road games in the week ahead. We had to make the long trip to Terre Haute to play Indiana State and then venture up north to St. Joseph in Rennselaer. We lost to the 7 and 4 Indiana State team 75 to 55, but I continued my good shooting streak scoring 16 points. Schurr added 12 and Davis 10. The Sycamores were led by Ted Dayhuff with 20 and Jim Bates with 17. Our team shooting fell to .268 against Indiana State and we only made 17 of 38 free throws.

Against St. Joseph we shot only .315 and lost 73 to 58. Diminutive Dan Rogovich killed us with 23 points and Bob Williams added 18 and George Lux 15. I again shot well making 14 points, but the 15 by Wilbur and only 11 from Mouse weren't enough for us to pick up a badly needed conference road win. Something had to be done since we were now 4 and 7 on the season and 1 and 4 in the conference.

During all of this playing I would still try to study and take Pat out for a pizza or a romantic interlude, be with friends or get some rest. Pizza was a new thing around Muncie. An ad in one of the game programs told people to come to about the only pizza place in town. The ad said: After the game it's The Italian Villa for Pizza Pie. I recall eating my first pizza here.

CHAPTER NINE
The Mouse that Roared

"MOST PEOPLE'S GREATEST REGRET IN LIFE IS THAT THEY DIDN'T GET TO FINISH SOMETHING THAT WAS REALLY IMPORTANT TO THEM." (NICK SABAN)

As mentioned, I had seen the team stats in the Evansville program that included games through Jan. 4th. It bothered me when I read that Mouse was shooting at only a .290 clip. He had taken 101 shots and made 29. I had taken 60 shots and made 26 to lead the team with a .435 percentage. Wilbur and Sully were right at .400. Terry had been shooting off foot and I thought it was limiting his production. He was not on balance and had shot well the year before and in the summer. I decided to approach him about it. He said he knew he was doing it, but "I can make them that way." His Sigma Phi Epsilon frat brother and team scorekeeper, Tom Hilgendorf, also spoke to Mouse about his shooting form. I didn't pursue it any further as Mouse was our leader. I didn't have the heart to mention that in the last eight games he was averaging about 10 points a game and getting good shots. That wasn't going to be good enough for us to put together the win streak we needed. Terry could do better, he had to do better.

We managed to beat Franklin 63 to 50. Terry played better making 17 points and Wilbur had 18 and Sully 12. Even though I played most of the game Franklin's defense limited my shots and I made only 6 points. I had several assists and I was pleased for Terry, although his bad habit still showed up some. This is the game that reserve guard George Taylor took two left footed

141

shoes with him and Jim made him wear them. When George got in the game it looked like he was turning left every time he ran down the floor.

Now we had to go play Evansville again in the spacious Roberts Municipal Stadium. The Purple Aces were now at 11 and 2 and leading the conference at 5 and 1. We were to stay at the Van Orman hotel in downtown Evansville. Just a couple years before the Ball State team had to stay fifty miles away in Vincennes, Indiana because black players on the team were not welcome in hotels in Evansville. It was mainly the racists in small towns who controlled the politics in Indiana and the bigger towns began to disallow segregation in establishments that served the public. Evansville was at least one town in Indiana making progress in racial relations and that was good to see.

Sully and I had our pictures in the *Evansville Courier and Press*. It was funny because when we arrived players started walking around the hotel and Sully and I just happened to get on the elevator together and laughed because we both had about three copies of the paper.

The newspaper noted how Sully and I had transferred in to Ball State and were "beefing up Ball State's basketball squad." Also mentioned was the fact that "Terry Schurr and Norm Jones operate at guard and work effectively around the head of the circle." Getting the attention of the players was the mention that over 6,000 fans were expected for the game in a stadium that could hold over 13,000.

I was thrilled to play in Roberts as it was a classy place where the Division II, or College Division championships were held in those days. A bus could be driven right up to the team entrance and a large door would automatically raise. The bus driver could drive right down a ramp to the floor only yards away from one basket. The place looked like Grand Canyon to me, but I did have thoughts of playing in similar surroundings at the Ft. Wayne Coliseum which had a well-lighted scoreboard overhead as Roberts did.

I was still in the starting line-up and was so pumped up to play I led the team out of the dressing room. I dribbled the length of the floor as some Evansville fans booed and rang cowbells. I thought, "I'll show them, I'll can a jumper from behind the foul circle and shut them up." I embarrassed myself as the ball almost went over the backboard. I figured I better do what Woody taught me... get in close to the basket and get a good feel for the rims before I started shooting out on the floor. As the game approached I was zeroed in on the basket...but as a team we were not. We were still having team shooting problems.

I think the spacious conditions got to some of the guys and we had our worst first half of the season trailing 48 to 25. Sticking to his philosophy, Jim told us at the half in the locker room, "We aren't this bad and our problems are not in here, they are with the baskets. I want you to go right back out and start in close and get the feel for the rims." I had already done that and felt OK with the baskets and shot well the first half.

Again coach Hinga's strategy paid off as we made what had to be one of the biggest come backs in Ball State history. We seemed to come together as a team in the second half, one I will never forget. We scored 57 points in the last half and actually had a chance to win as the score got to 76-68 with over five minutes remaining. Hal Cox had to make three free throws right at the end to bail out the Aces. They finally won in an 86 to 82 Indiana "barn burner." It was a great game that made the Evansville fans get quieter and quieter as the game progressed. Eleven players were in double figures. Six of us Cardinals were in that group as Terry led the way with 18 points and guard Larry Perry played well again netting 15. Still, we had lost and our playoff hopes didn't look good.

In another pleasant surprise in my basketball career, the Ball State student newspaper featured Terry and I right about the time we played Evansville. It was titled Cardinal Hardwood Stars Presented. In the first paragraph in the article I was pleased to read, as I'm sure "Mouse" was, the following excerpt:

> When a basketball team owns a pair of men who are capable of leading the squad in assists (helping teammates score points) as well as ranking near the top in the scoring department themselves, team success is usually the result. Ball State owns two such men.

The article was a long, detailed one and gave our backgrounds, season stats, even the names of our parents and addresses. Terry said, "I'd like to get in the NAIA playoffs again this year. We have the potential." I was quoted as saying, "I hope we can at least win the rest of our conference games at home and a couple on the road." It was nice to be referred to as "Cardinal Hardwood Stars." This article meant a lot to me as it seemed to verify that my long time dream had come true. I also knew I would call myself a Hoosier the rest of my life. Maybe the first black player to play Major League Baseball in Chicago said it best. One of my favorites, Minnie Minoso of the Chicago White Sox said, "Recognition makes you feel good, don't let anyone tell you different."

Also, about this time of the season an article appeared in the *Muncie Star* that listed me as the fifteenth leading scorer in college basketball in the state of Indiana. It had me averaging 15.2 points per game. I didn't think so and checked it out. Either it was a mistake or someone was trying to make me look good. What happened is, whoever put the article together used the seven straight games I scored in double figures from the Wabash game through the St. Joseph game which did figure out to 15.2. However, all games must be included for an accurate season average and the article neglected to state I played four games before that string. I didn't even cut out the article for my "grandkids to see" as I knew it wasn't true. I was averaging about 12 points per game at the time which might have put me in the top twenty. I was happy to be where I was at in state scoring after worrying about even making the Ball State team.

I was pleased when coach Hinga posted conference stats. I was seventh or better in field goals made, field goal percentage and total points. To be mentioned with names like Bobby Plump and Wally Cox from Butler, Ed Smallwood and Hugh Ahlering from Evansville and Dan Rogovich and Bob Williams from St. Joseph made me feel as though I had become an accomplished player and could lay claim to being a Hoosier! Tom Johnson from DePauw may have been up there by then as well he deserved to be with his ability. At this point in the season, no other Ball State player was in the top ten in conference scoring statistics. That would need to change as the season progressed.

Our next game would be at home with Manchester. I think coach Hinga decided a change in the line-up might be best. I had a bad defensive game at Evansville guarding Hal Cox so I went to the bench. The move bothered me some because I thought I had helped the team, especially since the team was not shooting a good percentage. I did, indeed, understand something had to be done and Larry Perry had been coming on strong. I think this shows how competitive college basketball can be. Just a few mistakes can make you a sub real quick. Even though it was embarrassing after all the nice publicity, I told myself that if someone had told me when the season started that I would be playing as much as I had been with this great bunch of guys I would have been happy. Of course, I was looking forward to playing against my former teammates at Manchester. We needed a win real bad.

I recall my friend, Troy Ingram, from Manchester and I meeting at mid-court during warm-ups and Troy asking me, "Are you starting tonight." I had to say no, but got in the game and made three buckets against my old teammates. Ron Stork, who was there when I passed out with my knee injury, and Mike Yoder both played well in the game. Ron made 18 points and Mike 14, but we won 83-67 as Mouse got his act together and made 22 and Larry Perry made 13. I think I am the only player ever to have played for Manchester and beat Ball State and played for Ball State and beat Manchester.

I saw coach Wolfe before the game and he congratulated me on the season I was having. He told me he was glad my knee healed up and I was able to play again. He was a nice guy and so were the players at Manchester, but I have always been happy with my decision to transfer to Ball State and grateful to Dr. Stauffer for his input in that decision.

Anderson College was our next opponent and they had been red-hot all year and now had a 17 and 2 record. This was the best record in the state including Indiana, Purdue and Notre Dame. We were now 6 and 8 and needed to put a win streak together in order to have any chance to make the playoffs. In those days if a school the size of Ball State, the fourth largest college in the state at that time, could reach the teens in the win column it had a chance to get in some type of playoff. We were eligible for every national tournament.

I knew after knee surgery that I could not jump as high and my lateral movement was affected a little. I had 154 stitches in my knee and it was cut down both sides. Once I started playing on it I realized I had to try hard to maintain good defensive position. I didn't want guys going around me. If they were going to score I wouldn't look as bad if they hit from out on the floor. I thought once in the lineup I could stay there with that philosophy, but it caught up with me as we entered the last third of the season. Don't think for one minute that scouts for other teams didn't notice I was a little slow on defense. There were just certain movements I could not make on the court and teams were beginning to exploit that deficiency in my game.

In the program for the Anderson game, season stats were listed again. Big Wilbur was leading in scoring with 169 points and a .410 field goal percentage. Terry was next with 149 points, but still only shooting at .320. Sully was at 143 points and a .380 percentage. I was next with 142 points and leading the team in field goals and a .420 percentage. Ted Fullhart had improved dramatically from a .280 shooting percentage to .333.

We mauled favored Anderson 84 to 70 before an overflow crowd of 4,000. We once led by 25 points and the game was never in doubt. Larry Perry took advantage of his starting assignment by scoring 20 points. It was good to see my friend John Lebo score 10 and reserve center Bob Crawford had 9 points. I thought the team was gaining bench strength and maybe we could make a run at the playoffs. I played some in the game, but did not score. We were now 7 and 8.

The *Muncie Star* articulated how crazy Indiana basketball could get with this report. The first half was interrupted with about 5:20 left by a scuffle at the Ball State bench, as an over-exuberant Anderson fan mixed it up with the Cardinal coaching staff. One person was ejected and order was quickly restored. At times, fans got too excited about winning.

Indiana State, who beat us soundly before, was coming to town and we had a chance to get our record back to 8 and 8, finish decent in the conference race and possibly qualify for a tournament. Mouse played by far his best game of the year as he shot the ball on balance and scored 31 points. Only eight of us played and I did not score and Perry made 7 points. Except for limited playing time, I enjoyed the team effort as we won in overtime 73 to 70.

In a game I was really looking forward to, we were to visit Butler Fieldhouse in Indianapolis to play the tough Butler Bulldogs. The Bulldogs, showing the strength of the ICC, had already beaten Indiana, Notre Dame, Michigan and Ohio State. Possibly no other conference in the country was as under rated as the ICC was in the late 1950s.

Butler Fieldhouse was the scene where the famous Milan-Muncie Central state final game took place in 1954. It was a dream of mine to play there. I had watched many All-Star and state final games there, saw Bevo there as well as the Indianapolis Olympians and Bill Russell and the U.S. Olympic team. It was no secret that most Indiana boys would like to have played on that magical floor. I don't know when I ever worked so hard in practice. I wanted to get back in the line up and play on that famous floor.

Upon arriving at Butler, I was told a reporter from Marion wanted to interview me. It was Bob Lee who wrote the nice *The Morning After* column when we lost to undefeated Mississenewa in the Marion Sectional. We had a nice chat in the bleachers before I had to get dressed for the game, but I don't know what sort of a write up he made about me in the *Marion Chronicle*. It was nice to be sought out by a reporter from my hometown. I wanted so bad to get some substantial minutes and give him something to write about. I did, as it looked as though Jim was giving me a chance to get my starting assignment back. Drawing some "time on the pines" is a great motivator for any player who has any pride in his game.

In a game I will never forget, we had five guys in double figures and Butler did too. Mouse and Bobby Plump, who hit the famous shot for Milan, went head to head. Plump had 24 points and Mouse was brilliant with 23. Wally Cox, a deadeye from Butler, had 21 before over 7,000 fans. Ted Fullhart had 13, Sully 11 and I was back in form with 10. It was a great game, but we lost 91 to 79 to put us below the .500 mark again at 8-9.

It was a thrill for me to play on the same floor with such great players from the state of Indiana. I did notice that Ray Craft, Plump's running mate at Milan and high scorer in the famed Muncie Central game, did not score in the game. I'm just not sure how much playing time he got at Butler, but he was and still is a big name in Indiana basketball. I had no regrets about not going to Butler.

I made five out of ten field goal attempts and loved the atmosphere at Butler. I recall the quickness of Bobby Plump when he went around me once so fast I thought I was going to get windburns. He was a great player and deserves the accolades he still gets. He once got a letter addressed: Plump, Indiana.

After the disappointing loss at Butler, we were faced with just trying to have a winning season and let the chips fall where they may as far as the playoffs were concerned. I would not be a part of it. Tuesday after the Butler game I was running down the floor in practice and my knee gave out. I limped to the sidelines in some pain, but not nearly like the first time I hurt it at Manchester. It was looking like I might regain my starting assignment after shooting so well at Butler, but all that excitement disappeared real fast. I would have to miss the last five games of the season and, worse, jeopardize my chances of being on the twelve-man squad if we did make the playoffs. I was as heartbroken that day as I was when Ginger didn't show up at the hospital in Ft.Wayne. It was almost too much to take after trying so hard during the season to become a good player, keep my grades up, earn a scholarship and help the team win. It was like my life was on a roller coaster, up and down, up and down.

In what is one of my fondest memories, and probably his too, I watched the last five games as Mouse put us on his back and almost single handedly drove us into the playoffs. We beat DePauw in Greencastle 77-66 and returned home to play St. Joseph. Mouse and Sully scored 22 and 26 respectively to win 83 to 76 to put us at 10 and 9 for the season. We avenged the earlier defeat at Wabash, 76 to 64, to go 11 and 9. However, we then had to go to tough Valparaiso who had beaten us in Muncie early in the year.

While sitting out I spent everyday in the whirlpool. I now doubt the whirlpool helped much, but it felt good. I was on crutches for just a few days, but still was not certain if I could return if we did make the playoffs. What made me feel better was being with Pat more often. I would go to practice, take the treatment and go to Elliot Hall to eat with the team. I got a lot of studying done and it helped my grades and Pat and I got to know each other better. She was supportive because she knew I loved to play. She had seen most of our games, but she was disappointed because we missed some big dances because of my injury. I was disappointed because I learned that, with hard work, dreams can come true, but in sports if they are not sustained for awhile it leaves a feeling of emptiness.

While I was injured, Pat and I would go to the Waymire's or a bunch of us would gather at our house on Wheeling Ave. to watch *The Ed Sullivan Show* on Sunday nights. I spent some time at the fraternity house and generally got to know more people. John Hevel and Judy Wall were getting more serious about each other. My brother was dating Pat's roommate, Jane Condon, from Westville, Indiana. We had a good group with whom to take a break from studying and generally had a good time. Still, my spirits were down, feeling unfulfilled.

During the injury period coach Hinga informed me I would have to get back on the practice floor before our last game against Butler or I would not be able to join the team if we got a playoff bid. I remember I came back and got in some practices on a limited basis and did some running a few days before the team had to travel to Valpo. I would not dress for the game… but I'm glad I went. Mouse sprained his ankle three days before the Valpo game. It was bad, it turned every color in the rainbow and he was on crutches. I thought our chances to beat Valpo were bad if he didn't play. He told me he was going to play "no matter what." He didn't get on the practice floor until the day before the game and was limping noticeably.

In what I think to this day was one of the most courageous athletic performances I have ever seen, Terry "Mouse" Schurr made 30 points against Valpo and we surprised them 80 to 75. After limping through warm-ups he made 12 out of 23 shots and 6 free throws and was all over the court. The team shot a sizzling .477 from the field as Wilbur and Sully made 27 points between them. Terry's performance reminded me of the night Donnie Butts made around 30 points against DePaul and coach Ray Meyer shook his hand after the game.

The *Muncie Star* said Terry played a "brilliant game" and he did. Indiana Governor Otis Bowen once said that, "Terry Schurr is the finest small man

I've ever seen play." Terry made it clear to everyone on the team he wanted to go to the NAIA again and had not given up. We needed the win as it lifted our record to 12 and 9 and were now in third place in the conference behind the good Evansville and Butler teams. There was a mouse in the Ball State gym... a mouse that roared.

Evansville won the conference with an 11-1 record and Butler was second at 9-2. This Evansville team would go on and win third place in the college division tournament held on their floor. Butler accepted an NIT bid to play in Madison Square Garden and this would be the first national tournament in which Butler ever played. Butler was sixth in the nation in field goal accuracy and fourth in free throws. Plump set a new career scoring record, replacing the one set by Ralph "Buckshot" O'Brien. Butler lost to St. Johns in the prestigious NIT field by seven points. Plump was named to the West All-Star team. There is little doubt that the ICC was not given its due credit in this 1957-58 season and many good players set their mark and will be remembered by fans across the state.

We still had to play Butler at home to finish the season, but we had already received a bid to play in the NAIA tournament to be held in Anderson, but at the high school Wigwam, not the Anderson College home court. Four teams from the ICC would play in national tournaments. In addition to the bids Evansville and Butler received, Indiana State would join us in the NAIA at Anderson.

In what the *Muncie Star* called "one of the most spectacular games ever played in Ball Gym, Butler's Bulldogs defeated the Ball State Cardinals in overtime 82-76." It was in front of an overflow crowd of over 4,000 that Mouse and Bobby Plump again went head to head. Mouse again was brilliant outscoring Plump 24 to 22. Ted Fullhart and Jim Sullivan both scored in double figures for Ball State as did Ken Pennington and Wally Cox for Butler. The loss gave us a 12 and 10 record, but we were in a tournament. We had come from behind all season to establish a winning record. I was extremely disappointed I could not play and had to choke back some tears as the team lost this overtime game.

Terry Schurr shot nearly fifty percent and averaged about 22 points per game his last five games of which we won four. This was a far cry from his early season streak where he averaged only about 10 points up to mid-season. In our last nine games we lost only twice, both losses to Butler, one in OT. In retrospect, I hope the talk that Tom Hilgendorf and I had with Mouse at mid-season helped him to shoot on balance because he proved near the end what a good player he was when he did things fundamentally correct.

I was a little on edge when coach Hinga called the squad together the day after the Butler game with the purpose of naming the tournament team. I was thinking that I had scored in double figures against every team in the conference, was still leading in field goal percentage and close to the top in other departments despite missing several games. I had accomplished my dream and was in the starting line up more than half of the season. I thought I deserved to be on the tournament team. I wanted to go to Kansas City and continue playing.

Coach Hinga read off some names and said about me, "Norm contributed a great deal in the early season and deserves to be on the team." I had shown just enough in practice that I could get back playing and it convinced Jim to put me on the twelve man roster. I was relieved. We would open the tournament seeking our 13th win with a team that beat us early in the year, Hanover. They were 14 and 8 on the season. We had a week to prepare, which was good for me as it gave me more healing time.

The first player I saw the next day was big Wilbur Davis. He asked me if I had my bags packed for Kansas City? He said his suitcase was packed and he was ready for the train ride to Kansas City. I did tell Wilbur the lyrics to the song *Kansas City* were rolling through my mind. One line in the song goes, *"Kansas City here I come."* We were a happy bunch, happy that Mouse got us where we wanted to go. It was nice to read in the Muncie paper that, "Norm Jones has rejoined the squad and is available for duty."

We beat Hanover 75-70 as George Taylor, just back after a bout with the measles, made two free throws with ten seconds to go to seal the win. According to the *Muncie Star,* Jim Sullivan had a "brilliant 30 point performance" and Mouse scored 16 and "set up many successful buckets." The team hit 21 of 23 free throws for a sensational .913 percentage. Coach Hinga surprised me and let me play a few minutes even though the game was close. I surprised myself and probably my teammates by making both of the jump shots I took. I loved the baskets at the Wigwam and felt as though I was again ready to contribute…and help get us to Kansas City.

Anderson beat Indiana State 82-77 to set up the title game. In one of the saddest moments of my basketball career coach Hinga told me after the Hanover game that he was not going to play me against Anderson. I guess he felt my knee might be taken advantage of and didn't want to take any chances. I was disappointed because I felt we might need some outside shooting since Anderson liked the zone defense, but understood where Jim was coming from. Larry Perry was a good player, but not as effective from outside as he was with his slashing drives to the basket. He had tailed off in scoring the last four games as he averaged only about 6 points per game. I thought we would need balanced scoring to beat Anderson this time around.

The game was, indeed, a "barn burner" but we took a 30 to 24 lead at the half and moved that out to a 13 point lead with about seventeen minutes to go. Anderson regained the lead and actually led 61 to 56 with 1:48 to go. Sully and Ted Fullhart fought back and made baskets that got us to within 63 to 62. We grabbed a missed Anderson free throw and called time out with two seconds to go. Here is what happened as described in the *Muncie Star* the next day:

> The ball was thrown in to Jim Sullivan, who got off a jump shot from the left side, but the shot struck the left side of the backboard as the gun sounded.

Our season was over. We would not be going to Kansas City. On the bus home all I could think about was how I got runner-up to Sharon, runner-up to Mississenewa, runner-up to Ginger and now runner-up to Anderson. I was wondering if I would have to endure getting runner-up to Pat in the near future. I also thought about how good a year it had been for me and how not being able to contribute near the end of the season made any success I had bittersweet. I felt as though I had let the team down, by getting hurt, especially since in the Anderson game Larry Perry, John Lebo and George Taylor only made 6 points between them and Larry made all of those. My fear about balanced scoring and outside shooting came true as Anderson placed all five starters in double figures and we only had Fullhart with 21 and Mouse with 18. Ted played his best game of the season on this night. I could see the determination on the faces of Ted and Terry and was disappointed for them. It was frustrating to me to not be able to help.

Both Terry and Ted made the NAIA District 21 Honor Team and Sully made honorable mention. As the season ended, The Mouse was still roaring as he was voted the Most Valuable Player in the tournament.

It was sad for us to lose to a team that we had beaten soundly during the year, but such was life in Hoosier Hysteria. Adding somewhat to the sadness, it was announced that for the first time since its inception the NBA would not have a team in Indiana. The Ft.Wayne Pistons moved to Detroit and disappointed many Indiana basketball fans. One bright spot for Hoosiers was that transplanted Hoosier Oscar Robertson became a consensus All-American in his sophomore year at Cincinnati.

CHAPTER TEN
A Forgettable Senior Season

*SOME PEOPLE IN INDIANA THINK THE
STATE BIRD IS LARRY.*

Jim Hinga was very fair with me and told me my Pepsi Cola scholarship would be honored for my senior year, the 1958-59 basketball season. Scholarships were not guaranteed in those days if a player sustained an injury. I checked with my academic advisor and he told me I had caught up on my credits and I would not have to go to summer school in order to graduate in May of 1959.

Pat and I were hitting it off better than ever and I was beginning to feel as though she might be the right woman for me. After her telling me she needed some breathing room I was very careful how I approached things with her in fear of losing her. I even remember asking her if she would be comfortable with me working in a summer job as athletic director at Camp Crosley since it was just a short distance from her home in Pierceton. She would be working as a telephone operator. Pat didn't seem to mind so I took the good job offer at the camp. I didn't have a car, but would manage to scrounge up rides to her house and back. Unfortunately, the camp job didn't last long as the camp director began to lose his staff by demanding too much out of them. He lost me when he told me to mow an area over a quarter of a mile square...with a hand mower.

I told Pat about the situation and she understood. I had to go back to Muncie and would see Pat sparingly until school started. I got a job at the Pepsi Cola Company in Muncie. While at Pepsi Cola I met two great African-American guys. Jim Nettles and Norm Wilson were football players at Muncie Central. Jim was an all around athlete. He and Ron Bonham had played

153

basketball in the Indiana Final Four when Central lost to Crawfordsville in March. We were all working to try to stay in shape. We would have to fill wooden cartons with glass bottles of Pepsi and load them on trucks for the next day delivery. This was before soda was ever put in cans. We would have to lift the heavy cartons over our heads, stand on our tiptoes and flip them up on top of the trucks. We all thought this was good exercise for our arm and shoulder muscles and even our legs. I would assimilate flipping the cartons to a jump shot and follow through as I placed the cartons on the truck. A lot of the work was at night so there wasn't much time to do other things.

During the previous school year I had become friends with several Sigma Phi Epsilon guys one of whom was Ted Fullhart, my varsity teammate. Others were Larry Yazel, Jim Horein and Don Clark. Don "Cookie" Clark played briefly on the Ball State varsity and was tall. Jim Horein had played high school ball and was a good rebounder and could score some. We decided to enter the North Webster, Indiana outdoor basketball tourney. Larry's dad would coach the team. Terry Schurr, also a Sig Ep, did not play as he had graduated and was getting married. We had some other good players and won our first two games in the tourney. We then had to play the tourney favorite sponsored by the North Webster Bank.

The tourney was good experience for Ted and I as we would be returning lettermen for Ball State. We lost to the Webster Bank, but in a way Ted and I won't forget. I made three quick jump shots to start the game and they quickly put a guy on me who had played for the NBA Milwaukee Hawks. He was by far the best defender I ever had guard me. I couldn't even move, let alone get a shot. Mr. Yazel took me out. We talked on the bench and the guys decided that since the pro player was also their best rebounder it might be smart to put me in and if he stayed on me he would be away from the basket in the back court and it would help our rebounding game. The plan seemed to work as we caught the Webster Bank at the end of the game.

Somehow I got the ball when we were down by one with seconds to go. I went up for a jumper and saw Ted wide open underneath and I passed it to him. He made the lay-up. The ball went through the net, bounced on the court at least once, maybe twice and the buzzer went off. We thought we had upset the tourney favorite. Not too surprisingly in Indiana, the referee signaled the basket didn't count. Ted and I, my brother and the Yazel's and most everybody else argued, but to no avail. It was the worst call I had seen since the eighth grade when the ref called a foul on me and I wasn't anywhere near the action. The Webster Bank hired the refs so what else could anyone expect in a state where it was important to win in basketball even in the summer?

I played in a couple more tournaments, but mainly pick-up games around Muncie the rest of the summer and my knee seemed stable. I thought I was getting better and worked hard at the game because we had Ted, Sully, big Wilbur, Larry Perry, George Taylor and John Lebo coming back on the varsity and some good freshman would be moving up. I remember one pick-up game at the Muncie Central Fieldhouse court that had so many well-known players on the court the game drew a crowd of fifty to a hundred people. We could have sold tickets and made some money. Hoosier Hysteria was alive in Muncie as Ball State had made the college playoffs for the second straight year and Muncie Central had reached the Final Four. The Bearcats had several underclassmen and were obviously building a state contender.

Coach Hinga sent out letters in the summer to each returning varsity player. In the letter he talked about how, "We had a fine basketball season last year, and with so many of last year's squad returning, plus several fine new prospects becoming eligible for our varsity team, I think we can look forward to a fine year if we all pull together." Jim said, "I admired Wilbur Davis for having his suitcase packed for Kansas City last year. I've got a spot picked out in my office for the ICC basketball trophy. Evansville can't be much better than last year, but I know we will be and we were within a basket of them this year." He encouraged all players to run some in the summer and practice basketball hard, "Then come into my office the first week of school and get a locker and shoes." He enclosed a schedule and mentioned that, "We have a week in Washington, D.C. and play tough Dayton then our tough conference schedule. We must be ready."

Jim Hinga ended his letter by saying, "Give your girlfriend a squeeze for me and I'll see you soon. Might send some play diagrams later. Read them and study them." The letter got me fired up because I had been worrying about what Jim would be thinking about my injury and I was concerned that he chose not to play me against Anderson. The letter made me feel as though I was part of the team again and I would be allowed to play out my dream to play well and on a winning team. I couldn't wait to get started. There would not be the pressure of tryouts as I was a returning letterman on scholarship and that was a great feeling. That fact alone made me feel as though I had accomplished some goals and had every right to call myself a Hoosier.

Giving my girlfriend a squeeze was not going to be a problem, but I was not getting to see Pat as often as I would have liked. By the end of the summer I had visions of graduating in a year, getting a good job and asking Pat to marry me. I had come close to meeting the goals I set for myself while in St. Joseph's hospital and I figured I might as well set some more goals.

I had a little money in my pocket after working all summer and, being on scholarship, I didn't have to worry about paying for my education except for books. Often the frat house had used books donated by graduating fraternity brothers. When Pat got back to campus I recall taking her to a nice restaurant in Anderson and she seemed impressed. We talked a lot about plans for our last year together on campus. She would be a junior and would be living in a girls' dorm named Wood Hall. I would be a senior and still be living at home.

I didn't have a problem keeping busy before basketball started. The football team went 6 and 2 under coach Jim Freeman and surprised a lot of people. Many people in our group knew the players and attended games not too far away. The games made for great weekends. Bob Million, a lineman from South Bend, Ed Corazzi, the ICCs best quarterback and elusive halfback Tim Brown led the football team. Tim, a good-looking African-American, was an orphan from Morton Memorial High School near Knightstown, Indiana.

There were fraternity and sorority activities to keep Pat and I busy. I was in the "B" club having earned a varsity letter. My classes in my senior year were more to my liking as I had classes that would prepare me to coach and teach. One class, titled Team Sports, was with assistant football coach and head baseball coach, Ray Louthen. I wrote a fifty-page paper on the fast break in basketball and coach Ray told me I ought to try to get it published.

With so much experience and overall talent returning on the basketball team the campus was, especially after the exciting football season, abuzz about basketball. I remember picking up a national magazine that rated teams by what it called power ratings. Even though Evansville got runner up in the College Division and had the entire starting five coming back, the magazine ranked us right there with the Aces. We should be able, as coach Hinga said, to compete for the ICC title.

Jim wanted the returning lettermen to try weight lifting in pre-season practice. It was not popular and almost unheard of in those days. Sully and I tried it about twice and never went back to the weight room. Jim didn't force us to do it as it was looked upon as a fad at that time. We all felt we would get too muscle bound to shoot well.

We were introduced to Al Cook, an African-American player, who had impressed Hinga in tryouts. Al had transferred in from Tennessee State. He stood about 6'4" and had good credentials. He had played on the Tennessee State NAIA champions. As the season started, coach Hinga also allowed Tim

Brown from the football team to join the squad. Tim had played in high school and did have some basketball skills.

The *Muncie Star* had the following to say about the team as the season opened:

> "If things go right, Ball State's basketball Cardinals should give their followers some exciting moments before the campaign ends."

The article named me as a starter and mentioned that Al Cook might replace Sully since Sully had sprained his knee in practice. I did earn a starting position for our first game against Hanover and recall how thrilled I was to be back playing with a healed knee. However, for the first time in Ball State history we had a full-time trainer in Sayers "Bud" Miller. Bud told me he could support my knee and, hopefully, it would last through the entire season. He would wrap it in gauze, then tape it and then fit me with a brace lined with a steel rod on each side. It seemed heavy to me and slowed me down.

Although I was not at my best even in practice and somewhat discouraged having to wear the brace I reclaimed my starting position. We beat Hanover 72-60 in Muncie as Sully overcame his injury and scored 15 points. Larry Perry and I started at guard and he had 11 and Al Cook played well scoring 9. I made the first basket of the game, a driving lay-up, on a tip play we had run for two years. It was my only basket of the game. I found the brace to be cumbersome and restricting my movement. I could not make the moves to get open for a shot. It was like I was dragging my leg and I felt a little clumsy on defense.

The *Muncie Star* reported how we were to next play Dayton, a team that "sports height comparable to the New York skyline." I was told I would be guarding a player named Frank Case who was being touted by Dayton as an All-American. Pat would make the trip from Muncie to Dayton with my folks on a cold night. The heater went out in my dad's car and as it turned out, it was a miserable trip for everyone from Ball State.

When we got to Dayton we learned the game was going to be on television locally. I picked up a program and read about another good player for Dayton named Terry Bockhorn. The program wrote him up as the "Boy With The Bandit Hands" and told about how many steals he had made in his career. I told myself to watch out for him.

In front of about 6,000 fans, the starters were to be introduced by dribbling to mid-court, stop and pivot and pass the ball back to the next player. All this was to be done under a big spotlight as the gym was darkened. My brother swears I traveled during this routine, but I didn't think so. It was an exciting and proud moment for me as I acted as captain on this night and shook hands with Case and Bockhorn. During warm-ups some kids I had worked with at Camp Crosley came to the floor and asked me for my autograph. As I signed their programs I began wondering what it must be like to be a real celebrity. However, my flirting with stardom changed rather quickly.

I tried very hard and, I think, got lucky the first half and held Case to 4 points, but we were down 19 at the half. I think I took two shots. I won't soon forget playing against those giants, but their height didn't turn out to be the problem for me. The "Boy With The Bandit Hands" stole the ball from me so clean while I was dribbling up the floor he could have taken my pants and jock if he had wanted to.

Coach Hinga took me out after the steal and I was embarrassed. I couldn't move swiftly enough with the brace and knew when that incident happened that the heavy brace caused me to lose a step that I simply couldn't afford to lose. Dayton went on to beat us 75 to 43. The *Muncie Star* reported the next day that Ball State "learned how things are done in large cities." Case only made 13 points, but Bockhorn had 16 and I only made one basket…again. I was a little discouraged.

We moved on to beat DePauw 74-60 and move into first place in the ICC. Sully was away for a family illness and Al Cook scored 24 points in taking his place. Mike Henderson, who transferred to Ball State from DePauw played well, making 8 points as did Ted Fullhart. John Lebo started in my place and made 9 out of 11 free throws and three fielders for 15 points. It was John's best game since I had known him. I played some, but had the sinking feeling that since I wasn't getting shots and probably looked slow, the coaches decided other players could help the team better than me.

We next lost to Franklin College and didn't look good doing it. Al Cook scored 30 points, but we were suffering from a lack of balanced scoring. I don't think I played in the game as coach Hinga was probably having as much trouble forgetting the "Boy With the Bandit Hands" as I was. Our record was 2 and 2, but we were 1-0 in all important conference games. I began thinking that to play on a conference champ would be a nice way to end my college career regardless of how much I played.

As mentioned, Tim Brown had joined the squad. He had been named as an All-American halfback. Tim had talents beyond football. He could sing and I remember him singing to us as we returned from a road game. He had a pretty good rendition of *Sonny.* It was only after a few games that I found myself taking a shower at the same time as Tim and he said to me, "See ya' Jonesie, this is my last practice." I inquired why and he said, "I've been drafted by the Green Bay Packers and I'm headed for Green Bay to play for Vince Lombardi." I said, "Tim, that's great. Can I ask how much you signed for?" He said, "Sure, $8,900.00." I thought that sounded like a million in those days. Teachers were starting at about $3,500 in Indiana.

In those days the college All-Stars played an NFL team each summer in Soldier Field in Chicago. Tim was named to the team and made a long, impressive run in the game. From there Tim joined the Packers and had a rough first year and Vince Lombardi traded him to the Philadelphia Eagles. The Eagles went on to win the NFL title and Tim was their starting running back as well as their punt return man and kick-off return man. At one time he led the NFL in total offense and had an outstanding NFL career. Precious memories are made when teammates move on to successful careers.

Every player was looking forward to the trip that would have us play in the Quantico Marine Invitational Tournament. Quantico is a large Marine base just outside Washington, D.C. We were guaranteed three games in the eight-team tournament and everyone knew coach Hinga would be doing things to get the team ready for the big conference run. I told Pat I would be gone for an entire week and this would be the longest we would be apart for quite sometime. Those players making the trip besides returning lettermen and Al Cook were, Mike Henderson, Dave Horn, Dean Campbell, Ron Jenks, Bill O'Neal and Bob Stewart. Dean and Bill both played at Muncie Central. Wilbur, Sully, Al Cook and Bill O' Neal were our African-American players and, thankfully, no special accommodations would have to be made for them at Quantico.

We traveled by car to Richmond, Indiana and then had to catch a train to D.C. Our first game would be on Tuesday at the base after leaving on Sunday. We would have to try and get some sleep on the train, but did not have sleeping quarters. Transportation was provided for us to get from the D.C. train station to the Marine base. We checked in to the athletic barracks and tried to catch up on sleep. The barracks were guarded by Marines with rifles.

In thinking back and analyzing the culture in which I grew up in, it dawned on me that coaches and athletic directors were unnecessarily burdened with issues of racism when planning trips for teams. I recalled how, as a basketball team, it seemed safe to stay at government run places of lodging such as the

Purdue Student Union or Pokagon State Park so a discussion would not have to take place as to whether or not black players could stay. I noticed as we played in the Quantico Marine tournament that the barracks on the base were well integrated and the barracks assigned to the eight teams were integrated and it was not a problem.

It is easier to see now why our African-American players had the right to ride the train to Quantico. Rosa Parks saw to that in 1955 when her courage to maintain her seat on a bus in Montgomery, Alabama eventually made it illegal to segregate people on public transportation. It seemed to me that our basketball schedule was made out with the thought in mind to minimize the pain some of our black players might feel if they found out, like Oscar Robertson did, that they were not welcome in some public accommodations.

We were scheduled to play Westchester State from Pennsylvania at 2:15pm on Tuesday. We would play the next three days and move on to Washington, D.C. early Saturday morning before catching the train late Saturday and returning home on Sunday.

We managed to beat Westchester 75-73 as Jim Sullivan scored 26 points and Wilbur Davis controlled the boards. I thought the team looked better, but I didn't play as George Taylor and Larry Perry played well. Guards John Lebo and soph Dean Campbell, a baseball standout, played ahead of me since I had not done much in practice and played poorly in the first two games. I was miserable and had not even enjoyed the train ride to D.C. as it was uncomfortable rattling around on the rails.

Unbeaten American University out of Washington, D.C. was our next foe and they had a great player in Willie Jones who was an African-American. Only 5'9", Willie bombed us for 39 points and a 71-69 win for the Eagles. We then lost to Buffalo University 80 to 64. I played a couple of minutes. Big Wilbur was hurt during the game and had to go to the Marine Base Infirmary to get his back checked out, but it was nothing serious. The Marines upset American University 69-63 to win their own tourney. Jim Sullivan made the all-tournament team and Willie Jones was the tournament MVP.

The next morning the team went right to the capitol building for a visit that had been arranged by Indiana Congressman, Ralph Harvey. In the capitol coach Hinga looked at me and said, "This place would hold a helluva' lot of hay." Only a true Hoosier could come up with such a remark.

Once we finished the tour of the capitol we were given an envelope with money in it to spend however we saw fit before the train departure. I wanted to see all the monuments and the history and so did sophomore Dave Horn so we hired a taxi cab driver to show us around. It was a great way to spend a day and I still regard it as one of the best educational experiences of my life. We had to be at the train station by 6:30pm as the train was to leave Washington at 7:45. The Quantico trip was a good experience, but I didn't like the armed forces way of life...and not getting to play much.

After losing our last two in the Quantico Tournament we proceeded to lose our next four games which gave us a surprising six game losing streak. Three of those games were conference games. I played very little and, at a more mature age of twenty-two, I saw the handwriting on the wall. I thought back to Jim telling me I would not play against Anderson in the playoffs the year before. Looking back, I think Jim starting me the first two games of this year was a gift to a returning letterman who had some success the year before. I simply could not move with the heavy brace on my leg.

The trainer told me I would not finish the season if I didn't wear the brace so I had little choice. Coaches simply do not want to take a chance on a player who might be in the lineup one minute and not the next. It was hard to take, but I tried to cope. Dreams seem to shatter a lot faster than they are fulfilled.

The team record went to 3 and 8 and then 4 and 10 real fast. The spot for the ICC trophy Jim had picked out in his office could now be used for something else. There were some good individual performances as Dave Horn scored 34 points in a double overtime loss to Valparaiso and late in the season made 31 against Butler. Mike Henderson came on strong after mid-season and had some good games. I knew we were in serious trouble when Manchester beat us 86 to 60. It was obvious this team did not have the cohesiveness the team had the last season. Home crowds dwindled and the spirit was soon gone. There would be no playoff bid. We missed the leadership and competitiveness of Terry Schurr. We finished at 7-15.

In less than a year, I had gone from having fun chasing a dream as a starting guard on an exciting team to an also ran on a ball club that had great individual talent, but struggled to win. We lost our last four games by a total of 75 points. I wasn't even dressed for our last home game against Butler as my knee did finally give out while wrestling in an Individual Sports class. Seniors were introduced, as was the custom, at the last game. It was embarrassing for me to go to the middle of the court on crutches. In fact, the 1959 Ball State yearbook shows me sitting on the bench and my crutches can be seen under the bench. A team picture in the year book with me standing there with my big brace on has reminded me through the years how my playing days resembled the ups and downs of a yo-yo. I enjoyed a brief stretch of glory and then became an also ran.

I have often looked back on my playing days at Ball State and am proud how I met my goals after serious knee surgery in Ft.Wayne. I walked on, beat out a lot of good players then won a starting position, played well for about a dozen games, earned the Pepsi Cola scholarship and then got hurt, ending my career. It has always bothered me that I started out playing so well while Terry Schurr was struggling somewhat. Then, just when Terry started playing on balance, I got hurt and never played much with Terry after the injury. It would have been nice to have us both play well at the same time. I think the team record might have been a little better since we did lose several close games during that time frame. And we might have been able to get to Kansas City.

To my mind, not knowing how good I could have been if I had been blessed with strong legs haunts me even now. I think for any athlete to taste the limelight and be called a "star" then have such glory days come crashing down is a difficult thing to handle. The situation handed to me is always in my memory, but I have learned that it is not how many times you get knocked down, it is how may times you get up that shows character. I tried to apply Mr. Mason's words to myself after getting hurt and I give his advice credit for helping me to move ahead and make good decisions about my future.

Coming back on the train from Quantico I played Checkers with assistant coach Fred Kehoe and during quieter periods thought a lot about Pat, my future and how to finish my years at Ball State. I decided it was time for me to find out just how much Pat cared about me because I was always somewhat apprehensive about getting serious about someone and getting hurt...again. I decided to see if she would accept my fraternity pin. Many people held candle light ceremonies to celebrate getting pinned and most of them got married after graduation. It was considered something just short of getting engaged.

Maybe my timing was right as Pat did seem to miss me while I was at Quantico. She did accept my pin right about the time basketball season ended, but we didn't talk much about getting married. We just told each other about our goals. Such things as finishing our degrees would be important before discussing anything else. Pat was of the Catholic faith and I was Episcopalian, but we decided that would not be a problem if we did move ahead and get married. Cardinal teammate Ted Fullhart was not Catholic, but was to eventually marry a Catholic girl named Rosi Fisher. Rosi was the 1958 Homecoming queen and a varsity cheerleader. Ted and I talked some and he told me the story about when he first went to mass with Rosi. She genuflected right in front of him when he wasn't looking and he tripped right over the top of Rosi. He reminded me to be careful if I married a Catholic girl.

Jim Hinga surprised me after the season and asked me if I wanted him to write a letter to the NCAA and request that I be granted another year of eligibility. I was shocked by his question. I had made less than 10 points my entire senior season, didn't feel as though I contributed anything at all to the team and wasn't sure I could ever reach the level I had reached in 1957-58. I thought about his question and it quickly ran through my mind that I would be on campus with Pat. Maybe I could have more surgery and play without the knee brace and contribute, etc., etc.

Jim was thinking that I had been injured so much that the NCAA might grant me another year. The rules were a little bit unclear in those years and Jim wanted to at least get clarification. The letter came back from the NCAA making it perfectly clear that a player would lose a year of playing time upon transferring to another school no matter what happens to that player during his remaining eligibility. That letter officially ended my playing days at Ball State. It was just as well as the team went 5 and 17 in 1959-60. Even with my arms wrapped around Pat, I would not have been happy to be a part of that season.

I had made plans with my academic advisor to do my student teaching in my last quarter in college at Newcastle Junior High School in Newcastle, Indiana about thirty minutes south from Ball State. My folks also planned to visit with my aunt and uncle in Clarksdale, Mississippi during spring break. I decided to make the trip and the only thing I recall about it was my uncle's reaction when I showed him pictures of the Ball State basketball team. He said to me, "Now Norman, when these black boys pass you the ball, do you try to catch it?" I told him it was a little difficult to keep an offense moving if a player didn't catch the ball. Of course, he was telling me in his way that something might just rub off of the ball on to me and damage me for life.

It was just amazing to me how many people could believe that black people were so dirty that white people had to work to keep them "in their place" for fear of being contaminated. It just never made sense to me that to keep the blacks in the balcony of a theatre helped prevent them from contaminating white folks when the same whites would eat the food cooked by black chefs in the fancy restaurants the whites enjoyed. If they could not see the blacks cook the food then everything was OK, but if they would have to sit beside a black person in an integrated theatre that was different.

I learned more about racial injustice from the way my uncle spoke about it than I did from any professor or from reading a book or news reports on TV. It has also added to my understanding of the segregation and integration issues since I have figured out the reasons we stayed at certain places and ate in certain restaurants with the teams I played on during my time growing up in Indiana. Racism was simply part of the culture in which I grew up.

As if I needed any more let downs after the horrible basketball season Pat informed me just before spring break that she was returning my pin. She tempered the move with words designed to soothe my already beat up soul. She explained she was going to Florida with some sorority sisters and didn't think it would be right to go out with some guy while being pinned to me. She did say she didn't anticipate finding anyone, but her initial words devastated me so much that statement didn't make much difference to me. All I could think about was...getting runner-up again. We were at my house and I will never forget her walking out just after a nice romantic afternoon with her. I got a little choked up by telling myself I had been through this many times.

While Pat was gone I did have a date or two, but always was thinking about what was going to happen when Pat got back from Florida. I didn't want to go out with anyone more than once or twice since I didn't want word to get back to Pat that I might have found someone else I was interested in. I cannot recall how Pat and I got back together, but I know I found out through her girlfriends that she did not find a sub for me while in Florida or early in the fall. I thought that was a good sign for me.

In my last year at Ball State, Indiana high school basketball had a year never to be forgotten by fans who lived anywhere near the era of the 1950s. On Feb. 20, 1959 Mr. Basketball to be, Jimmy Rayl of Kokomo and Ray Pavy of Newcastle engaged in one of the most amazing high school shoot-outs ever played in Indiana. Pavy's team won 92-81. Playing in the cracker box Church Street gym in Newcastle, Pavy outscored Rayl 51 to 49 to total 100 between them. Pavy hit 23 of 36 field goals and Rayl hit 18 of 28 and both added free throws to their totals. I remember anticipating the shoot-out and reading about it in the newspaper.

Indianapolis Crispus Attucks beat Rayl's Kokomo Wildcats in the state final game in Butler Fieldhouse. That game may also have helped to move integration forward in Indiana. Still an all black school, Attucks won the admiration of many fans as the players conducted themselves in a classy fashion. There is no question that the championship teams from Crispus Attucks High School in the 1950s played a part in promoting integration in Indiana.

Rayl and Pavy were selected as the #1 and #2 players on the Indiana All-Star team. They split two games with the Kentucky stars. Both went on to Indiana University where Rayl twice scored 56 points in Big Ten games and became an All-American. Pavy had his playing career ended by an automobile accident that paralyzed him from the waist down. Both players are in the Indiana Basketball Hall of Fame.

I finished the last quarter at Ball State doing my student teaching in the legendary Church Street gym in Newcastle where the famous Rayl-Pavy 100-point shootout took place. In my junior high class I had a student by the name of Butch Joyner who later made Newcastle proud by being named to the Indiana All-Star team. He then played for Indiana University and made the Indiana Basketball Hall of Fame.

I did have to attend summer school because my advisor made a mistake counting my credits. I took an art class to complete a minor and survived a driver's education course in which I taught older people how to drive. This would give me credentials to teach driving to high school students and later in my career it did help me obtain a teaching position.

Trying to get away from the shattered dreams of a miserable basketball season and still reeling from Pat's decision to possibly search for my replacement, I took up golf. My fraternity brother, Earl Yestingsmeier, who made some of the basketball trips with us as scorekeeper, was a good golfer. He helped me a great deal and, in fact, he later became a successful golf coach at Ball State. Learning about golf was a good way to pass the spring months while student teaching and getting things in order to graduate.

I attended graduation ceremonies, but could not pick up my degree until the end of summer school. Pat had returned to Pierceton to work for the summer and I did not yet have access to a car so I didn't see her much. I got a job at Warner Machine in Muncie and met a fellow who had a beautiful Plymouth convertible he wanted to sell. It was green and white with the big fin like fenders in the back. My dad told me he thought a bank would loan me money to buy the car once I signed a contract to teach.

I got lucky and the Ball State Placement office called me by mid-summer. I went for an interview and signed a contract immediately after it to teach and coach in North Vernon, Indiana located about seventy-five miles southeast of Indianapolis with a population of about 5,000. I was hired to teach junior high health and high school art classes, supervise the yearbook and coach two sports…for $4,700. I was to be head baseball coach at the high school and eighth grade basketball coach. The schools were combined…and integrated.

Pat and I were not at the point yet where we were seeing only each other. However, while I was completing summer school I would take my new car to see her and she seemed impressed. I sensed we were back together and I was on firm ground with her once again. I would do my studying and my factory job and go see Pat on weekends.

Romance seemed to be blossoming.

Later in the summer, just a few weeks before I was to report to North Vernon I returned from seeing Pat and my mom and brother told me my dad was in Ball Memorial hospital. He had suffered a heart attack. I went right up to see him and he was doing OK. In a few days he asked me if I could help pay some medical bills so I went to the bank again and obtained five hundred dollars and gave it to him and told him not to worry about paying me back since he had been a big help in helping me make decisions in my college days. He recovered quickly and I was pleased to be able to help in that process.

As summer school ended I was ready to head for North Vernon with a great deal of excitement about my first job and happy to be in good standing with Pat. I said good-bye to Ball State as far as undergraduate work was concerned, took my convertible and belongings and moved to North Vernon to begin my coaching career in the delirious world of Indiana basketball.

CHAPTER ELEVEN
Bolden Is Golden

"FOR A COUNTRY BASED ON INDIVIDUAL FREEDOMS, WE SURE ARE FULL OF LOOPHOLES." (BILL RUSSELL)

North Vernon was just a little different than most Indiana towns. When I arrived there one of the first things I heard about was the great football teams they had at the high school. The team was so successful for a few years fans would take several passenger cars from the local railroad and travel to the next game. The head football coach then was also the head basketball coach and favored football so much he bought *eleven* basketball uniforms. In some Indiana communities he could have gotten fired for doing that sort of thing. On the other hand, people liked to win so bragging rights could be enjoyed.

In fact, it wasn't hard to get fired in Indiana if you chose to coach basketball. If anyone doubts the importance of basketball in Indiana, keep in mind that when little Milan pulled the upset over much larger Muncie Central that inspired the movie *Hoosiers,* over 40,000 people came to Milan the night school boy legend Bobby Plump hit the jump shot in Indianapolis. If he had missed there might have been that many people celebrating in Muncie.

Ralph and Millie Jordan rented me a room in the middle of North Vernon. I had a bed and a place for my clothes and that was about it. I bought myself a TV right away mainly so I could watch the Indiana Hoosiers and any other games I could get.

The first days in North Vernon I met Walter O'Brien and wife Katie and Don Pelkey and his wife Suzie. The O'Brien's had cute little twin daughters which was not surprising since Walter had a twin brother, Waller. Walter was to be the head basketball coach and Don the head football coach. Walter was also a brother to the well-known Ralph "Buckshot" O'Brien who, as mentioned earlier, was a star at Butler and then with the Indianapolis Olympians. I figured I could learn some basketball from coach O'Brien. These two couples would have me over for dinner once in awhile, which I appreciated because I was eating out every night and missed "home cooking."

I enjoyed my first job, but could not wait to get back to Ball State and see Pat on weekends. I wore out my new car, but it was worth it as Pat and I became serious about each other as we rolled into another basketball season. There were times I would go pick her up and drive the couple hours to North Vernon for a game. I had become friends with Dr. Calli and his wife as their boy Jim was a good athlete at the school. They insisted Pat stay at their home when she visited and Pat did like it there. In what amounted to a lot of driving for me, I would take Pat back to campus on Sunday and return to North Vernon that night.

I spent a lot of time watching the football coaches teach and try to motivate our young players. I needed to learn as much as I could about coaching before starting with my eighth grade basketball team. O'Brien, as expected, had all kinds of stories coming from a legendary basketball background. He played some for Tony Hinkle at Butler and knew the ropes in basketball. He had coached before and I was interested in hearing about his experiences in coaching in small Indiana towns. I guess he must have been fired once because I recall him telling me, "In Indiana, you haven't coached if you haven't been fired." He also said, I think with tongue in cheek, that he knew a coach who had an irate mother of a player come down on the floor during a game and yell at him, "If I was your wife I would feed you poison!" Supposedly the coach responded, "If I was your husband I'd take it!"

O'Brien wanted me to do some scouting for him and I was elated because that meant I would be seeing some of the best coaches and best teams in Indiana. We had big school teams like Madison, Columbus and Seymour on our schedule and played famed Milan. My friend Julius "Bud" Ritter who had owned the A & W root beer stand in Marion while coaching at Peru High School now coached Madison. Bud played at Purdue and then started coaching. At one point Bud set a state record at Madison by winning 61 consecutive regular-season victories. Bud, my high school coach, Woody

Weir, Larry Hedden and Ball State coach, Jim Hinga, are all in the Indiana Basketball Hall of Fame.

I figured with my playing background and having had two Hall of Fame coaches in Woody Weir and Jim Hinga that I knew enough about basketball to coach an eighth grade team. Early in my basketball practice sessions with the eighth graders our high school principal, Mr. Livingston, came by. After the kids left the floor to shower he said to me, "Man you don't have much talent do you?" I said, "I don't really know because this is my first coaching job and I don't have anything to compare it to. All I know is I have a guard who is quick as a cat, a black kid who can really jump and some decent shooters." Luke, as everyone called him, said, "You can't win half of your games. In fact, if you win half of your games with that bunch I'll treat you and your kids and their parents to a spaghetti dinner in the school cafeteria." I said, "I think the kids would like that and that is real nice of you to offer us that challenge." I told the players about the offer.

We had a fourteen game schedule. It was a great experience. I loved those kids and they hustled their tails off...and they all liked spaghetti! I got so fired up I even scouted eighth grade games. O'Brien and Pelkey thought I was crazy as no one ever scouted junior high games before. I wanted to do the best I could with what I had. I wanted to give the kids every chance to win that spaghetti dinner.

We went to Madison to play and they had a great player named Howard "Bugsy" Humes who was only a seventh grader. Bugsy would later make the Indiana All-Star team. Bugsy was running through us like a chain saw. I put forward Tom Gegax in the game and told him to foul Bugsy. Bugsy quickly made two more baskets. I took Tom out and said, "Why didn't you foul him?" Tom said, "I couldn't catch him." I learned as a young coach how to size up match-ups a little better.

The season got down to the point where we were 6 and 7 and had to go play Greensburg on their floor. We had to win to lock up the dinner. Jim Calli, the quick guard and Terry "Teko" Colbert, the African-American lad, played great games and we upset Greensburg to win the dinner. The kids were so happy, it was like we had won the state championship. Luke paid off and it was a happy time for everyone involved.

To be sure, one of the things I was looking forward to was winning the Sectional tournament. North Vernon had tough kids and had won the last two Sectionals. I had not cut down any nets in high school or college and it was almost like I wasn't going to become a complete Hoosier if I didn't get to perform that Indiana ritual. Jim Sullivan, Carl Miller and Bob Crawford, my teammates at Ball State, had cut down so many nets in high school they could have started a clothing factory.

The way the varsity was going under O'Brien it looked like we had a shot at winning the Sectional. The only problem was we had to play it at Greensburg and they had a good team under coach Rex Wells. Walt went 11 and 7 on the season. We had some good players and one, Donnie Hearne, went to Ball State and played freshman ball there. I did scout a lot and once Walt said, "I want you to scout our team." I scouted North Vernon and recall giving a player named Bill Bolden a tip. I told him if you don't rebound get an outside lane on the fast break and you can get some easy buckets. He did that the next game and made seven lay-ups and 18 points, his best effort of the season. Both he and O'Brien thanked me for the tip. Late in the year Walter's team looked good in beating Salem 90 to 55. However, we lost the Sectional to Greensburg 78-68.

I was excited to attend the Indiana high school Final Four at Butler Fieldhouse in March because my fellow worker at Pepsi Cola, Jim Nettles, would be playing for Muncie Central. Also, Ron Bonham, the tall blonde kid I had watched workout in the summer of 1957, was named Mr. Basketball. Ball State players could get in a pass gate to watch Muncie Central games. I was curious, after seeing Bonham that summer, about how he would develop, and attended a few games his sophomore year. Bonham and Nettles would try to help Muncie win another state championship. It wasn't to be as East Chicago Washington, led by enthusiastic coach Johnny Baratto, beat undefeated Muncie in the title game, 75 to 59. Bonham scored 40 points and broke Oscar Robertson's Final Four single game record as Muncie scored a record high 102 points in upending Bloomington in the afternoon game.

Ron Bonham joined Oscar Robertson as a multiple award winner when he was named Mr. Basketball and Star-of-Stars in both of the Indiana-Kentucky All-Star games held that summer. Indiana lost in Butler Fieldhouse, but won in Freedom Hall in Louisville. Bonham was Muncie Central's second Mr. Basketball as Tom Harrold won the honor in 1951. Bonham later played on NCAA championship teams with the University of Cincinnati and made All-American. He also played on NBA championship teams with the Boston Celtics. He is in the Indiana Basketball Hall of Fame. Jim Nettles went on to the University of Wisconsin where he played in the Rose Bowl and then became a defensive back for the Los Angeles Rams.

Although I was on a basketball court just a few minutes with Oscar Robertson it was something special to see him finish up an amazing career at Cincinnati. He was college player of the year three times and led the nation in scoring all three years. He led Cincinnati to the NCAA Final Four in 1959 and 1960. In his career, Oscar played in ten games in the NCAA tournament and averaged 32.4 per game, once scoring 56 points against Arkansas. He co-captained the U.S. Olympic team in 1960. In the NBA he is the only player to average a triple double. He teamed up with Kareem-Abdul-Jabbar to help the Milwaukee Bucks win a NBA title. He is in the Indiana Basketball Hall of Fame and the National Basketball Hall of Fame. Oscar helped to bring about needed social change and his efforts earned him the honor to become the first basketball player to ever be pictured on the cover of *Time* magazine. He was, as Jim Barley predicted, a great one, but in more ways than just basketball.

I didn't have much time between basketball and baseball, but did manage to get back to campus and see Pat. One night we were parked behind Ball Gym and serious talk about our future together took place. I don't remember making a marriage proposal and Pat can't remember one. We worked out a plan for her to select an engagement ring.

A few days after we got engaged we told our folks and friends and set a wedding date for June 18, 1960. I would have completed my first job by then and Pat would have graduated with a degree in elementary education.

I went back to school and started coaching the baseball team. I know I was happy as the team turned out good and most players would return next year. Making me even happier was the fact that Pat had agreed to marry me.

Some former basketball players around North Vernon entered a team in the state AAU tournament right after my eighth grade season and they asked me to play. They had been playing together all winter and had a decent team. I didn't have time to play while coaching, teaching and scouting. O'Brien, Pelkey and some of the assistant coaches and faculty members and I often shot around on week-ends, but seldom could find enough players to play full court games. As a result, I wasn't sure about my conditioning or the stability of my knee. It was for certain I would not wear the cumbersome brace and tape job I wore at Ball State in order to play. I would just play and have fun and if my knee popped I would quit. I had the feeling of being unfulfilled on the basketball court after my terrible senior season at Ball State. I just wasn't ready to give up the thrill of playing basketball in Indiana.

We played the AAU tourney at the nearby Brownstown High School. Brownstown, Indiana was the central location in Indiana for the AAU. I practiced with the team only once and didn't know many of them well, but they were nice guys. We won our first game and I tossed in 43 points against a team of mainly former high school players from the area. The guys on my team recognized I was in a "zone" that day and fed me the ball. Being fed like that I think I might have made 50 points if it hadn't been for a couple of breathers I had to take. Our next game would be against a better team that had as its main players two guys who had played at Indiana University, but I can't recall their names. Although we lost, I made 33 points in that game for a total of 76 for two days. I even surprised myself with my conditioning and the point totals. After these games I thought maybe it had been a mistake to wear the brace at Ball State since I moved around so much better without it.

After the last game the elderly score keeper came over to me and said, "Just want you to know that I have been keeping score at these AAU games since they started years ago and I think your 76 points in two games is a state record." I told him that was good to know, thanked him and turned to head for the locker room. I was stopped again by a man who said he represented the state AAU. He explained they still had spots to fill on the Indiana State AAU team that would represent the state in Bartlesville, Oklahoma in the national AAU tournament. He said, "If your teammates could have gotten you a few more shots you could have won that game." He told me he was looking for a shooter and thought I could fill the bill. I explained I was working. He took down some information about me and explained that employers were usually good about letting players off work to represent the state in basketball. In Indiana, that was not hard to believe. I considered it an honor to even have my name discussed, but I never heard from the man again.

In the spring, Walter coached golf and Bud Ritter came to town with the Madison golf team. The three of us played together and I remember Bud saying to me, "If you are going to coach, don't go to tombstone territory." By that comment he meant go to a school where you had a good chance to win, one with basketball tradition.

Right before school was out in late May, Walter O'Brien announced that he had been hired as the head basketball coach at Salem High School. That meant the head job at North Vernon was open and I applied. It was just after school was out that Don Pelkey and I were doing some painting at a local elementary building when news came over the radio that Orville Bose from Butler had been hired as the new coach. I knew the name as we had played against each other in college. It was a very disappointing time for me as I wanted to be a head coach in Indiana. O'Brien had left a good team of players coming back and it would not be "tombstone territory" as Bud Ritter had advised me to avoid.

I found out why I didn't get the job. Butler coach Tony Hinkle had called the superintendent and pushed to get Orville Bose the job. Jim Hinga told me later that "when Hink called for his players it was like God calling." Tony Hinkle was such a legend in Indiana even then that school administrators would be in awe if he called them. (Tony Hinkle won 572 games in basketball and had winning teams for years in football and baseball at Butler. He is in the James Naismith Basketball Hall of Fame, the Indiana Basketball Hall of Fame and was once president of the National Association of Basketball Coaches and served on the NCAA rules committee. He was an All-American basketball player in 1920. Butler Fieldhouse became known as Hinkle Fieldhouse).

A North Vernon school board member phoned me and she said she was sorry I didn't get the job as she had supported me. She pleaded with me to stay and see what might happen and maybe things would be different next time around. I did briefly inquire about some jobs around the state and followed up leads in the newspaper when guys got fired, but nothing seemed available that fit my credentials. I decided to stay and coach with Orville Bose and it was a good decision.

I worked through the disappointment by telling myself that I didn't have time to run around the state all summer looking for a job because I was getting married and looked forward to taking the summer off. I figured it would be best to stay and coach with Orville Bose. I had a contract that moved me up to assistant varsity coach and I knew my baseball team would be very good. I also thought it would be best for Pat and I to start our teaching careers together in a place where we knew people and were comfortable. Also, former Ball State friend Bronson Blackwell joined the faculty.

Pat came to North Vernon right after she graduated and we looked around at area schools and talked to people about an elementary teaching job for her. We didn't have much time before the wedding. I knew the elementary principal and the superintendent rather well, but they both said nothing was available in North Vernon. In those days, trustees ran the schools in rural southern Indiana and, with nothing available in North Vernon, it looked like we would have to contact these people and that would take time we didn't have. We would have to find Pat a job after arriving back from our honeymoon.

Even though Pat did not have a contract we turned our attention to finding a place to live and finalizing wedding plans. We found a nice little furnished apartment within walking distance of North Vernon High School. It was so small our bed was a pull out couch in the front room. It had a kitchen and a bathroom and little else. It would be convenient because I could walk to school. Since cars averaged about $3,000 then, Pat would need to use the one car we could afford when she did find a job.

We were married in Pierceton, Indiana on June 18, 1960. We honeymooned in Chicago, Milwaukee and at the Wisconsin Dells. We saw Major League Baseball games in Chicago and Milwaukee where such stars as Willie Mays, Hank Aaron, Warren Spahn and Ted Williams played. The baseball program in Milwaukee cost fifteen cents and Schlitz "the beer that made Milwaukee famous" was advertised. Hot dogs were thirty cents. In Milwaukee we saw the first heavyweight fight ever shown on a big screen in a movie theatre. African-American Floyd Patterson knocked out Ingemar Johansson of Sweden to become the first man to regain the heavyweight crown.

Slowly, but surely, American black athletes were helping to overcome discrimination, but incidents in Aaron's career were shocking. Most sports enthusiast know that Hank Aaron, from Mobile, Alabama, broke Babe Ruth's record of 714 homeruns by hitting 755. Hank came up through the southern minor leagues where racism was the most visible. One author, in mentioning Hank's days in the bush leagues, wrote, "Hank led the league in everything except hotel accommodations." As he closed in on Ruth's record Hank Aaron received over 3,000 letters a day, mostly hate mail. One letter helped describe how some people in the American culture went out of their way to make African-Americans feel unwanted in their own country. The letter stated:

> "Dear Nigger Henry-You are not going to break this record established by the great Babe Ruth if I can help it. Whites are far more superior than jungle bunnies. My gun is watching your every black move."

The 1950s and 1960s were some of the most turbulent years for racism, but such letters to Hank Aaron prove that hatred and bigotry were well entrenched in the American culture.

After visiting Milwaukee, Pat and I went to the Wisconsin Dells and then headed back to North Vernon. Pat had a memorable interview with a trustee who was plowing a field on a tractor. After plowing a few rows, he offered her a job. She turned it down as she already had an offer for a hundred more dollars in a school in DuPont, Indiana, not far from North Vernon.

I had to report to North Vernon a little before school started since I was asked to start up the first junior high football team that would play four games. The school was barely able to supply uniforms for the kids. We had to use United States Air Force fighter pilot helmets for some of them. I didn't know much about football, but got the program started even though we lost all four games.

I was excited about being on the bench with the varsity basketball team and coaching the JV team because it would involve me more in Hoosier Hysteria than being an eighth grade coach and scouting. The 1959-60 season had been a fun year, but I wanted to get closer to high school basketball and real Hoosier Hysteria.

Orville Bose was a good player at Butler and we had a lot in common having both played in the ICC. He was everything I had hoped for and he and his wife Dixie became good friends of Pat and I. Once basketball started I could sense I was back in the pressure cooker as expectations for the varsity team were rather high. Orv worked hard to install "the Butler system" and I could help with that because I had learned it under Walter O'Brien. Orv was pleased with the things I knew about the system and we ran the same offense on both the JV and varsity teams.

I had an average JV team, but the varsity was an unexpected 2 and 9 more than halfway through the eighteen game schedule. Orv and I had a discussion about how to prepare for the all important Sectional. We decided not to change anything as we thought we were getting better. We proceeded to win the next 7 games and got our record to .500. A winning streak like that in a small town in Indiana in this pressure packed era of Hoosier Hysteria was just what the doctor ordered.

We won our first two games in the state tourney to stretch our streak to 9 straight, but had to play Greensburg on their floor in the Sectional final. After winning the traditional Saturday afternoon game we returned to our hotel where we had reserved two rooms for the team to take it easy if we did have to play again that night. As we came out of the gym that afternoon, we witnessed the beginning of one of the worst snowstorms in southern Indiana history. Over a half-foot was already on the ground and all we could do was get to the hotel, rest some, eat a light meal and get back to the gym for the title game.

When the referee tossed the ball up to start the title game little did fans know that this was going to be a night Ray Bolden and the people of North Vernon would never forget. Ray was our best player and it looked as though he and his mom were the only black people in the gym. Ray was omnipotent as he scored 38 points to set a new Sectional record and lead his Panthers to victory. Ray displayed more courage that night than I had ever seen in a high school player. I would like to have seen the newspapers run a story about his game titled Bolden is Golden, but the ones that were written did him proud. The school year book, *The Panther*, did single out Ray for special recognition in setting the record. Tragically, Ray Bolden was killed in an automobile accident several years ago.

Orville Bose was a classy man and thanked me for my help on the bench during the game and did so even before we cut down the Sectional nets. Little did Orv know that this would be the first time I would get to climb up the ladder and cut down the nets. It was a nice feeling as the fans applauded and made me feel more like a complete Hoosier.

When we came out of the gym there were seventeen inches of snow on the ground and the state police had closed all the roads. No one could leave town and that set in motion many problems. We got the team back to the hotel and learned that a Greensburg city ordinance prevented black people from spending the night in Greensburg. This type local law, not uncommon in Indiana, was known as the "sunset law" where blacks were "not allowed to let the sun set on their heads." It was a pathetic law supported by the Ku Klux Klan and winked at by local officials seeking re-election.

Don Pelkey, who had just become athletic director, Orv and I and our wives had decided we should just keep the team in the hotel until morning. Fans were safe from the storm as they stayed in the gym and the local YMCA. However, the hotel manager reminded us of the "sunset law" and told us Ray Bolden could not stay. Orville and I got into a discussion with the manager. What were we to do? Was Ray going to have to sleep in a snow bank...after scoring 38 points? It was a ridiculous discussion. The manager was afraid to violate the law, but finally relented and allowed Ray to stay.

This "sunset ordinance" situation was just another incident while growing up in Indiana where I learned how deep racial prejudice had set in amongst some people. All I could think about was how Ray might feel humiliated if he knew what the discussion was all about. I know I thought back to Oatess Archey swimming in the Matter Park Pool, the Purdue Student Union situation as well as rooming with Wilbur Davis at the Pokagon State Park. I remember thinking to myself...what is wrong with our society?

We learned right after the championship game that we were going to have to play Bud Ritter's undefeated Madison team in the State Regional tournament in Columbus the following Saturday. That team had junior Larry Humes on it. He was so good he would be named Indiana's Mr. Basketball the next year.

In preparing for the game, which was to be played before over 4,000 people, I suggested to Orv that we play a box-and-one defense where one player would guard Humes while the other four played a zone. This defense sometime worked to hold down a star player. Orv decided against it. We played a good game, but lost to Madison. That night in the Regional final, Columbus, under the brilliant Bill Stearman, upset Madison by playing a box-and-one and gained a spot in the coveted Sweet Sixteen. Orv told me on the ride back to North Vernon, "I guess we should have played a box-and-one, huh, Norm?" We didn't have the player talent Columbus did, but it was the right defense.

Orv, in showing great patience, had turned the season around by winning our last ten games and the Sectional tournament. It was a fun time for me as well as our staff at North Vernon. Later, in the spring, my baseball team, loaded with talent, went 17 and 3. Someone told me it was the best baseball team the school ever had, but we did not play in a conference and there wasn't any state tournament in baseball in those days so no one will ever know how good that team really was. Ray Bolden was on the team, but there weren't any racial remarks directed his way that I knew about and we did play several schools that did not have black players.

My hometown of Marion, Indiana was so basketball crazy at the time that the city officials invited the NBA champion Boston Celtics to play an exhibition in town in the spring of 1961. The Boston Celtics had already set into motion their dominance of the NBA. They won their third straight title in 1960-61 with players like Bill Russell, K.C. Jones, Bob Cousy and Bill Sharman. The dominance was so much so for fans in Indiana that it was like the Celtics had taken the place of the NBA teams that had left Indiana.

During a ceremony before the game, Marion's mayor presented the Celtics the key to the city. After the exhibition the Celtics could not find a restaurant in Marion that would serve their black players. Later that night, to protest the discrimination and the loopholes in the laws in many Indiana towns, Bill Russell and some of his black teammates returned the key to the city to the mayor. Despite U.S. Supreme Court rulings that seemed to be clearing the way for an integrated country, much prejudice remained in Indiana...and in my hometown. The Celtics later became the first team in the NBA to start five black players. To his credit, coach Red Auerbach declared the move was not a political statement because he always started the five best players.

Near the end of the school year in North Vernon Walter O'Brien called me and asked me to become his assistant at Salem High School. I had never been to Salem, but Pat and I decided it couldn't hurt anything to visit. Once we saw the facilities at Salem we were very impressed with the community attitude about having the best it could for young people. The high school building was one of the most impressive in southern Indiana at the time with outstanding athletic facilities. The beautiful gym would seat about 3,500 in this town of about 5,000 people about an hour from Louisville, Kentucky. Pat signed a contract to teach fifth grade. I would become the assistant basketball coach, teach Drivers Ed. and Health and be backfield coach for the varsity football team. I went to summer school at Ball State and then rented a truck and moved our belongings to Salem to begin football with head coach Dale Scrivnor who was a Ball State graduate.

CHAPTER TWELVE
Tombstone Territory

*THE RICHNESS OF LIFE LIES IN THE
MEMORIES WE HAVE FORGOTTEN.*

In talking with Walter O'Brien, I did learn that Salem did not have a winning tradition and the basketball record the last ten years reflected that problem. Walt had been there a year and told me we had good players coming up and he thought we could win the Sectional within a year by playing all underclassmen this year. After Walt told me about the lack of winning at Salem, I thought back to Bud Ritter warning me about going to what he called "tombstone territory" to coach. Salem seemed like such a nice place to be I dismissed the tombstone territory advice. I told myself that adversity had to be overcome to solve most problems. I thought I had handled adversity rather well up to now in my life and wasn't afraid to face it again if it arose.

Most of the excitement in Salem my first year was outside of basketball. One of my fraternity brothers at Ball State, John Fultz, was from Salem. He was a teacher and single and was at our home on a regular basis. Pat, John and I and the rest of the town marveled at the fact that CBS television was coming to Salem to film some material for a program titled *Eyewitness to History* anchored by Walter Cronkite. The purpose of the program coming to Salem was to film the daily routines of people in a small town in the mid-west. The Vietnam War was imminent as our troops occupied that country, the Berlin wall went up in East Germany and President John F. Kennedy was about to be inaugurated. CBS wanted to let the rest of the country know what people were doing in small town America around Thanksgiving time while tension mounted around the world.

The CBS television crew came into the high school and even filmed portions of one of our varsity basketball games. The television crew had heard about Hoosier Hysteria and knew their program would lack something if they didn't include clips of a high school basketball game in Indiana. When the program was shown a few weeks later it was possible, if one didn't blink, to see Walter O'Brien and I standing by our bench. The entire community enjoyed seeing the film clips of the time CBS spent in Salem.

There was, however, one incident that will remain memorable to many basketball fans and one CBS cameraman.

The Salem Lion cheerleaders had constructed a large paper hoop for the players to run through. I was standing right there as the team came out of the dressing room. As I remember it forward Tom Knight, who played fullback on the football team, led the Lions through the hoop. Suddenly, at the last second, a cameraman knelt down just in front of me in front of the hoop. Tom Knight burst through the paper hoop and ran right over that unsuspecting cameraman. The man got up with a little cut on his nose and retrieved the expensive camera and was OK. He told me he had no idea anyone was going to run through the hoop, he thought the cheerleaders were showing off their handy work to support the team. No one in the history of Indiana basketball ever got a better introduction into Hoosier Hysteria, but that part didn't make the national showing of *Eyewitness to History* with Walter Cronkite.

The basketball season went along as could be expected with underclass players. The usual rumblings about a losing team in Indiana were kept to a minimum as Salem fans seemed to accept the fact we were building a team for the next year. We lost in the Sectional and that intensified the need to have a good record and win the Sectional in the next season.

There were a couple memorable things for me concerning basketball that happened during this season. One was that Wilt Chamberlain became the only NBA player to score 100 points in one game. The other was that Bugsy Humes played as a freshman for Bud Ritter's undefeated Madison team in the Indiana Final Four. They lost, but Bugsy's brother, Larry Humes became Mr. Basketball and I thought back to my days at North Vernon and coaching against these two great players.

Once again I attended summer school at Ball State and the warm months went by fast. I was constantly thinking about the good athletes we had returning in Salem and that coach O'Brien had told me we could win the Sectional.

This 1962-63 season would, indeed, be a good one for Salem Lion fans and coaches. The football team assembled by Dale Scrivnor and assisted by Max Bedwell was the best in school history. A seven game win streak gave the team the Mid-Southern Conference championship and an 8-2 record. I learned a great deal about football as coach Scrivnor made it easy for me to be backfield coach.

Before basketball practice even started there was another racial incident of nation wide importance. There had been rumors that James Meredith, a black student from Mississippi, would try to enroll at the University of Mississippi in Oxford. His application to Ole Miss was rejected and a suit was filed, seeking an injunction. Governor Ross Barnett did what he could to keep Meredith out and the application helped to enrage prejudice students.

President Kennedy let it be known on national television that Meredith would be admitted to Ole Miss in accordance with the federal law. When Governor Barnett personally went to campus to protest and President Kennedy ordered U.S. Marshals to escort James Meredith to class, one of the worst nights ever to take place on a college campus drew the attention of most Americans. Swarms of people tore up the campus, army tents went up and chaos ruled.

The explosive situation got so bad that eventually two people were killed and close to 300 were injured. I remember seeing President Kennedy make a plea for calm on national television, but it took 20,000 Army troops to restore order. It was a tension filled time for our country and for the state of Mississippi. Ole Miss officials made good decisions during this time and many of them centered around the football team that was trying to become the top ranked team in the country. As fate would have it, the Homecoming game was scheduled to be played against Houston on campus.

The United States government decided that to have thousands of people in one place on a Saturday afternoon in the small town of Oxford, MS might be asking for more trouble. The government told Ole Miss officials that the game had to be moved to Houston. The University of Mississippi administration thought the game should at least be played in the state of Mississippi. There was a big stadium in Jackson and it was finally agreed that the game would be played there. This would draw students and other fans away from the campus. The plan worked as calm prevailed. Ole Miss won 40 to 7.

A few troops remained on campus until November as the anger of people slowly subsided. The Ole Miss Rebels went undefeated and many people believe that the exciting football team helped to draw attention away from the racial conflict. It helped that the football team qualified to play in the Sugar Bowl and finished the season ranked third in the nation after defeating the University of Arkansas. Even with the volatile admission of James Meredith many southern states still refused to accept the court decisions that declared equal treatment for all people.

Once basketball got underway in Salem it was obvious that the same boys who won the conference in football would lead the school to a good basketball season. Although we did not win the conference in basketball the team did go 15 and 7. This was the best record in over ten years and we went on to win the Sectional. I did not get to cut down the nets because coach O'Brien decided that I was the best person to scout our next opponent. I did scout a good Seymour team and told O'Brien we would have to play our best game of the year to beat them. They ran over us in the Jeffersonville Regional, but all in all, for a school not used to winning, it was a good year in sports for Salem High School.

The 1962-63 basketball season was also interesting to me because the Muncie Central Bearcats won their fifth state championship, the most claimed by any school. I noted that only 639 teams entered the state tourney. I remembered that 751 teams started when I was at Marion High School in 1954. The consolidation of schools was beginning to cut down on the number of teams entered in the state tourney.

After basketball ended, superintendent Dr. Jack Davidson asked me if I would like to coach golf. I accepted the assignment to become the first golf coach at Salem High School. It was nice being on the golf course after being cooped up in the gym all winter.

Dr. Davidson was a former coach and loved to play basketball and stay in shape. In the middle of the basketball season he closed all the schools because of another near record snowfall. Once he did that he called up a bunch of the coaches and strongly suggested we play some basketball. We would meet mid-morning and play, play, play. Finally, Dr. Davidson, who was a good player, said, "I have to call the bus drivers and see if we can have school tomorrow." He came back from the calls and told all of us that we would have school.

After getting the news they would have to go to work the next day all the guys headed for the locker room. Jack, as he wanted to be called, said, and this stands out in my mind, "Where are you guys going?" We told him we were going to get dressed. He said something like, "Just because you have to work tomorrow you aren't going to play anymore?" Most of us indicated that was the case. He said, "OK, wait a minute, let me check with a couple more bus drivers and see how the roads are." We all waited while he made the call and he came out and said he had called off school for tomorrow. With revived spirits we played the rest of the day. Everything revolved around basketball in the 1950s and 1960s in Indiana, even closing schools so grown men could play the game!

As most coaches did following being eliminated from the Indiana tournament I relaxed and watched the rest of it and any games I could in the NCAA tournament on TV. It was startling to hear about a racial incident in the usually racism free NCAA tournament. It began when Mississippi State, located in Starkville, Mississippi won the Southeastern Conference. They had an automatic bid to the tournament. In protest to the 1954 Supreme Court decision to integrate schools, Mississippi State had refused bids three previous times because they would have to play against integrated teams. Other SEC teams, like Kentucky, had played integrated teams in past tournaments.

The state of Mississippi was one of the last to defy the 1954 federal law and had not integrated even its elementary or high schools. When the president of Mississippi State University gave the OK for the team to play in a early round game in East Lansing, Michigan against Loyola of Chicago and its four black starters, tremendous backlash took place. Newspaper editorials from key cities in Mississippi made it clear how attitudes of segregation still permeated the south. Most newspapers had no qualms relaying the biased opinions of those who owned and operated them. For example, one quote from an editor of the *Meridian Star* appeared in the *Jackson Clarion-Ledger* and seemed to add fuel to the fire by making a clear statement for the legions of segregationists in Mississippi. The editor said the following about Mississippi State accepting the NCAA bid:

> "Especially in these times we should make no compromise regarding our Southern way of life-we cannot afford to give a single inch."

In showing its true colors, the state of Mississippi had, since the 1954 *Brown v. Board of Education* decision, passed fourteen separate laws designed to circumvent the federal mandate. One law allowed the governor to abolish all of the state's public schools, including colleges, rather than submit to integration. It was thought by some people if the governor had acted quick enough he could have made it so Mississippi State didn't exist and therefore could not play in the NCAA tournament.

The college officials stood their ground and the state legislature got involved to try to maintain "the Southern way of life." The newspapers did all they could to influence the politicians to stop the team from participating. Finally, the same legal official who issued an injunction against James Meredith at the University of Mississippi issued another temporary injunction against Mississippi State University. The team was not to leave the state. However, the college officials devised a clandestine plan to get the team out of Mississippi before the injunction could be legally served. Many people thought there would be monumental problems in East Lansing. Although the game would have been played anyway, the injunction was lifted by a justice from the Mississippi Supreme Court. The historic game was played without incident in front of 12,143 spectators. Loyola won 61 to 51 and players got along well and it was a well-played game.

Loyola players did later reveal that they had received cards and letters designed to intimidate them. On March 15, 1963 the *Chicago Daily News* ran a story that told how Loyola players were told to "bring their shoe shine kits" to the game, or "come down here and pick some cotton." Some of the letters were signed, "KKK." It was similar to the harassment that Oscar Robertson courageously endured just a few years before even in the regular season when his team ventured into the southwest and Dixie.

Despite the congenial outcome to the game, powerful voices continued to oppose integration in the south. The 1960s would become one of the most volatile eras centering on racial issues in American history and sports would become instrumental in bringing about change...and basketball, with good black players developing fast, took center stage.

While coaching in Salem I can recall seeing TV newscasts where powerful fire hoses were used to control blacks as they protested in public places. Attack dogs and tear gas were used to disperse those protesting. There is no question that the well-publicized discrimination in sports helped to intensify the efforts of African-Americans to gain the freedoms the laws of the land granted them.

Civil rights leader, Dr. Martin Luther King, Jr. became very active in the south and had the backing of President Kennedy and his brother, Attorney

General Robert Kennedy. On the heels of James Meredith, Dr. King visited hot beds of segregation such as Birmingham and Montgomery, Alabama. While working at Salem High School I vividly remember Birmingham being referred to as "Bombingham" because it had so many violent racial incidents. It is not easy to forget the face and voice of Governor George Wallace of Alabama as he pledged on TV "Segregation forever" when he was inaugurated.

Dr. King went to Birmingham and was jailed for marching in protest on Good Friday. This was one of the twenty-nine times Dr. King would be jailed for his efforts to overcome segregation and bring people together. While in jail in Birmingham he was told "to wait for equality." He wrote the following which told America that he too held bad memories of the atrocities perpetuated upon his fellow African-Americans:

> "When you have seen vicious mobs lynch your mothers and fathers at will and drown your sisters and brothers at whim... when you suddenly find yourself tongue twisted and your speech stammering as you seek to explain to your six-year-old daughter why she can't go to the public amusement park that was just advertised on television, and see tears welling up in her little eyes when she is told Funtown is closed to colored children... then you will understand why we find it difficult to wait."

On June 11, 1963 Governor Wallace tried to block the integration of the University of Alabama. He failed, but the next day civil unrest was escalated as Medgar Evers, an NAACP leader, was shot and killed in front of his own home in Jackson, Mississippi. He was 37 years old. It took thirty-one years to convict his killer. Sporadic incidents of violence linked to racism continued in the south even though more federal legislation was passed to outlaw segregation.

Following this racially charged school year I again attended summer school at Ball State and completed requirements for a Masters degree in Guidance and Counseling. I would return to Salem for the 1963-64 school year to coach and teach Physical Education and Health. My goal now was to become a guidance counselor and a head basketball coach. I also thought it was possible to win a conference championship in golf.

We lost most of our good players on the varsity basketball team and my JV team had won only half of its games so coach O'Brien and I knew we had our work cut out for us for the 1963-64 season. We had played only a game or two when a shocking event took place. I learned about the assassination of President Kennedy in Dallas on November 22, 1963 as I was walking in the halls of Salem High School. A fellow teacher informed me and the events that took place the next few days are some of the most vivid ones etched into my memory.

Our basketball game was cancelled the evening of the Dallas tragedy and weekend college football games were postponed, although the NFL did play games the weekend following the shooting. Pat, John Fultz and I watched television accounts of the assassination as two days later Jack Ruby shot and killed suspect Lee Harvey Oswald in the Dallas police station. Salem streets were vacant and the nation mourned the passing of a popular president.

To add to the already troubling year the varsity basketball team almost reversed the record of the year before as the team won 5 and lost 17. My JV team made a good account of itself and I gained valuable coaching experience.

At the end of the season it was apparent that even though coach O'Brien had won a Sectional just the year before, it wasn't enough to save his job in a hot bed of Hoosier Hysteria. He resigned to become a principal near Indianapolis. Of course, I was interested in the head coaching vacancy and I applied. I had recalled that Jack Davidson had made some nice comments about my playing ability and he and my principal had told me they liked the way I motivated the kids to play hard. Still, I didn't have any head basketball coaching experience. I wondered what kind of a chance I would have against the many outstanding applications flooding in from around the state.

I am certain Dr. Davidson went to bat for me and this time I didn't get runner-up and was named head coach late in the 1963-64 school year. I would also become a full time guidance counselor. It was a good job. Now all I had to do was win!!!

About the same time I was named head coach, I was informed that I would be supervising a student from Indiana State University by the name of Marc Denny who would be doing his student teaching. In reviewing Marc's background I noted that he was from Bedford, a town not far from Salem and was a basketball star there. In fact, he was named to the 1960 Indiana All-Star team that featured Mr. Basketball, Ron Bonham from Muncie Central. The first time I ever saw Marc Denny he was playing basketball on TV for Indiana State in Roberts Stadium against Evansville University. He was going up against Larry Humes from Madison and Jerry Sloan who would eventually become an NBA legend. I was impressed as Marc, who was 6'foot 8", made a good account of himself scoring 14 points. I figured we had a great deal in common.

Marc Denny took over three of my classes so now I was only responsible to teach two classes. It was a relaxing time for me after a trying basketball season and being named head coach of the Salem Lions. Near the end of the school year Dr. Davidson needed to sign some teachers for the next year. I let him know that Marc seemed to me to be a born teacher. Within two weeks Marc signed a contract to teach at Salem High School and his wife, Mayme Jo, would teach elementary school.

It had already been determined that the new football coach, Verne Ratliff from Butler, would be my varsity assistant. Marc would help in football. John Fultz would be taking over the baseball team left vacant by coach Scrivnor. My golf team finished well over .500 in our matches and we positioned ourselves for a run at the conference title in the next year or two.

Head basketball coaches were closely scrutinized by the Indiana High School Athletic Association (IHSAA). I was paid to work with boys in grades five through eight during the summer, but no coaching could be done with high school players in those days. I had not had the head job more than six or eight weeks when Dr. Davidson paid me a visit and wanted to know if I had been working with any of the varsity boys? I said no, only grades five through eight. I was told that someone had reported to the IHSAA in Indianapolis that my car was parked behind the gym on a daily basis and I was practicing illegally. It was Dr. Davidson's duty to make a report to the IHSAA and tell them what was going on.

It was suspected that a female relative of one of the applicants who didn't get the job lived near Salem. She was disappointed her relative didn't get the job and proceeded to try to get me in trouble. Nothing ever came of the incident, but it made me very wary of how important it was to follow the rules when coaching basketball in Indiana. Hoosier Hysteria could get vicious in many ways. When coaches had bad seasons, disgruntled fans would send U-Haul trucks to their homes to make it look like the coaches should move. Notes were sent saying, "There is a train leaving town at 3:00pm, be UNDER IT." I was told that one coach in a small town experienced an explosive device hurled through his front room window. Sometimes "For Sale" signs would be planted in the yard where the coach lived.

I taught Driver Ed. and worked with the elementary basketball boys for a summer job. This was the summer where people from the north would organize themselves and go south to help register black voters. Segregationist were doing all they could do to keep blacks from voting. One tactic used was to have blacks take literacy tests. One sample of a question was, "How many bubbles in a bar of soap?" Many of the so-called "Freedom Riders" left northern towns to go to southern towns to register blacks to vote to prevent such crimes against humanity. The summer of 1964 became known in American history as Freedom Summer as the riders for freedom invaded the south.

There is no question that cases such as the incident at Matter Park pool, the Celtics being turned away from Marion restaurants and the horrendous murder of Emmett Till motivated African-Americans to fight for their rights. The cases of Rosa Parks, James Meredith and Medgar Evers can be added as well as the vulgar harassment of Oscar Robertson. The attempt to keep Mississippi State University out of the NCAA basketball tournament gave national attention to segregationists and no doubt helped to motivate freedom riders. The denial of black students being admitted to the University of Alabama by Governor George Wallace and Orval Faubus stopping blacks from entering schools in Little Rock, made blacks feel they had waited long enough for equal rights.

How well I remember when President Lyndon Johnson was able to get through to the 88th Congress in July of 1964 and the Civil Rights Act was passed a full ten years after the *Brown vs. Topeka School Board* decision was made by the U.S. Supreme Court. The 1964 Civil Rights Act was passed to provide access for all Americans to public accommodations. This included all public facilities such as hotels and motels, restaurants, lunch counters, motion pictures, concert halls, sports arenas and stadiums. The Act included education, employment and voting rights and outlawed all discrimination based on race, color, religion, sex and national origin in public accommodations and employment. Passage of the Act would later provoke even more racial unrest in the country.

The 1964-65 school year just had to be better all the way around, or at least it would seem so. Pat announced that she was pregnant. She quit smoking for good. It looked as though our first child would be born sometime during the state basketball tournament. However, there were signs in the summer that bad luck might be part of the upcoming equation for my head coaching debut. The best player returning on the varsity severely injured a finger in a boating accident in the summer. Luck plays a big part in coaches surviving in Indiana high school basketball. Observations around town this particular summer made it clear to me that Salem certainly wasn't like Marion or Muncie as far as boys playing during the summer to get better.

As our troops became bogged down in an unpopular war in Vietnam, the school year began and I enjoyed my work as a guidance counselor. I had time to talk to players about the upcoming season. I had completed a basketball notebook for the players and gave each player a copy of the *Lion Log*. Early practices went well and I was confident we could win the Sectional to be held on our floor.

It seems serious injuries plagued either me or my players throughout my years in Indiana basketball. In our first game, against state powerhouse Madison, my best player fell on his left elbow after rebounding and suffered a compound fracture. It looked as though he would be out for the season. It was a crushing blow. We lost early games and got behind on the record and this helped to create attitude problems. Despite my pleas to the team to hang in and do a Mr. Mason and "do the best we could, with whatever we had, wherever we are," losing our best player deflated the team. My second best offensive player hurt our chances when he decided to quit the team because I decided to spend more time on defense. A good defense can be a great equalizer in sports. It is the element that usually wins championships and I tried to get that across to the players.

About halfway through the season I noticed a man standing in the shadows behind a glass door watching my practice. I recognized him immediately, but let on like I didn't know he was there. It was Everett Dean who had coached Stanford to the NCAA title in 1942. Woody Weir was his assistant at Stanford and I had met coach Dean since he had married a woman from Salem and lived in the area. I did learn that he told friends of mine that it looked like I knew what I was doing. It was nice to get feedback like that from a legendary coach, but I couldn't count on him convincing the whole town that I knew basketball. We were below five hundred at the time and I figured the way our season was going I could get fired if we didn't win the Sectional. I was concerned about our level of experience.

During this season our freshman team was running over every team they played. They were well drilled by coach Charlie Hunt and played with a lot of poise and determination. Dr. Davidson's son, Bill, was leading this team and showed tremendous leadership and poise. One of my problems with Salem basketball was that teams from the ninth grade on down didn't play the bigger schools. I told people, "If you want to be the best, you have to play the best," but the lower level schedules remained the same. I thought it hurt in preparing boys to play against some of the best schools in the state when they reached high school. I knew for certain that the competition in the North Central Conference helped me develop as a player. At Marion I had played against the best players in the state. I always thought that playing against that type competition game in and game out helped me to survive a treacherous tryout period at Ball State and eventually become a starting guard and a scholarship player.

With the approval of Dr. Davidson, we moved the first five of the freshman team to the JV team with just a few games left in the season. We needed players and they performed well. Bill Davidson performed so well I decided to put him in some varsity scrimmages. He surprised everyone with his skills and poise. I decided to play him on the varsity. I knew the parents of upperclassmen who would miss some playing time would be upset, but I was doing what I thought I had to do to have a chance to win.

Shortly after moving the junior high boys, a well-respected judge in Salem called me and asked to visit with me in my home. His boy was a starter on the team and a great kid with whom to work. The judge asked me if I would consider taking back on the team the senior boy who was the second leading scorer? I told the judge I didn't kick the boy off of the team, he had quit the team evidently because we were working harder on defense than he wanted. The judge was taking part in Hoosier Hysteria because he would like for his son to be able to play on a Sectional champion and was pressuring me to get the team both he and his boy wanted ready for the Sectional.

The request of the judge put me in a bind because I wanted the boy to come to me on his own and ask to be reinstated. I didn't want the judge or his son to tell the boy who quit that if you go see the coach he will put you back on the team. I told the judge I wasn't going to take the player back. I knew if the player didn't come back our chances of winning the Sectional were slim. I didn't want to sacrifice my principles to keep my job. I thought to myself that I could not live with myself if I succumbed to the pressure of the judge. I also figured I would get fired if I didn't win the Sectional even though it was my first year as the head coach.

I was, indeed, witnessing Hoosier Hysteria from a rather ugly perspective. The principal's two sons had been on my JV teams, now the superintendent's son was on the varsity and a state judge was asking favors. What more could a coach ask for in his first head coaching job in Indiana high school basketball?

While coaching the varsity at Salem one incident has always stood out in my memory. During a time out I asked a player if he knew who he was guarding? The boy replied, "I've got the nigger." I said, "You mean number thirty-four?" All of the players in the huddle just looked at each other. My comment was my way of telling the team that we should treat people the same way we would want to be treated...with dignity. The player's comment revealed how prejudice and bigotry could be implanted in young people. Keep in mind that Salem was one of those communities that implemented the "sundown ordinance" against blacks just as Greensburg had done.

My first varsity team won only about as many games as the year before and we drew the Sectional favorite, West Washington High School, for our first game. It was my first game as a varsity coach in the Indiana state tournament. I never had one thought that if I played the superintendent's boy that it would save my job. I was going to continue to do what I thought best to win the Sectional. I am certain that many people in Salem believed I was playing Jack Davidson's son in hopes of Dr. Davidson convincing the school board to keep me on as coach. Not once did that thought enter my mind. Bill Davidson had shown me in practice and in the few games he did play on the varsity that he could play with poise and help the team. My best player who had injured his elbow did return late in the season. I still had confidence we could win the all-important Sectional.

I don't recall if I started Bill in the West Washington game, but I do recall that he came through with what has to be one of the most remarkable performances by a freshman in Indiana state tournament history. Bill scored 21 points in front of 3,500 screaming fans and we upset West Washington and looked good doing it.

My best player was still rusty, but with the addition of Bill Davidson, I thought we had a one-two punch that could pull us through the next game. It wasn't to be. We had a young back court and a very experienced coach from Milltown High School played the right defense and pressed us the entire game. We turned the ball over too many times and lost by one point in the Saturday afternoon semi-final. I was heart broken because I so much wanted to win the Sectional my first year as a head coach and it was a good opportunity. It was little Milltown that beat us the year before and Salem, the bigger school, had now won only one Sectional in the last thirteen years...on its own floor. The good people in Salem deserved better than for the town to become known as tombstone territory for coaches.

Sure enough, within a couple of weeks of our loss, Dr. Davidson paid me a visit in my counseling office. He informed me that the school board didn't want me back as coach, but I could stay as a counselor and golf coach. He said if I wanted to return as basketball coach he thought he could persuade the board to give me another year. He said that before I made that decision he wanted me to know that he would be moving to Oak Ridge, Tennessee to be the superintendent there and Bill would not be on my team.

I told Dr. Davidson that I didn't want to coach if Bill wasn't going to be on the team. He said he would announce to the newspapers about him leaving and that I had resigned as coach. He told me it had been a difficult year for me and that I did not have much luck in my first year. I told him I had some thinking to do and thanked him for all he had done for me in Salem. I was young and figured with the background I had in basketball that my coaching days were not over if I didn't want them to be.

After the turmoil surrounding my first year of being a head coach settled down an organization at the school announced an interesting money raising project. Members had contracted a farm team of the Harlem Globetrotters to play a Salem High School faculty team. The team was known as the Harlem Magicians. The Trotters would use a Magician player when they needed a player to fill in because the Magicians performed the same routines as the Trotters and, in fact, wore uniforms similar to the Globetrotters. To have an all-black team come to Salem didn't happen often. Where would they spend the night?

Although I did have some trouble with my knee from time to time, it seemed healed and I decided to play against the Magicians. I was always restless about my playing days because there was a sense of not being satisfied since I had missed so many games after being injured at Ball State. It left me with an unfulfilled feeling after fighting so hard for playing time. I got a mind set that if I really focused maybe I could show people I could play the game even though they didn't think I was worthy enough to be their coach. I got myself psyched for the Magicians game.

Marc Denny was our only experienced player and John Fultz loved to play so we took on the Magicians as best we could. Spanish teacher Frank O'Leary gave us a rousing pre-game motivational speech...in Spanish! In front of about 1,500 to 2,000 people who came to support the school organization, I again surprised myself. Someone told me I had made 11 out of 12 shots for 22 points in the first half. I do recall missing only one shot. We were in the game with the Magicians.

In the second half the Magicians started rolling down my socks on free throws and flipping my jock and trash talking to me to try to cool me off. Their tactics didn't bother me and I finished the game with 35 points, but we did lose as expected. Marc Denny made a comment to me after the game that I wasn't expecting when he said, "I've never seen anybody shoot like that." Coming from an Indiana All-Star the remark meant a lot to me after all the trials and tribulations I had been through in Indiana basketball. Marc had seen plenty in the basketball wars in Indiana, both in high school and college and I was taken back by his kind words.

The game against the Magicians would be the last basketball game I would ever play in Indiana. It was a memorable one as I received nice comments from people in Salem and around the school for the next few days.

Our first child was born in Salem on March 21, 1965 the weekend of the Indiana high school finals. Pat's room was at one end of the hospital and the only TV set was a good walk from the room. We arrived at the hospital before noon on March 20th, but she did not deliver our baby girl, Denise Marie, until about 3:00am that night. I ran back and forth to see the afternoon games televised from Hinkle Fieldhouse in Indianapolis and even for the championship game that night. Indianapolis Washington became the second Indianapolis school (besides Crispus Attucks) to win the state title, but I don't remember much about basketball that day as Pat had a very difficult time in labor. I had asked our Dr. Apple what would have happened if Pat had the baby while I was coaching during the Sectional? He said, jokingly, "We would have just set up shop in the locker room."

I found that it was nice to have friends who understood how vicious things could get in coaching in Hoosier Hysteria. Ralph "Fergie" Ferguson, my friend and Woody Weir's assistant at Marion High School, called me after he learned I would not be coaching at Salem and offered me the head basketball job at Wakarusa High School. Fergie was the athletic director and had convinced the school board I could do the job. I made a mistake and told Fergie I wasn't interested. I should have at least gone to the school located in northern Indiana for a look-see.

I guess I was rather soured on coaching at that time and didn't want any part of another tombstone territory. In fact, Pat had just given birth and I was trying to sort out what to do. I didn't know if I would miss coaching or not. I had spent more than half of my life in gyms either playing or coaching.

Even before Fergie called I had interviewed for a head basketball position at Veedersburg, Indiana near Lafayette. I was offered the job, but turned it down because I would have to teach World History on a permit. That would be a tough job as compared to being a counselor and golf coach and no teaching assignment. I decided to stay at Salem for several reasons. First, we had a baby girl to think about and I wasn't enthralled about moving into un-chartered waters again. I had good friends in Salem such as Marc Denny and John Fultz and dentist Dr. Gene Hedrick who had taken Pat and I to the

Kentucky Derby. Jerry Hoover, who played at Purdue and had some luck as a young coach replaced me and I thought it might do me good to take a year off from basketball and see what someone else could do in a situation such as Salem found itself in.

Since I would not be involved in basketball I had plenty of time to myself when the next school year came around. I wrote an article for a magazine called *Athletic Journal.* I had remembered what coach Ray Louthen had told me at Ball State about publishing part of the paper I had written about the fast break in basketball. I condensed it and sent it to *Athletic Journal* and got lucky as the magazine published the article in the September issue of 1965. The school librarian put the magazine on display in the school library and I got some nice feedback.

Some feedback created a memory from growing up in Indiana that I was not expecting. It came from a strange source in…Accra, Ghana. It seems that *Athletic Journal* was quite popular wherever basketball was played around the world. I received a letter written in broken English from a young boy in Ghana who had seen my article. He said he needed "sox", some shoes, maybe a jersey and listed several things a basketball player might need. He said he was very poor and needed help so he could play basketball. The letter brought tears to my eyes as I could not imagine anyone being so poor they could not play basketball.

Salem had a Bata shoe factory not far from my house so I decided to go there and show the letter to someone in management. The manager thought the letter was as amazing as I did. He said he would give me a pair of shoes if I would get some socks, pay the postage and send the equipment to the boy. How could two Hoosiers turn down any boy wanting to play basketball?

I got the socks and mailed the package. In those days it cost me somewhere around ten dollars to send the package to Ghana. Several weeks later I got the package back. The post office explained there had been an uprising in the part of Ghana where the boy lived and he could be dead or at least the post office could not get the package to him. It cost me more money to get the package back, but I paid it and kept the shoes. At least I tried to further the career of a basketball player.

Jerry Hoover didn't have much more luck than coach O'Brien and I did as he also lost the Sectional in Salem. We became friends and I scouted some for him and this helped keep me a little involved in basketball. I did coach the golf team and that helped to keep me busy. My luck in coaching didn't change much as Salem lost the conference golf championship by one stroke when my best player somehow lost his ball in the fairway on the last hole. I got runner-up again! The match was held at a course near New Albany, Indiana where Masters champion Fuzzy Zoeller played while growing up.

Of course, I followed basketball other than at the high school level. Since Bill Russell left an impression on people in my hometown of Marion it was interesting to learn that his legendary Celtic coach, Red Auerbach, had resigned. It was a step forward in racial relations in sports when Auerbach named Russell player/coach. Russell would become the first black head coach to lead a major sports franchise in American history.

In the NCAA tournament in 1966, Texas Western, now known as UTEP (University of Texas at El Paso) became the first college team to start five black players. Some of them were from Indiana and further stamped the Hoosier state as a breeding ground for good basketball players. Texas Western upset a favored and all-white Kentucky team 72-65 to go 28 and 1 on the season. Many people believe that this game moved the NCAA tournament ahead of the NIT in popularity. More importantly, the upset victory by Texas Western was a milestone in the culture of college basketball. It helped advance the acceptance of blacks and made more people aware of the changes that needed to take place after the adoption of the 1964 Civil Rights Act.

Watching the Salem team play during the 1965-66 season I guess I got the itch to coach again and as jobs began to open up in March I began to apply. My brother, who later became a State Senator in Illinois, tipped me off to a job near him in Palatine, Illinois and I set up an interview. On the same trip to Illinois I arranged for an interview at the new Cascade High School near the West Side of Indianapolis. Both jobs would get me back into basketball, but at Palatine High School I would be a head coach and a counselor. I would have a full teaching assignment and be an assistant under a good former Indiana University player at Cascade High School.

I think my seven years of coaching experience, my playing back ground under two Indiana Hall of Fame coaches, good references and the article on the fast break impressed those who interviewed me. When I returned to my office on Monday morning at Salem High School I was offered both jobs. To my mind, I had overcome tombstone territory. I chose to go to Palatine, Illinois and try once again to be a head coach. I was elated that my fellow Hoosier Marc Denny agreed to become my assistant at Palatine High School. It was good-bye to Hoosier Hysteria and hello to March Madness in Illinois.

Looking back on growing up in Indiana I have no doubt that making two baskets in front of 5,500 fans in the sixth grade had a profound effect on me. It is said Hoosier Hysteria gets a grip on people without them knowing it. Hearing the crowd roar started what became almost a constant dream for me to become the best basketball player I could be. Little did I know at the time that thousands of other Hoosier boys were solidly woven into the same dream and the competition in fulfilling that dream was almost overwhelming.

In retrospect, I was luckier than most of those attempting to live out their dreams in basketball in the era of the 1950s. I was fortunate to have played in what are arguably two of the most legendary communities in Indiana basketball history...Marion and Muncie. More good fortune came my way as I was coached by two Indiana Hall of Fame coaches. I had wonderful teammates and many friends and relatives who attended games.

What youngster remotely interested in basketball would not have been smitten by the events that took place surrounding basketball in the late 1940s the 1950s and early 1960s? A few of those events that made a big impression on me while growing up were: The arrival of three NBA teams in Indiana. Marion High School going to the state finals in 1947 and again in 1950. One hometown player made the Indiana All-Star team and another even became Mr. Basketball. In 1951 and 1952 Muncie Central won the state championship and I would later play with and against many of the players on these famous team.

In 1953 Indiana University added to Hoosier Hysteria by winning the national championship. In 1954 I played in the state tournament. I then attended the famous Milan-Muncie Central game and later played against and with several players from this game. That same year Indiana University won the Big Ten title and I was allowed in the locker room and met great players Don Schlundt and Bob Leonard. Death threats and betting scandals in basketball took place during this era. In 1954-55 and 1955-56 the fabulous Oscar Robertson, whom I briefly played against, dazzled Hoosiers with his amazing skills while playing for Indianapolis Crispus Attucks. In 1955 and 1956 Bill Russell and K.C. Jones won the NCAA tournament at San Francisco University and then played in Indiana on the United States Olympic team. As Boston Celtics in 1961 they came to Marion to play and were refused service in Marion restaurants. As an adult coach in the world of basketball I saw ugly discrimination take place after a state tournament game when a black player I coached was denied access to a hotel.

The last two incidents mentioned above show why basketball was only one part of my life as I grew up in Indiana. There is an ugly side to the culture in which I was raised. It has been alarming to me as I have grown older to gradually learn that the prejudice, hatred and bigotry that existed was partially hidden from me and my white friends while our African-American friends felt the full force of discrimination.

The culture in Marion, Indiana while I was growing up there was really a reflection of that which was transpiring throughout America. I now know the culture I observed while growing up in Marion was more pleasant for me than for my African-American friends. It is difficult for me to imagine what it was like for Pop Gates when he visited Indiana. I wonder more now what it was like for Jumping Johnny Wilson, Bill Garrett, Oscar Robertson or even my teammates Oatess Archey, Tommy Nukes, Wilbur Davis or Jim Sullivan when they were youngsters growing up in Indiana.

One of my favorite players, Frankie Brian of the Ft. Wayne Pistons, once said, "Whenever I hear the song *Back Home Again in Indiana,* I get real nostalgic. Even though I was a transplanted Hoosier, I also get sentimental since there are so many good memories to hang on to about growing up in Indiana. It seems sad that as the stories are told about racial tensions of the 1950s and 60s that memories for African-Americans cannot be as nostalgic as they should be.

THE END

REFERENCES

References are organized in the following manner: When a source (book, periodical or web site) is used in a chapter, the author and title, etc. are listed. Then under that listing the page number in that chapter on which the material appears is shown to the left just before the referenced material (quote or paraphrase). At the end of the referenced material is the page number on which the material can be found in the actual book or periodical. For example, in Chapter One on page 3 the following quote is found from the book A Lynching in the Heartland. (Note just the first few words and the last few words are used as this is enough to identify the material). "The first sounds the prisoners heard...along the riverbank...press stories reported." p-5. (This quote is found on page 5 in A Lynching in the Heartland).

CHAPTER ONE

Madison, James, H., *A Lynching in the Heartland: Race and Memory in America*, Reproduced with permission of Palgrave MacMillan, 175 Fifth Ave., New York, NY 10010 and Houndmills, Basingstoke, Hampshire, England, (c) 2001.

Page-3- "The first sounds prisoners heard...along the riverbank...press stories reported." p-5.

TM 2005 Jesse Owens Trust by CMG Worldwide/www.JesseOwens.com

Page-4-(Material about Jesse Owens was obtained and permission for use was granted from this Web site).

Gould, Todd, *Pioneers of the Hardwood: Indiana and the Birth of Professional Basketball*, Indiana University Press, Bloomington & Indianapolis, (c) 1998.

Page-8- "The volcano of bigotry...dead when we got back." p-26. Ibid: "We looked forward...in the country at the time." p-26-27.

Bates, Don, M., *All-Star Memories: A History of the Indianapolis Star's Indiana-Kentucky High School All-Star Basketball Series (1939-1989)*. Published and copyrighted (c) 1989 by Indianapolis Newspapers, Inc. Indianapolis, Indiana.

Page-9 -(Records of All-Star games and player participation are paraphrased here)-Kentucky didn't beat Indiana...Ralph Beard and Wallace "Wha Wha" Jones...beat Kentucky All-Stars in Louisville. p-16-20.

Page–10 -Paraphrased-Bill Garrett was named Mr. Basketball... win 86–50.

Weagley named to All-Star team. Clyde Lovellette...led team to a 70-47 rout of Kentucky. p-20-22.

CHAPTER TWO

Gould, Todd, *Pioneers of the Hardwood: Indiana and the Birth of Professional Basketball*, Indiana University Press, Bloomington & Indianapolis, (c) 1998.

Page-17- "I had pretty good success...high school tournament." p-37.

Page-24- "I think the Olympians---took Indianapolis by surprise. P-170.

Page-25- "On May 25, 1950...goes to Knickerbocker Five..." p-177. Ibid: "Clifton, Cooper and Lloyd...society in 1950."

Sachare, Alex, *100 Greatest Basketball Players of All Time*, Byron Preiss Multimedia Company, Inc. 24 West 25th St., New York, NY 10010, (c) 1997.

Page-26- "It was during this time...all of my shots were jump shots." (On Paul Arizin) p-6. Ibid: "territorial draft pick." p-6. Ibid: "He led the Warriors...won NBA scoring title." p-6.

CHAPTER THREE

Bates, Don, M., *All-Star Memories: A History of the Indianapolis Star's Indiana-Kentucky High School All-Star Basketball Series (1939-1989)*, Published and copyrighted (c) 1989 by Indianapolis Newspapers, Inc. Indianapolis, IN.

(This book includes box scores of All-Star games mentioned in Growing Up in Indiana especially games in 1945 and 1946-47 and 1952). p-16-18-20-28.

Page-35-(All-Star Memories discusses Indiana beating

Kentucky 86-82 in first OT game-Jim Barley plays-Kentucky coach Ed Diddle calls thirteen time outs). p-28-29.

Gould, Todd, *Pioneers of the Hardwood: Indiana and the Birth of Professional Basketball*, Indiana University Press, Bloomington & Indianapolis, (c) 1998.

Page-36-(paraphrased comments about the Olympians taking a side trip to Chicago ... arrest of Beard and Groza. p-189-190.) Ibid: Players paid large sums of money to keep spread under eleven points.

Page-36- "As long as I live...shave points in that Loyola game." p-192.

Page-39- Paraphrase-NBA All-Star game in Ft. Wayne... first coast to coast. Marty Glickman and Hilliard Gates. Governor declares Indiana Basketball Week. p-207.

Raisor, Philip, *Outside Shooter: A Memoir*, University of Missouri Press, Columbia, MO, 65201, (c) 2003.

Page-42- "When we traveled...because we had black players." p-44.

CHAPTER FOUR

Madison, James H., *A Lynching in the Heartland: Race and Memory in America*, Reproduced with permission of Palgrave MacMillion, 175 Fifth Ave., New York, NY 10010 and Houndmills, Basingtoke, Hampshire, England, (c) 2001.

Page-46- "Adults didn't need to explain ... innocent to understand." p-143.

Newt Oliver, *Basketball and the Rio Grande College Legend*, (with Dr. Danny Fulks) (c) 1995. (Comments about "Bevo" Francis on page 41 were verified mostly through this book sent to me by coach Oliver).

Roberts, Randy, *"But They Can't Beat Us."* Sports Publishing Inc., Champaign, IL. Indiana Historical Society, (c) 1999.

Page-55-"Huff...cut him wide open." Ibid: "I didn't think much about it. " p-56.

Page-55-"most publicized game..." Ibid: Five players

threatened...police guarded...FBI involved." Ibid: "10,000 fans...season game in Indianapolis." p-57-58.

Raisor, Philip, *Outside Shooter: A Memoir*, University of Missouri Press, Columbia, MO., 65201, (c) 2003.

Page-62- "Losin' tonight, son, will hurt you all your life." p-8.

CHAPTER FIVE

Gould, Todd, *Pioneers of the Hardwood: Indiana and the Birth of Professional Basketball*, Indiana University Press, Bloomington & Indianapolis, (c) 1998.

Page-68- (Paraphrased)-Addition of the 24 second clock... stall tactics. p-182.

Madison, James H., *A Lynching in the Heartland: Race and Memory in America*, Reproduced with permission of Palgrave MacMillion, 175 Fifth Ave., New York, NY 10010 and Houndmills, Basingstoke, Hampshire, England, (c) 2001.

Page-74- "In the 1940s..polluted by their blackness." p-131.

Page-75-"All persons... entitled...Constitution of the United States" p-136.

Page-78- "A reminder...how far Grant County had come." p-150. Ibid: While it may have been an ordinay place...had faded." p-152.

CHAPTER SIX

Raisor, Philip, *Outside Shooter: A Memoir*, University of Missouri Press, Columbia, MO., 65201, (c) 2003.

Page-92- "Get them niggers, Phil." p-57.

Roberts, Randy, *"But They Can't Beat Us."* Sports Publishing Inc., Champaign, IL. Indiana Historical Society. (c) 1999.

Page-92- (paraphrased) "although the mayor led the parade...at Monument Circle." P-115. Ibid: "stopped briefly downtown." p-116. Ibid: "The mayor...key...to coach Crowe. Ibid: "When Milan ... all the squares in Indy."

Page-92- "Dad, they don't like us do they?" p-117.

Gould, Todd, *Pioneers of the Hardwood: Indiana and the Birth of Professional Basketball*, Indiana University Press, Bloomington & Indianapolis, (c) 1998.

Page-93- Paraphrased- The first...nationally televised...NBA game...on Nov. 6, 1954. Pistons defeated the Knicks...1,000 fans showed up. p-215.

Page-93-(Paraphrased)- No home gym for the Pistons. p-217.

CHAPTER SEVEN

Hoose, Phillip, H., *Hoosiers: The Fabulous Basketball Life of Indiana* (2nd Edition), "Guild Press Emmis Books, Cincinnati, OH (c) 1995."

Page-113- "Almost all restaurants...bottle caps...Polk Milk company." p-179.

CHAPTER EIGHT

(No references used in Chapter Eight)

CHAPTER NINE

Caldwell, Howard, *Tony Hinkle: A Coach for All Seasons*, Indiana University Press, Bloomington & Indianapolis, (c) 1991.

Page-146- (Statistics and scores about the 1957-58 Butler basketball team can be found in this book).

CHAPTER TEN

(No references are used in Chapter Ten)

CHAPTER ELEVEN

Caldwell Howard, *Tony Hinkle: A Coach for All Seasons*, Indiana University Press, Bloomington and Indianapolis, (c) 1991.

Page-173- (The excerpt about the career of Tony Hinkle is organized from the facts about Coach Hinkle found on page 143 in this book).

Schwartz, Larry, *Hank Aaron: Hammerin' back at racism.* This is a four-page article written as a special to ESPN.com. It can be found on the web site at http://espn.go.com/sportscentury/features/00006764.html.

> Page-174- "Hank led the league...hotel accommodations." p-2. Ibid: estimated 3,000 letters. Ibid: "Dear Nigger Henry... My gun is watching your every black move."

Chapter Twelve

Thomas, John C., *Forty Years Ago Today*, (This is an article found on the web site at http://www.ramblermania.com/1963/31563.htm. It describes what happened just before and on Friday, March 15, 1963 when Mississippi State was to play Loyola of Chicago in the NCAA tournament in Lansing, MI).

> Page-183-"Especially in these times...we cannot afford to give a single inch." p-1.

> Page-183-(Paraphrased)-Since the 1954 Brown v. Board of Education...to circumvent the federal mandate. Ibid: Finally, the same legal official...issued an injunction against Mississippi State. Ibid: The injunction was lifted by... Mississippi Supreme Court. Ibid: The Chicago Daily News..."bring their shoeshine kits." Ibid: Some of the letters were signed "KKK."

The Kennedy Administration and Civil Rights-This is an article found on the web site at http://www.historyforum.150m.com/kennedycivilrights.htm. The following is directly quoted from that web site. (Free web site hosting).

> Page-185- "When you have seen vicious mobs lynch...can't go to the public amusement park ... see tears welling up in her little eyes...then you will understand why we find it difficult to wait." p-1.